LOST
AND
FOUND

LYNDA BELLINGHAM

LOST
AND
FOUND

MY STORY

EBURY
PRESS

1 3 5 7 9 10 8 6 4 2

First published in 2010 by Ebury Press, an imprint of Ebury Publishing
A Random House Group company

The Random House Group Limited Reg. No. 954009

Addresses for companies within the Random House Group can be found at
www.randomhouse.co.uk

A CIP catalogue record for this book is available from the British Library

The Random House Group Limited supports The Forest Stewardship Council
(FSC), the leading international forest certification organisation. All our titles that
are printed on Greenpeace approved FSC certified paper carry the FSC logo. Our
paper procurement policy can be found at www.rbooks.co.uk/environment

Mixed Sources
Product group from well-managed
forests and other controlled sources
www.fsc.org Cert no. TT-COC-2139
© 1996 Forest Stewardship Council

FSC

Designed and set by seagulls.net

Printed in the UK by CPI Mackays, Chatham, ME5 8TD

HB ISBN 9780091936402
Export-only TPB ISBN 9780091936464

To buy books by your favourite authors and register for offers visit
www.rbooks.co.uk

To Michael, my husband,
and my sons, Michael and Robert,
who saved my life

CONTENTS

PROLOGUE

I T WAS A crisp, clear October morning in Montreal, Canada. The sun glinted on church spires. The trees on the hills round the city were a blaze of red and gold against a clear blue sky. A young woman, clutching a bundle in her arms, climbed into a yellow cab. She seemed to be talking to herself.

As the taxi made its way through the morning rush hour, she gazed out of the window as though seeing her life flashing past outside. Then her eyes turned down to the baby in her arms. She drank in every feature of the upturned face. She counted the tiny fingers curled round her thumb. She whispered urgently to the little face gazing at her intensely, 'I love you, dear. Remember, I will always love you. No matter what. You will always be loved. Keep that thought with you always. I do love you.'

The cab stopped suddenly and she struggled out and paid the driver. She turned and climbed the steps up to the front door of a large town house – a doctor's surgery. The door opened and the young woman was swallowed up inside.

Anyone watching the door would not have long to wait before it opened again and the girl reappeared. As she paused on the top step, it was clear she was no longer holding the baby and that her whole demeanour had changed. She seemed bereft. Lost and defeated. Her small frame seemed to have shrunk into her coat. She moved down the steps and crossed the road, looking neither right nor left, taking cover from the seasonal wind in a bus shelter. The sun was still shining but the winter wind that would soon bring the snow was teasing the litter on the street, reminding folk to wrap up warm. The young woman waited.

A few minutes later, across the street and round the corner came a couple. He was handsome, wearing a pilot's uniform. Tall and ramrod straight, with a classic RAF moustache. The young woman was beautiful and very elegant in a fitted suit, with a neat hat set at a jaunty angle. She had her arm through his and they were laughing. They looked happy and so full of hope as they entered the house.

As the girl waited, pulling her coat round her for warmth and comfort, the big door opened again and the young couple emerged from the house, engrossed in the bundle held between them. The man helped his wife down the steps while she carried the baby, their faces shining with love. They walked to a car parked just round the corner and the young woman carefully handed the bundle to her husband before she got in the back, then her husband handed her the baby. She was smiling as he shut the door, first carefully arranging her coat inside. He walked round to the driver's side and got in the car.

As he started to move slowly out into the traffic, the young woman in the bus shelter stepped into the road and, as the car passed her, she began to run after it. The young husband caught the movement and looked back at her in his driver's mirror. The girl was standing with her arms stretched out towards the departing car. She was howling with grief.

I was that baby. She was my mother.

I was lost.

Then she was found.

PART ONE
LOST

CHAPTER ONE

GETTING TO
KNOW THE FAMILY

There was a little girl
And she had a little curl
Right in the middle of her forehead.
And when she was good
She was very, very good
And when she was bad
She was horrid!

I N NOVEMBER 1948, Don and Ruth Bellingham flew back to England with their new baby girl. How excited they must have been. My dad was actually piloting the plane so it was an even more auspicious occasion. Quite early on in the flight, however, an engine caught fire and my father had to take the decision to turn round and go back to New York to land. So I was causing trouble from day one!

In those days it was a big deal to fly the Atlantic, and I was presented with a certificate pronouncing me a member of the 'Honourable Order of Pond Hoppers'. It is signed by my dad, Captain D J Bellingham, and hangs in my lavatory. This always made my dad smile, because he felt it should have been hanging somewhere more salubrious, but I would tell him that I wanted everyone to see it.

My dad was the youngest of four boys. The other three were farmers, but my dad was able to use the Second World War as an excuse to learn to fly, which he wanted to do very much. During the war my father was posted just outside Oxford. My mother was working in a factory in Headingly, near where she lived. Their courtship was conducted in the local pub and riding their bikes down long country lanes. It was only much later, when he retired from BOAC (now British Airways), that he went back to his roots and took up farming.

But when my parents came back to the UK in 1948, we first stayed in a little cottage on the farm owned by my paternal grandfather, at Great Kingshill, Buckinghamshire. I don't remember much of my early days at the farm, but there are photos of me with my grandfather sitting on a large carthorse, and it was the beginning of my love for the country and life on a farm.

We used to visit all the time after we moved to Bristol, and I have such fond memories of Sundays spent at Kingshill. My nan used to take me out to a huge cherry tree in the garden in the summer and I would help her pick cherries. We would make a picnic and have our tea under this beautiful spreading tree. Then in winter, we used to have our tea round a big table in the parlour. I always wanted to watch *Robin Hood* starring Richard Greene and my mother would say 'no' but my nan would say 'yes'. Guess which one I listened to! My nan was quite plump and had snowy white hair. She had an aura of calm about her. She never raised her voice in anger and I was always respectful of her. She was forever working in the house. She never sat down: even when we were eating our tea she would hover to make sure we all had everything we might want.

I used to go out with Grandad to bring the cows in for milking. I would scurry along beside him as he strode forth with a big stick in his hands. I had a little stick to match, and rather oversized wellies, as I recall. He owned a very ferocious bull that was infamous with the locals, but Grandad was frightened of nothing: I heard stories from my dad that they would let the beast out to service the cows and could only get him back in his pen again by being chased in a pony and trap by my grandfather. On several occasions disaster struck, the trap tipped over, and Grandad was deposited in the mud; twice he was actually gored by the bull. I used to stand in the bull pen and watch him pawing the ground: he really was scary, snorting and banging his horns on the railings. And that was just Grandad!

AROUND 1950, we moved to Bristol. I must have been about two or three. It was a brand new council estate. During this time I didn't see much of Dad as he was flying for BOAC on long-haul flights. I had Mum pretty much to myself, and it was a shock when my sister, Barbara, arrived in February 1951.

My parents had decided to keep my adoption a secret to all but close friends and family: people just assumed I had been born in Canada while Dad was working there. So it must have been very strange for them, especially my mother, when she fell pregnant with Barbara. Of course, she had to tell the midwife eventually, because the assumption was that my mother knew what she was doing for childbirth, as she already had one child. Nothing could have been further from the truth!

Barbara was followed very quickly by Jean in 1952. I really don't remember being jealous, but there is a photo of me looking at Barbara in her cot with a look of horror on my face. I do recall going into her bedroom once, when everyone was downstairs, and staring at this peacefully sleeping creature in its cot, and I believe I gave her a poke or two, which resulted in waking her up, and caused her to burst into very loud screams. This, of course, brought Mother running up the stairs, to see me backing hurriedly out of the room and trying to disappear.

Because my sisters were close together in age, it set a sort of pattern for life. Me and them. Which was slightly ironic, given that I was adopted. Yet as you will see from the early photos of us all, at one stage we looked liked triplets. But to me, the most telling photo of all shows Barbara sitting on Dad's knee and Jean with Mummy. I am standing to the side, on my own, defiantly striking a pose. Slowly, over the coming years, I would begin to wonder: where did I fit in?

But I had an idyllic childhood. In those early days, I was educated at home. This was quite unusual in those days and I think my parents may have got the idea from other couples who were with BOAC, who had similar problems of moving house frequently or being abroad.

After Bristol, we went to Limerick, in southern Ireland, for a year in 1954, as my dad was training pilots at Shannon Airport. Our house was on a very new residential estate; I remember seeing ditches everywhere that were the foundations for other houses. It was a great place to play in but not much fun on my own, and I was desperate to meet and play with the local kids, who never seemed to go to school. Truancy was rife. Limerick was quite rough in those days and very anti-British. I found this out to my cost one afternoon. My dad tells the story of coming home one day and seeing me in the distance, pushed up against a wall and surrounded by a group of children who were all shouting abuse at me, while I was singing 'God Save the Queen' at the top of my voice. Not a good idea! I must have won them over, however, because I was invited to join the gang on a trip across the river, one day. The river in question was the Shannon, and near the estate it was very deep and fast flowing. Early on in our stay, my parents had taken me aside, and explained to me that on no account must I EVER go near the river, or on it, for any reason whatsoever. So there I was, one sunny afternoon, dressed in my favourite pink and white spotty dress, being rowed across the Shannon in a little round craft made by the locals, bobbing up and down and shrieking delightedly. I was to find out later, to my cost, that I was also very visible. I had a wonderful afternoon and returned home for my tea in blissful ignorance of what was awaiting me. I was greeted by both my parents in the front room. Had I had a nice day? I nodded. Where had I been? Around. Why didn't I tell anyone where I was? Don't know. Did I know that a little girl in a pink and white spotty dress had been seen on the island this afternoon? Gulp. I have never again seen my father as angry as he was that day. Obviously, he was worried and frightened for me, but he chased me upstairs to my room – where I hid under the bed, to no avail, as he grabbed my leg and pulled me out – and spanked me with a hair brush (this was the good old days). I was locked in my room for the rest of the night without any tea.

After Limerick we went to live in Sunningdale, in Berkshire. It sounds very posh but we had to be on a route to Heathrow for Dad. I had my first taste of real school there; I was about four and it was horrible. The local primary school turned out to be a bit like Limerick: I wasn't welcome. I sat in the classroom that first week and sobbed and sobbed. I was so frightened: the windows seemed very high up the walls; it was like a church hall with a vaulted ceiling. When we were let out for break, I suddenly found myself pushed to the ground with a big fat boy on top of me, shouting into my face. I didn't go back.

Instead, I was sent to the Marist Convent School for Girls. Yes, a convent! I loved it. I loved the nuns. Well, that's not quite true: I loved one nun and hated another with a passion. We were taught by extremes: the really good and the really bad. Sister Mary Benildus was the good nun. She was the gentlest soul in the world and we adored her. In the classroom next door was Sister Louis, who also taught us. She was the classic bitter-and-twisted nun. I can only think that she must have been jealous of Sister Mary and her little band of adoring students as she gave us all endless detentions for no particular reason and plotted to get rid of Sister Mary. Which she managed in the end. We were all devastated when Sister Mary left. (Amazingly, thirty-odd years later, when it was my turn to be confronted with the big red book on *This Is Your Life*, my lovely mum managed to track Sister Mary down. She was working in Harrow, still as a nun, but no longer from a convent. It was so wonderful to see her again after all those years.)

While I was at the convent, my parents decided to move house, and I became a weekly border for a couple of weeks. I was very excited about the prospect of staying until, one night, one of the other girls in the dormitory came to me and insisted that I had been abandoned by my parents. I hadn't actually been told they were moving house, but this girl had got to hear it somehow and tried to convince me they had moved away and left me behind. I would not be consoled and spent the night in floods of tears. My mum had to be summoned to the school, and explained to me that I was only boarding for a bit because they needed time to prepare the new house for me.

Although my parents were Church of England, the convent was, of course, Catholic, and had lots of different practices, in terms of worship, that I didn't understand. In the dormitory, for example, there was always a nun on duty, so she had a special corner that was screened off from us girls to give her some privacy. My first night I was awoken by the sound of an earnest nun going through her Hail

Marys as she undressed. Each article of clothing was thrown over the screen as she finished a prayer. I remember lying there listening, in the half light, watching the shadows from the little night lights flickering on the walls. More scarily, when I went to the toilet there were statues round every corner that seemed to jump out at me: gruesome images of the Madonna holding her dead son in her arms; or Jesus on the cross with copious amounts of blood dripping from his wounds. Not great images for a young girl to fall asleep with in her head. One night, we were woken up by Reverend Mother. She had just returned from a trip to the Vatican and had pictures of the Pope to hand out to us all. We were told to keep them under our pillows.

But these moments were a small price to pay for being in lovely surroundings with mostly lovely teachers. I went from that convent to another one called St Louis, in Aylesbury, Buckinghamshire. That was also OK, except that, again, religion was apt to get in the way of the teaching and the good will of the nuns. The policy was that no Protestant pupil could go to the catechism classes. I went along the first time and sat enthralled at the stories being told to the children, but I was very upset by the notion that if you were born without being baptised you went to a place called Limbo, and couldn't go to heaven. When all the children were being taught about confessing their sins, and doing penance, I was first in the queue to give it a go, but given my Protestant status was told to leave immediately and never come back. I was very disappointed, as being with nuns all the time actually encouraged me to go through a very religious period in my life. At the age of nine I think the drama of it all appealed to me, and I was very keen to change my name to Mary and become a nun. I have never completely lost my faith and still call myself a Christian.

This was encouraged by my maternal grandmother, Granny Carter, who was herself very devout, and consumed with the guilt of having given birth to her child, Ruth, illegitimately. I adored her. She had amazing black hair that reached down to her waist, which she wore in plaits round the top of her head. I never saw anyone else ever wear their hair like that, except Heidi the goat herder! She used to let me sit on her bed in the mornings and brush it for her. She brushed it a hundred times a day and would only wash it twice a year, which seems strange in this day and age, but it never seemed greasy or dirty and was always shining. To the day she died, in her late seventies, she hardly had a grey hair. When I realised the implications of what it meant to be adopted, it was Granny Carter who really helped me understand it all. She always tried to make me feel special. She must have felt a special affinity with my birth mother who had given me up.

Brought up in a household full of men, Granny Carter had three brothers and a very strict Victorian father. She had got pregnant by a soldier at the end of the First World War. He was married, but his wife would not give him a divorce. I don't really know the ins and outs but my grandmother decided to keep the baby. When the father offered her the money for a termination, she refused and went and threw the money in the river. It must have been a very brave thing to do in those days. She subsequently married Charles Carter, who was 'prepared to take on' her and her baby. From what I can gather from my mum, he was not an easy man to live with, and my grandmother did not help the relationship when she refused to have any more children. Her husband's disappointment manifested itself in his dislike of her daughter and I think my mum had a really hard time with him over the years. Then my grandmother became very religious, which isolated her even more, so it was never a very happy marriage.

I knew nothing of this at the time, however, and used to love going to stay with Granny and Grandpa Carter in my summer holidays, although I was aware that my grandfather was quite stern and that I had to behave to keep him sweet. One of my enduring traits is the desire to please, so I worked on winning him over. I know he was very fond of me and, when I stayed for holidays, he used to devise an egg hunt for me every morning.

They lived in a suburban street in Worthing by the Sea. All the houses in the street looked the same. Their house was rather dark inside with lots of leather chairs and dark wood. At the back they had what my granny called a loggia. It was a bit like a conservatory but not nearly so grand. It was full of plant pots with all kinds of plants, and lots of cacti. Both of them loved gardening. Theirs was a classic English garden, full of blooming flower beds of many colours, and lots of shrubs at the far end, leading to a small vegetable patch, and rows of runner beans and sweet peas. Grandad had a garden shed that was kept immaculately tidy and, beside it, a small greenhouse for tomatoes. I can still recall its musty, woody smell mixed with the scent of summer lupins.

The garden was perfect for an egg hunt because it had so many nooks and crannies. I would crawl around under the bushes, fearful of any creepy-crawlies that might be lurking. Oh, the sheer joy of spotting my lovely brown egg nestling under a mossy stone, waiting for me to carry it gently and proudly to the stove, to be popped in the boiling water for my breakfast! Then dipping soft white buttered bread soldiers into the golden yolk and watching it dribble down the side of my egg cup. Magic days.

Often the days would be filled with us taking buckets and spades up the long, wide avenue to the sea. The beach was all stones there, but I never cared. It was part of the fun, trying to run into the sea barefoot. Picnics were conducted like military operations in the trenches. Towels were attached to poles stuck in the stones to act as windbreaks, but provided poor cover against the English summer winds. I loved the whole camping element. We had plastic cups and plates so all the drinks tasted of plastic, and all the food slid off the plates into the salty piles of seaweed. Which just added to the flavour, my grandad would say. I believed him! Then we would find a sandy patch and make a sandcastle or he would bury me in the sand to look like I was in a car. Such simple pleasures. In the early days we had donkey rides on the beach: I have a photo of me by the sea on a horse, which was so fat I can still remember the discomfort in trying to stretch my legs across its back.

I'll always remember how the walk to the beach was so easy, but how the return lagged! God, it seemed to go on and on. Tired, grumpy and often with a bit of sunburn on the tops of my legs, which stung when they rubbed together, I would trudge home along Worthing's avenues, which seemed to be immensely wide, and all lined with tall pine trees like the kind one always finds by the sea. Some were bent and gnarled against the winter winds, and curled over the pavement like an arch.

One of my granny's brothers was called Row Harvey. He had a daughter called Gillian who is a year younger than I am, and we would often all be there together. Uncle Row was quite strict with Gillian but he really adored me, so I got away with murder. When Gillian and I would get a fit of the giggles at the dinner table, Uncle Row would tell Gillian off, which would make me laugh more, and then he would have to forgive her or tell me off as well. He would drive us to Brighton to have a day on the pier, or to Hove, where there was a brand-new swimming pool where we both learned to swim. I was so proud of myself. I loved going there because after we finished swimming we got enormous mugs of hot chocolate to drink and would sit and warm up before the car ride home. I would always sing very loudly from the back of the car and annoy everyone. When we got home Granny would give us meringues with whipped cream, eaten in the loggia so as not to make a mess inside on the carpet.

CHAPTER TWO

MY LITTLE PONY

I N 1958, when I was ten years old, we were living just outside Aylesbury in a little village called Weedon. But Dad had found the farm of his dreams in Aston Abbotts, the next-door village, and was making plans for the big move. Meanwhile I was enjoying a life without care.

The riding stables next door was providing me with endless hours of joy. It was more a livery stable, really, where people kept their horses. I would spend all my free time there helping to muck out the loose boxes (that's professional horse-speak for stable), walking the horses round and cleaning the tack (the reins and saddles, etc.) There was a very famous show jumper of the day called Pat Smythe, and I wanted to be her. Acting was not even an idea, then.

One day, a lorry pulled into the yard with a new recruit. The lady who owned the stables, Pat, introduced me to Tiddlywinks, a bay (that's brown to the uninitiated) pony, with a beautiful black shiny mane and tail, and the biggest dark brown eyes you have ever seen. It was love at first sight for me, though Tiddlywinks looked decidedly suspicious, and was reluctant to come out of the trailer. She was very nervous and jumpy, and Pat explained she was a rescue pony who had been badly treated by her owner, and would need lots of love and care to put her back on the road to recovery. No problem. This was my mission. I applied myself with gusto.

It took several weeks for me and the pony to bond. In the early days it was hard work. Every time I went near her she swung round and tried to kick me. She would flash the whites of her eyes and bare her teeth. I was pretty nervous myself, which is the worst thing to be around animals. I would try to sneak up on her to get her saddle on, and she would lash out at me and send me scuttling into a corner. We must have looked a strange pair: the jumpy pony and the little girl talking nineteen-to-the-dozen, as she tried to get near. But I persevered and slowly Tiddlywinks began to relax. One of the memorable moments for me was when I went to the field and called out to her, and instead of running off she came up to me at the gate and nuzzled my hand, looking for her daily apple. I would groom her until her coat shone and the thick wiry hair of her mane and tail started to become soft and silky. I loved her with a passion.

Riding her was more of a problem. I was a competent horse-woman, well, girl, but still quite nervous, and Tiddlywinks could sense this and gave me hell. She was very devious as well. One morning I was with my dad, who had come to watch me ride out. I was showing off to him, but should have remembered that pride comes before a fall... I mounted OK, and gathered up the reins, gently kicking her to go forward. Up until this point, Tiddlywinks had been as good as gold, standing quietly, swishing her tail and looking like the perfect pony. Suddenly, up came her rear end as she kicked out her hind legs, and she let out a squeal of indignation as she bucked me off. I cannot tell you how humiliating it is to land on your arse in the mud, look up, and see your mount standing there quietly nibbling the reins you are still clutching. I made things even worse by bursting into tears. What a wally.

Dad decided to help. He took the reins from me and mounted Tiddlywinks. Of course, the pony was only little and my dad was six foot, so when he sat on her his feet touched the ground. Tiddlywinks did not like this at all. She looked round at the lump on her back and went to buck him off just as she had done with me. Nothing happened. She could not lift her hindquarters because of the weight. It was so funny – you could actually see her straining to kick her legs out, but to no avail. She kept looking behind her at my dad, and eventually almost seemed to shake her head in defeat, and give up. Dad then made me get back on, much to my dismay, but nothing happened. Tiddlywinks was so relieved to get rid of the big heavy man, she behaved like a dream and never gave me grief again.

One morning, I arrived at the stables to start the day with my usual routine, and found the yard was blocked by the horse box. The ramp was down, and Pat was leading Tiddlywinks out of her stable towards it. Panic took me over. Where was she going?

'We're taking her for a check-up because we may have found a buyer for her,' Pat told me.

A buyer? It had never occurred to me that Tiddlywinks was for sale. I had just assumed she would stay for ever. I ran home in floods of tears. I begged my mum to stop them selling my pony.

'But, love, she's not yours. She belongs to Pat, who can do what she likes with her.' My mother's gentle response didn't help.

'But Tiddlywinks loves me,' I sobbed. 'She trusts me, Mum. If she goes to a new owner she'll be upset all over again. You can't let her go. Please stop them!'

It was like *Black Beauty* in spades. But my pleading fell on deaf ears, and I watched the lorry disappear over the hill. I was beside myself and, to make matters worse, the following day we were going on holiday, so I had no idea when I would see my precious pony again.

The holiday was to be a big event in the Bellingham calendar. We usually stayed in the UK but this time we were off to Italy. Rimini and Rome. I couldn't have cared less where we were: I just wanted my pony back. However, we arrived at the Trevi fountain and I suddenly perked up. One of the big successes in the cinema, then, had been the film *Three Coins in the Fountain* where the heroine throws a coin into the water and makes a wish, and lo and behold, it comes true. Could this be my moment? Would my wish be granted and Tiddlywinks be mine? It was worth a punt. I closed my eyes tight and prayed with all my might. I promised God all manner of good behaviour if he granted my request.

How fickle is youth? I forgot my promise so quickly that, half an hour later, when my good humour had left me once more, and we were traipsing round the Vatican, I did a terrible thing. I feel obliged to share it with you, dear readers, at the risk that you may be so disgusted with me you throw this book at the wall. But confession is good for the soul and we are talking about being in the Holy City. Anyway, Mum had bought us all an ice cream in the hope it would cheer me up. As we continued round the great works of art, I was now struggling to eat it all before the ice cream melted down my hands. The exercise was becoming very tiresome, and I was getting stickier and crosser, when we passed a letter box and I decided to post the whole creamy pile. Yes, I posted my ice cream! Presumably into the very letter box used by thousands of tourists to send letters to loved ones all over the world, from the ancient Holy See. What kind of vandal am I? I have kept that secret all these years and I am still truly ashamed of it.

On arriving home after the holiday, I rushed down to the stables to see if my beloved pony had returned. No. I was plunged into despair once again. To add to the gloom I was about to take my 11+ exam, which would gain me entry to the Aylesbury grammar school if I passed it. I knew my parents wanted me to get this exam and I was filled with foreboding. Not that my parents pushed us girls in any way. They did not pressurise us, but always said you must try and do your best. My best could have been better, quite frankly.

My parents had engaged a maths tutor (well, start with the weakest link). He was a beady little man called Mr Nuttall; even the name makes me shudder. He had slicked-back hair with a middle parting, and black-rimmed spectacles. He had the neatest, most anal handwriting you have ever seen. He would purse his lips as he showed me how to draw a margin with a ruler, and those lips would stay firmly pursed for the rest of the hour. It was torment. I can only assume I was being punished for the ice cream incident.

My eleventh birthday dawned bright and sunny. I ran into my parents' room and jumped on the bed. My father got up and went over to the window.

'What's going on next door?' he said. 'Lynda, pop out and see what's happening, will you?' Rather grumpily, I made my way downstairs and outside to the bottom of the garden. I could see a brown rump through the bushes and strode towards it. Suddenly, from above the hedge came a flash of black hair and a welcoming whinny. No. Oh my goodness, it can't be…! It is! Running now, I jumped the gate and fell on Tiddlywinks's neck. My pony! The dreaded buyer had actually been my mum and dad. You cannot begin to imagine my joy. That had to be one of the great moments of my life. Not passing the 11+. Which I did, much to everyone's surprise, in particular mine and Mr Nuttall's.

As far as I was concerned, Life was now perfect. I spent the summer of 1958 riding Tiddlywinks round country lanes and going to gymkhanas. I tried very hard to become the next Pat Smythe but, much as I loved my pony, I did not love the hard work and dedication that is needed to make it in the competitive world of horses. Nor did I take to the people. In the main they were rather upper class and a bit snotty.

My parents were preparing for the big move to the next village, and the farm that was to be our home for the next forty years. It was in a terrible state, as the owner was on old boy who was quite ill, and had to keep going into a mental institution. He kept pigs and sheep in the kitchen on a regular basis and none of the bedrooms had been used for years and were full of rubbish. Every room was painted a dark brown colour. Out in the yard, all the buildings were crumbling and the focal point was a huge pile of manure. It was as high as the telephone wires, and when we started to clear the manure, it was so hot in the middle you could fry an egg!

The farm was a mess but it was in the middle of the Vale of Aylesbury, and the land was very sought after. There was no way my father could have afforded a farm like that if it had not needed so much work. He was a man on a mission. My poor, dear mum had her work cut out. She had never lived in the country and knew nothing about farms. The house was potentially really beautiful, though, so she set to, with all her tremendous energy, and turned it into a gorgeous home.

When we first arrived we all ran upstairs and chose our bedrooms. There was a long corridor and our three bedrooms were all in a row. Each about the same. Then there was a huge room at the end, which was over the dairy downstairs. It was amazing. It could fit a full-size table-tennis table. And because we were in the middle of nowhere we could play our music as loud as we liked. It made me very spoiled for future places!

It was near Christmas, and we begged Mum for a Christmas tree. She was reluctant because there was so much mess every-where, but we persuaded her to agree, if we promised to paint the little study so we had one room to sit in. Dad gave us a paintbrush each and we were soon splashing away happily. It was tiny but we made it very cosy. It had a real fire and all winter the flames roared.

There was no central heating in the house, and I remember that winter was bitter. We would all sit in a row, in front of the TV, facing the fire, and get absolutely roasted, but our backs remained freezing. I would come in from school and sit in front of the fire with my feet practically in the flames and give myself chilblains. I don't think they exist any more. They are bumps that itch really badly and are created by your feet being very cold and then very hot. They were murder. Snow fell and the windows all had ice on them. I used to wake up in the morning and study the patterns on the window made by the frost, and then breathe on it to clear it. If we were feeling cold we just put another layer of clothing on. We were hardy little souls.

We all worked together on the new house. To clear the pile of manure, Dad gave us all a spade and instructions to just dig. There were rats and fleas all over the place. At night we would queue up to get in the bath, almost crying with aches and pains and flea bites. Talk about abuse! When Dad first got the farm it had everything. Pigs, sheep, cows and chickens. I helped him castrate the little baby pigs. That was quite something: if you were not careful with the knife, you could lose your fingers. Every morning I was up with the lark, bringing in the cows on a cold, frosty morning, keeping warm by staying close to their bodies, and watching the warm, creamy milk fill the machines. Then into the dairy, which was wet and cold all the time from sterilising the equipment, and pouring the milk into the churns, to be picked up by the lorry later. After that I had to feed Tiddlywinks and muck out her stall. It was hard work but I loved every minute.

Collecting the eggs was a major joy and my sisters and I would fight for the pleasure. They often won that battle as it was something they could actually do, bearing in mind they were still quite young. Then there were the calves that were fattened up and then sent to be killed. It is such a strange world to the uninitiated. To care for these lovely animals, only to send them off to their death. Many times during the lambing season I would sit with a new-born lamb and feed it by hand to revive it, only to see it off to the butcher a few weeks later, or worse, have it end up in front of me on my plate!

Living on the farm shaped my life in so many ways. I was so lucky to live that life. For children it is perfect. We were outdoors all the time. We ate wonderful fresh food and understood how food is produced and where it comes from. It would be so great if all children, when growing up, were given time in the countryside on a farm. They would learn so much, and have such respect for life and living things. That is how I was brought up and I can see that it all has a natural order. Dad always said that all the animals in his care had a good life while they were alive. He loved them and cared for them.

After all the morning chores were finished, Dad and I would cook a huge breakfast together on the Aga. In those days, Agas were not very common, and certainly not the trendy objects they are in today's Chelsea kitchens. They were functional, and provided much-needed heat for the water, as well as cooking facilities. Break-fast is still my favourite meal of the day, and although I am not really allowed a big fry-up any more, every now and then I make one in homage to dear old Dad.

I'm reminded here of how I learned the facts of life. It was rather graphic, to be honest. When Dad bought the farm the purchase also included a bull called Bill. Unlike the one on my grandfather's farm, Bill seemed to have lost his *joie de vivre*, especially where the ladies were concerned. One day, I was helping Mum wash up. The kitchen looked out over the yard and that day it was full of heifers (young female cows that have not yet had calves). Today was to be their lucky day if Bill took a fancy. My father was in the yard with a couple of local farmers, and they were all standing round waiting for Bill to see the light of day. But Bill just didn't want to know and no amount of shouting and arm-waving could stir him into action. All the heifers were mooing in their most seductive tones, but to no avail. Then, suddenly, everything changed, and Bill was up for it. Literally. It's quite a frightening sight, believe me. I was watching it all, open-mouthed, and, as the bull charged past the window, I nudged Mum and pointed at the now very amorous Bill who was doing what he was supposed to do to one of the heifers.

'Is that it?' I asked, aghast.

'Yes,' came the reply from my mother. 'But it's very lovely when you're married!'

Another time we had been to church on Sunday morning, and invited the vicar back for a sherry. It was the lambing season and we had left a lamb, which was rather poorly, lying in a box in the bottom of the Aga. The bottom oven was only ever just above room temperature and was the perfect place to put ailing animals. As we sat round the kitchen table, Mum turned to the vicar and asked him if he would like to stay to lunch, just as the little lamb began to feel better and bleat out its desire for food. The vicar nearly jumped out of his skin. He saw the lamb in the oven, went white, and hurriedly made his farewells before we could explain!

That first year on the farm was magic. Full of new experiences and happy moments. But the end of the summer was looming, and my first day at the Aylesbury High School for Girls was a cloud in my blue sky.

MY FIRST DAY at the high school dawned. I went to say good-bye to Tiddlywinks and told her not to worry as nothing was going to change in our lives together. I went back home and put on my new uniform. Everything smelled new. We had to wear navy-blue serge tunics; mine was way too long and flapped against the back of my legs. I had a navy rain coat that was also ill fitting. Like most mothers, mine had gone for the 'get it a size too large' option, so it lasted longer. We also had to wear berets. I was dying by the minute as I regarded myself in the mirror. I had an all-consuming sense of doom. I looked like such a nerd. I was very short and had very short hair and looked like a boy. The white ankle socks made my legs look fat and the beret made my ears stick out.

Mum dropped me off that first day. I watched her disappear round the corner with a sinking heart. I was actually shaking as I set off up the drive to the main entrance. The school was brand new with bits still not finished. Classic sixties architecture – all brick and glass. I arrived at the front entrance only to be told to go round to the side and come through the playground to the side entrance. I joined the stream of laughing and chatting girls as we poured into the door. Just as I was about to go in there was a loud whoop and a rush of air and I felt my beret leave my head. I turned and saw the said headgear being mutilated by a blonde girl. She threw it to the ground, where she and another girl trod it into the damp forecourt. This caused much hilarity all round. I picked it up, shoved it in my pocket, and went inside. A teacher was crossing our names off a list. She looked up at me and said, 'Where's your beret?'

'Here,' I replied pulling the hat from my pocket.

'Well, dear, it's no good having it in your pocket. It should be on your head. In future you will wear it or get a detention.'

I started to interrupt but I was dismissed into the river of girls, once again. We were all herded into the assembly hall and addressed by Miss Camp. Yes, that really was her name! Had I been in a better frame of mind, and known what I know now, I could have appreciated the joke. But that is life, is it not? Youth is wasted on the young, and that includes the jokes.

I know we all have to go through this horror of first day at school. But when it's happening to you, it's hard not to take it all personally. The blonde girl was called Sue, I found out later, and she was the class tart with a heart. Within the next couple of years she had got pregnant and was expelled. The sad thing was, she was quite fun really, and very pretty, but there was no way she was going to be allowed to stay in the school. Miss Camp was on a mission to make us the crème de la crème. Next door to our school was The Grange, which was the secondary modern. That was where girls got pregnant. Not our happy band!

My first class that day was marred by a girl called Pat Bell. I turned round to say 'Hi' and try a bit of friendly chat, only to be greeted with: 'Turn round and get on with your own work,' hissed at me from under her breath. We have laughed about it since, over the years, and we still keep in touch, but that day she was awful. I felt so alone. In the first week I was teased mercilessly about how I spoke.

'OOH, aren't we posh, then?' screeched Sue. 'Did Daddy pay for you to come to this nice school? I heard you failed your eleven plus but he bought you a pass.'

I couldn't believe this. How unjust was that? After all my lessons with bloody Mr Nuttall. But I kept my mouth shut. If it was known I had had private tutoring it would have made me even more unpopular.

I began to find a way through that set the pattern for the rest of my life. I started to make people laugh. What I failed to do by way of sporting achievements or after-school activities – like going out and snogging loads of boys – I made up for by being a clown. I would hide in a cupboard during the maths class. I would perform in the Library behind the book cases. I always acted the fool and, gradually, I was no threat to anyone and they left me alone. I would be exhausted at the end of the day, not from studying, but from entertaining all day and trying to make people like me. I would wake up every morning and beg my mother not to send me back.

Home was my haven. I would get off the bus and run straight out to the field to see Tiddlywinks. I would either go for a ride or sit in her stable while she ate her tea and tell her all my stories. Next, I would sit in the kitchen and have my tea with my mum and my sisters. Lots of toast and butter and jam. Then I would watch *Children's Hour* on TV and then do my homework.

As a mother myself now, I often wonder how my mother managed to keep that routine going for as long as she did. We never questioned the discipline. It was all just accepted. But I guess there were no other distractions then. Although, in the summer, it was much harder to have to stay in when the sun was still warm at five o'clock. Dad would come by with the tractor and trailer, and we would ride down to the fields to get bales of hay, and then ride home, sitting on top of the hay like kings. We also had our own little hideaway down in the fields. It was an old shepherd's hut, and used to be where the shepherd would sleep while the sheep were lambing. It was a proper little house made of brick and had a real range to cook on, very small, but still, a real fire-range and a stone floor and a little window. There was just room for a table and chair. Can you imagine three little girls playing house? We would take everything we needed down for the day. We were not allowed to make a fire but when we grew older we did actually spend a night down there, and had a fire and everything (I think I was smoking tea-leaf roll-ups by then). We got very scared halfway through the night and, when Dad came down to check on us, we decided to go home with him.

It's hard to believe that it was possible to leave children to play like that then. The most dangerous thing that could have happened to us was to have come across a badger in the night that might have attacked us. The worst injury we could sustain was to fall in a pile of stinging nettles. But then we knew the routine – get the dock leaves and rub them all over the stings. Such simple knowledge, but all going now.

One really bad winter we were snowed in completely. The drifts either side of the road were six feet high. Dad dug a single path through the snow to the village. It was nearly a mile and a half away, and I remember proudly riding Tiddlywinks to the village shop to get our groceries! It was like being a pioneer of the wild west. I was an ardent fan of westerns as a child and, in particular, a programme called *Bronco* starring Ty Hardin. I actually wrote him a fan letter explaining that I had a pony and was a good rider, and did he think there might be a part for me in one of the episodes? I got a card back with his signed photo and a note saying he was so sorry but there was no part for a young girl at the moment but he would keep me in mind. How cool was that?

CHAPTER THREE

FROM FARMYARD
TO SCHOOLYARD

THROUGH ALL THIS happiness, my days at school would punc-
ture the bubble. They were horrible times, until I began to
discover drama.

I was chosen to be in the school play and my first role was
very modest, as a servant in Shakespeare's *Anthony and Cleopatra*. Here began my love of all things theatrical. Plus, I fell in
love with the leading man. Our school had joined forces with the
boys' grammar school for the play, and Andrew Roberton was
the object of my desire. He was magnificent. So theatrical, with a
wonderful booming voice. He would later go on to the Central
School of Speech and Drama, in London, and was the reason I
chose to go there, too. (He later changed his name to Matthew
Roberton.) His Cleo was a girl called Stephanie Daniel, who also
went to Central, and later to Australia, where she then went into
the soap, *Neighbours*.

I was choosing to stay behind after school and act. I loved
everything about it. The rehearsals were thrilling. We had an
English teacher called Miss Cattell who directed our plays. I think
she was really rather good and she loved drama. Looking back, I
wonder if she may have had ambitions herself, years before, but

never had the chance. She was a spinster and lived with her sister, who was the maths teacher, but I reckon she would have made a good character actress. Sadly, I was overlooked for the next three years, she would never give me a decent role. In *Romeo and Juliet*, I played the nurse. In *Saint Joan*, I played her mother. I had to bite my tongue and watch a parade of useless girls get all the roles I wanted. It was harsh but probably held me in good stead for my theatrical career, where perseverance is the name of the game.

All my disappointments at school were forgotten when I got home to my pony. She was the focus of my world in those days. Then, one morning, I woke up with hay fever. No great shakes, I hear you cry, but actually it proved to be a disaster and totally changed my life. It was so bad I had to stay indoors with the windows shut. My eyes would swell up so they were nearly closed. I could not go near Tiddlywinks without breaking out in rashes and endless sneezing fits. It was a nightmare. I could only stand outside the stable and watch as my dad fed her. Sometimes I just couldn't bear it any longer and made the sacrifice. Giving her a hug for five minutes led to an afternoon of misery stuck inside with my eyes like golf balls. But it was worth it. My summer days were cruelly cut short. For the next forty years I would suffer so badly with hay fever it made my life a misery.

Tiddlywinks's place in my life was gradually replaced by boys. Well, one boy, really. Karel Falk. He was to become my *raison d'être*. I had recently started going to a café, after school, with some of the girls, and this was where I first saw him. The café was in the square where all the buses came to drop off. Normally, I would catch the 4.10 which took me straight home to the bottom of my drive. If I missed that one I could get the 5.30, but would then have to walk two miles from the crossroads where the village road joined the main road. If I was really enjoying myself I caught the 6.10

which brought me all the way home again. I give you these fascinating facts on the times of the buses because they formed a vital part of my life for the next five years. I worked out that over that period I spent approximately 2,000 hours in that coffee bar. What wasted hours! All for love. Well, mostly.

Karel was the local Romeo. He was a kind of Peter Pan really. When I first met him (in the Regent coffee bar), he was seventeen and at art school in High Wycombe. He was very cool and went round with a beautiful girl called Sheila. She was the classic sixties girl, all long blonde hair and heavily kohled eyes. She was so gorgeous, and Karel obviously loved her.

When you are a teenager, 'Love' is so painful. I spent most of the time in tears or trailing round all the haunts in town where the object of my passion might be hiding. This brought me into contact with the characters lurking in the Dark Lantern. Sounds like a B movie, doesn't it? This pub was the hub of all the action, legal or otherwise, in Aylesbury. It was one of the oldest buildings in the town, with low ceilings and beams and log fires. Everyone who was anyone congregated here. Angels and villains. I had begun to get friendly with a girl in my class called Jenny Stanford. She was into folk music and was madly in love with a singer called Rod Puddefoot (who was also a Morris dancer – well, nobody's perfect!) They eventually married, and are still married now, which is quite a feat. I would accompany Jenny to the local folk club to listen to Rod sing.

Folk clubs and folk singing go hand-in-hand with pubs and drinking. So it was but one small step from this to lunchtime drinking in the Dark Lantern. Underage drinking at that. We used to go into town on our school lunchbreak, roll our long skirts up short, take off our ties, and away we went. Half a cider and the world was our oyster.

From the end of the fifth form to going into the sixth form, I became a difficult teenager. Not really bad: it was all quite innocent compared to today's youth, but I stopped trying at school, and spent far too much time messing about and obsessing about Karel. He never stopped being with Sheila. She was the one he loved but she had another boyfriend so in the meantime he would see other girls on a kind of rotation basis. He used to pick up with me for a couple of weeks, when we would go everywhere together, but then he would move on to the next girl, and so it would go on. When I was in favour, I was in paradise. We would sit in the bus shelter at the crossroads and snog for hours. Just kiss. He was the best kisser ever. My father caught us once – he had been driving round for an hour trying to find me.

Another time, just before I had to give Tiddlywinks up for good because of the hay fever, I decided to run away from home. I think I had had one of my usual spats with Mum and Dad which always seemed to end with me being very dramatic and pronouncing that no one understood me and that they would all be better off without me. I rode into town on Tiddlywinks. Still only fourteen, I was like some demented cowgirl and hitched my horse to the fence of Karel's council house. His father opened the door and stepped aside as I rushed in, declaring I needed to talk to Karel. I ran up to his bedroom and sat on the end of the bed and sobbed my heart out. Poor Karel must have been terrified he was going to be lumbered with this nutter. Eventually his dad came in and said in his broken English (he was Czech): 'Don't vorry, Leeenda. It is never so bad it cannot be vorse.' Bless him! Then, to my mortification, my father appeared at the door to take me home. Tiddlywinks was tied to the back of the minivan and trotted home very happily. She had been very unhappy about coming in the first place: when we had got out of her two-mile radius of home she had been very tricky!

Like most teenagers, my sense of drama was beginning to develop and also my insensitivity and selfishness. I realise now that all children go through this period, but there is an element in my phase that was different for me. I seemed to have a need to impress myself on people, and to prove something, but I didn't know what exactly. At school I had finally found my group. We were now in the lower sixth. The main school building didn't have space for us so we were in an annexe up the road. It was a big house, and each group of girls had taken over a bit of the house and made it their territory. Our gang had the kitchen. We would gather round the kitchen table and talk about everything, but mostly about sex. There was about ten of us, and several of the girls were way ahead in the relationship stakes, and had already had sex. I was terribly impressed, if not a little confused by what went on. I remember one day one of our lot was describing how you lay on your back with your legs in the air and then wrapped them round the bloke's back. I was horrified! It all sounded way too athletic for me. I wasn't really bothered about my sex life. As long as I could snog Karel I was happy. The rest of the time, I was busy going to the pub and learning dirty jokes, and hearing tall stories. I was happy in my role as court jester.

I was always vulnerable to being teased or mocked, and I learned to mimic voices to fit in. During these years, several girls would have a go at me for one thing or another, but then give up because I made them laugh. One reason was my voice. I have no idea why but I did sound posh. My parents were not posh at all. My dad had a slight Shropshire lilt to his voice, and my mum spoke quite normally unless we had visitors or she was on the phone, then she did go a bit posh. So where I got my voice from, I don't know. It was also quite deep and a bit husky, even then.

I always felt that the girls thought I was a show-off and I never really fitted in, but over the years we have kept in touch and it is great now, because they come and support me. 2009 was the fifti-eth anniversary of the high school opening and us all starting out. The gang came to see me in the West End in *Calendar Girls*, and to the TV studio to see *Loose Women*. Jenny (my folksinger friend) has always stayed close, even though we came from such different backgrounds. She once came to the farm and remarked how differ-ent it was from her council house, but she was not being unkind and bore no malice. She is a very special woman and I am so proud of her; in 2008 she was made mayor of Aylesbury and is now a councillor. But it made me realise that perhaps my circumstances were different from most of the gang and it was better not to rub anyone's noses in my good fortune. My family was not rich, by any means, but farm houses are big, and farming was still regarded by some as a kind of 'landed-gentry' thing, rather than a job of work.

One afternoon, Jenny and I decided to play truant and go the pictures. This was unusual for us because although we would go to the pub at lunchtime, we always went back to school in the after-noon. Anyway, for some reason or other today was different. When I got home, Mum asked me about my day. I mumbled something and then she said: 'Did you enjoy the film?'

The word 'Yes' was leaving my mouth when I stopped and, in that crucial nano-second in these situations, made the choice between telling the truth or lying. Stupidly, I chose to lie. It was just like the pink spotted dress all over again! My mother then spent the next two hours trying to get me to tell the truth. She tried yelling and threatening and cajoling; she even cried. To no avail. I was locked into that lie and had to stick with it. It's a horrible feeling and one that most of us have experienced. And once you've been there, you realise it's so much easier to just tell the bloody truth, isn't it? Finally, my father came home and the interrogation continued. As a parent myself, now, I know the frustration. You don't care what your child has done, you just want them to tell the truth. Dad was pacing back and forth, alternating between shouting at me and pleading with me. I just wanted it all to stop – I wanted to tell the truth but my mouth just would not engage with my brain.

Suddenly, Mum blurted out, 'The trouble is, Lynda, we just don't know who you are any more. God knows where you come from. We'll never know. We've dreaded this moment.'

Everything stopped. Silence. We all looked at each other.

I was so disappointed in myself. I so wanted to do the right thing, even then, and when I did something I knew was wrong I just felt such disgust with myself. As far as my parents were concerned I just wanted to make them pleased they had adopted me and now, of course, I was so frightened that they would reject me.

'You're right,' I said. 'I am horrible and I don't belong. I did go to the pictures. I'm sorry, and I'm sorry you got me.' I ran from the room, up the stairs, threw myself on my bed and cried my heart out.

It was a relief, in a way, to get it out in the open. Mum and Dad must have been going mad trying to understand the situation. I was the first child. The first teenager in the family. I was no longer a little girl who did what they wanted. They had to learn with me all the things that kids go through. But there was something else with me. I had started to look completely different from Barbara and Jean: I was turning into someone they could not recognise. The questions hung in the air. Who was I? What had they adopted?

I HAVE NOT FULLY brought up the subject of my adoption until now because it was never important until that moment.

I cannot remember exactly when my parents told me I was adopted, but I have a feeling it came out of a conversation I had with my mother after I had heard all that stuff at the convent school, about babies going to Limbo if they had not been baptised.

I vaguely recall a conversation about how they had chosen me especially, and that I had flown on a plane from Canada with them to England. I can honestly say it didn't mean a thing to me; I just accepted it and went on with my life. It was never mentioned because there was no need to mention it. I was part of the family: I had my sisters and Mum and Dad. No one knew any different. At least, until the incident of the cinema, when we all seemed to take a breath and shift position.

As I was growing up, I had of course become more aware of myself and I noticed differences between me and my sisters. We were all still similar in hair colour and style but I had very olive skin and my nose was very prominent. Oh, my nose! What grief it was going to give me! Of course I would experiment with different looks while the girls were still only quite young. I think they were much more traditional than me though. I went through all kinds of phases like the Cleopatra look when the film with Elizabeth Taylor came out. I was also a token Mod during the early sixties. Barbara and Jean were quite shy so when we were all together I rather took over!

I think I must have seemed worse than I was to the family not only because I was such an extrovert but also because I was the eldest and had to do everything first. By the time Barbara and Jean were going out Mum and Dad had mellowed somewhat in their attitudes.

Looking back, I hate to admit it, but I gave my darling parents a hard time. I was beginning to develop my dramatic side and my imagination started to work overtime. I started to ask questions about my real mother and the circumstances of my adoption. But my parents were always incredibly open about everything. They gave me my birth certificate, with my original name, Meredith Lee Hughes, and all the papers relating to my adoption and citizenship of the UK. They really knew very little about my birth mother, as it was a private adoption and they never met her.

When I think about it now, the whole process was just so lucky. For me, anyway. Mum and Dad had only been married a few months when Dad had got the chance to go to Canada and train pilots for BOAC. What young couple wouldn't have embraced the gift of exploring another country and having a good time? After all, they had just been through a war and rationing, and here they were in a wonderful city with the world at their finger tips.

The one cloud on the horizon was the fact that nearly a year later they were still trying to start a family, something they wanted badly to do. So much, in fact, that they went to see a Dr Gordon in Montreal to ask his opinion. It was he who suggested adoption, as he knew about my case. He sent my mum to visit me. I was in a big house, on the outskirts of town, run by a lovely lady from Yorkshire. Mum fell in love with me and took my dad back the next time for a second opinion. Apparently, I had looked up at him and given a big smile and that had sealed the deal. They came back to the UK with their new baby and everyone assumed Mum had had me out in Canada. I became a Bellingham. It was only now, as I was growing up and developing a personality, that questions were starting to hang in the air. But we talked it through and we all moved on as a family, and life took over again.

I took my 'O' levels at the end of the fifth form year. I failed maths. Well, there's a surprise, but I did not do too badly in other subjects. I was beginning to form a plan to go to drama school. My parents were not overly delighted by my career choice but, as ever, they were supportive and tried to help. In order to go to drama school, though, I was going to need to get a council grant, as my parents could not afford to support me financially. This meant I had to get some 'A' levels, as the Central School of Speech and Drama (where I had chosen to go) was regarded as a university in terms of funding. So whether I liked it or not – and I didn't like it

– I was going to have to stay on at school for another two years. My parents must have breathed a sigh of relief and prayed the whole idea would die a death.

I would love to tell you I worked hard to achieve the grades I needed, but it would be untrue. I worked very hard in my drama club and I won several competitions in the county for drama, and a couple for public speaking, but they were never mentioned in assembly at the end of term. I don't know why anything theatrical was regarded by the school as the lowest of the low: whenever a pupil won a hurdle race or did well in netball their names were read out to the school.

I don't know whether it was as a result of this lack of encouragement, but I did as little study at school as possible and instead continued to frequent the Dark Lantern in my quest for local knowledge. I made some wonderful friends there, from all walks of life. I suppose the actor in me just loved to study human beings. As far as the villains were concerned I was a scatty, upper-class bird who was good for a round of drinks and a laugh. I was like their mascot. Occasionally, one or other of the group would disappear for a while and then return and it took me ages to realise that these absences were due to prison sentences. In the main, they were a fun bunch of guys. I was still saving myself for Karel, who was showing scant signs of interest, and on the odd occasion I did bring a bloke home, often late at night, my dad would greet us, waving his shotgun from his open bedroom window: he was always concerned about burglars. Years later, he confessed that he was quite grateful for my dodgy friends because when all the other farms in the area were broken into, ours was left alone due in part to my association with the criminal fraternity!

My time spent in the pub was a different kind of social life from the one I had at school. It is strange, looking back, how I divided my social life into compartments and dipped in and out of each. I still do now. Maybe it is the gypsy in the actor that makes him flit from scene to scene. The gang at school were all now established in their love lives. Jenny was with Rod, and some of the other girls had regular boyfriends. And then there were the parties. I dreaded them because I felt so out of place. I just wasn't into the whole going-off-to-the-bedroom-for-a-grope business. At one party I found myself on a bed with a bloke from the boys' grammar school. Every time he made a lunge for me, I either fell off the bed or told a joke. That was my defence: I fended off unwanted advances with a steady stream of banter. He gave up in the end, and word went round the boys' school not to bother trying to pull Lynda Bellingham because she never stopped talking! One evening, at another gathering with the group, they decided to play Postman's Knock. For the uninitiated, this is a game where you take turns to be the postman. You have to go outside and wait while everyone else is left in the room and given a number from one to ten. Then the 'postman' knocks on the door and is let in and calls out a number. Whoever it is had to go outside with the postman and snog them! I prayed not to be chosen. But, horror of horrors, I got a bloke, Kevin. It was obviously a disappointment to him as well, because he was very offhand with me. We stood in the hall and because he was so tall and I was so short I had to stand on the stairs. We had a very wet, soggy snog and as he went back into the front room he very obviously wiped his mouth with the back of his hand. I was so upset; we never spoke to each other again. This may have been the defining moment in my life where I vowed I would not only be a star but the best kisser in the universe.

CHAPTER FOUR

AN ACTOR'S LIFE FOR ME?

M Y PASSION FOR acting had increased in leaps and bounds. There was a lovely man called Alan Garrard who worked for the Bucks County Council and organised my drama group to visit Germany. He was a great encouragement to my dreams of a theatrical career and I was chosen to make the speech in each town we visited on our tour.

I had also made friends with another future student of Central, Penny Casdagli. She was at the Arts Educational School in Tring, in Hertfordshire, and was everything one imagined an actress should be. Beautifully spoken and tiny boned, with long dark hair and gorgeous features, she was everything I longed to be. I first saw her playing Desdemona in *Othello* at a Shakespeare festival, held every year at Pendley Manor, in Tring. It was run, strangely enough, by the well-known commentator, Dorian Williams, who was famous for his television commentaries at the *Horse of the Year Show* and at Badminton. Now here he was running an outdoor theatre company in a beautiful country manor house. After seeing Penny that year I vowed I would join her the next. I only had a small part in Macbeth with the classic one line 'They are, my Lord, without the palace gate'. I loved every minute of it. The whole experience was heaven to me.

The following year, in 1966, I landed the part of Puck in *A Midsummer Night's Dream*. At one point in the play, I was required to run like the wind down to centre stage through a wooded glade. A local critic remarked that if I didn't make it as an actress I could always apply to run the 100 metres! I was well and truly struck by the bug.

As the end of school was nearing, everybody was very busy going to see the careers officer, except me. Nobody could help me. I applied for the Central School of Speech and Drama because that was where everyone else I knew had gone.

I went to see them in 1965, towards the end of my first year in the sixth form. I prepared a speech with the help of Mrs Maclaughlan, a wonderful geography teacher who was my only champion, and was thrilled to be asked back. In my interview, the staff asked me what I was doing. I explained I was doing my 'A' levels. That was fine by them, and they suggested that I return the following January and they would consider me for the 1966 year, which would start in the following September. I was over the moon, and told everyone that I was going to Central when I left school. My parents suggested it might be a good idea if I took a secretarial course that summer, as acting was such a notoriously precarious profession. I queued up at the local college to enrol and then suddenly, just as I got to the head of the line, I walked away. I decided if I couldn't work as an actress then I would just do anything to fill in the time. But I *was* going to make it, so there would be no problem.

I was used to doing rubbish jobs anyway. Every holiday I worked as a cleaner at Stoke Mandeville Hospital. In fact, it became rather an interesting job because as they were so short-staffed, I often ended up working on the wards a good deal of the time, performing tasks that should really have been done by the nurses. My other job was working in Moorhouse's jam factory. My friend

Jenny and I got jobs there, as did Stephanie Daniel (Cleopatra) and, I think, at one point, so did Penny Casdagli. It was while we were all bottling marmalade that Stephanie filled me in on life at Central, and she was the one who made me audition.

That factory was something else. The tedium of sitting staring at rows and rows of jam jars, for hours on end, made me realise I had to succeed as an actress, because I wasn't fit for anything else, and I certainly wasn't going to spend my life in the jam factory. It got so boring sometimes that we used to tip the jars upside down so all the marmalade or jam spilled down the sides from the machine. Then the alarm would sound, the conveyor belt would stop, and we would have a few minutes for a fag or a short break while someone cleared up the mess. One day, the manageress came to me and suggested that as I spoke nicely, she was going to put me in charge of bottling the Queen's gooseberries. I was by Royal Appointment! So, there I was, bottling away, when I noticed one of my fellow workers spitting into the jars. I asked her what on earth did she think she was doing as, for goodness' sake, these goose-berries were going to Buckingham Palace.

'I hate Royalty,' came the reply. 'I spit on Royalty.'

Well. She had to be reported, and she was, and she left. There's nowt so queer as folk.

On my second visit to Central after Christmas, as requested, I was full of confidence as I climbed the steps to the entrance. After all, this was just a formality. They had already said yes.

I did my speeches and the teachers asked what I was up to now. I explained that I was taking my exams in June and, hopefully, I would make the grades to get my grant to come to Central in September, as they had told me. There was an ominous silence. Then the principal, George Hall, delivered the rather unnerving verdict that they would like me to come back and do a workshop, with other students, before they could give me a final answer on my suitability for the course.

I was so disappointed, but I had no choice.

The college invited me to the workshop in April. There were quite a few of us and we all huddled in the corner like sheep. It was a very long day. We had to do movement and voice and improvisation. God, how I hated it. I still hate improvising now. I just felt so stiff and self-conscious, and my body felt heavy and cumbersome. I made friends with another girl and we went to lunch together. We tried to understand what it was they were looking for in us as actors. It was all very foreign to us.

I came home feeling very despondent. My 'A' levels were looming and the future was not looking quite so bright. Then I got a letter explaining that the staff at The Central School of Speech and Drama were very sorry but they did not feel I was right for the September intake of students. If I wished to ring them at the beginning of September, before the term started, they would review the situation, and there may possibly be a chance of a place.

My whole world seemed to cave in. It just had not occurred to me that I would not have a place. I hadn't even bothered to apply anywhere else. Now I was facing the prospect of a summer in the jam factory, and possibly the rest of my life. No. No, this was *not* going to happen.

I rang the girl who had been at the audition with me. I dreaded hearing that she had got in. But she was inconsolable as well, as she had had a refusal She read me the letter over the phone. Basically, it was very similar to mine but, and this was a big but, she had not been invited to call back in September. There was a glimmer of hope! I was going to do this. I began to form a plan. There was a small chance and I was going to grasp it with both hands. I decided I needed a second opinion about whether I had any talent or not, and I decided to talk to the lovely Mrs Maclaughlan about it.

Mrs Maclaughlan was a member of a theatre club, and often went up to Nottingham to see productions. She suggested she take me there to try and meet John Neville, who was the director of the Nottingham Playhouse. I knew nothing much about theatres then, but I soon discovered that the Playhouse was one of the finest repertory theatres in England at the time, and its reputation was solely due to the work of the director. John Neville became very famous for his work as an actor and director. He went to Ontario, Canada, and founded the Stratford Theatre there, which became very well known throughout the world, thanks to his productions. He also had great success as an actor and was knighted. The last film I remember seeing him in was *Baron Munchausen*, the Terry Gilliam film.

So off Mrs Maclaughlan and I went to Nottingham. What I did when I got there was up to me. We arrived at lunchtime and she dropped me at the theatre bar, with the agreement of meeting again later that day. It was packed with people waiting to go into the matinee. I cruised round, looking for the director. I had seen photos of him so I had a vague idea what he looked like. Then I heard a voice at my shoulder ask, 'Need any help?'

I looked at the guy who was talking to me. He was in his thirties, wearing jeans and a T-shirt. He seemed friendly and there were loads of people around so I thought I would be safe enough.

'I'm Lynda Bellingham and I am looking for John Neville,' I replied boldly. 'I have an appointment.'

'Really? Well, he'll be around soon. He's just broken for lunch. Would you like a drink while you're waiting? I'm Patrick, by the way.'

'Why not?' I said. We spent the afternoon talking. He was an actor with the company and told me fabulous stories about the company and life in rep. Several other members of the company came and said hello as the day wore on. I was in my element, telling everyone about my audition for Central, and how I had come to see John Neville to get his opinion on my acting abilities.

'If he tells me I am no good I'll give up,' I announced to the group.

'Well, young lady, that's a big responsibility. I hope I'm up to the job.' Oh, hell! John Neville was standing right beside my chair! I leapt to my feet.

'I am so sorry, sir,' I stammered. 'It's just I really need you to audition me and give me your opinion. I must know if I have any talent.'

I explained to him that my geography teacher had brought me up to Nottingham and that she was coming back to pick me up at six o'clock.

'Well, there could be a problem, then,' he said. 'I can't see you today as there's an evening performance. What about tomorrow morning?'

'That's fine,' I replied, without a thought. 'Thank you, thank you so much.' But he had disappeared into the crowd. I turned to the actor beside me: 'What am I going to do? I have nowhere to stay.'

That was a step too far. The actor looked at his watch, made his excuses, and left. I sat in a daze trying to decide what to do. Then I saw Mrs Maclaughlan coming towards me. I explained my dilemma, but she was completely unfazed.

'I can ask one of my old students to put you up for the night on their floor. Don't worry. I'll stay with some friends and we can drive home tomorrow after you've seen him.' And that was that. She took me to supper, and then dropped me off at a house full of students. I can hardly remember that night. I know the floor was very hard but I didn't care about sleep. I just kept running my speeches through my head and praying that John Neville would think I had talent.

Bright and early the next morning I turned up at the stage door. So early that no one was there. I sat out on the step and waited. It was quite a long wait and I began to think it was never going to happen, but eventually a lady came out, and asked me if I was Lynda Bellingham, and to follow her. I walked on to the stage and gasped. It felt so good to be there. I looked round and just wanted to open my mouth and perform. Which was just as well, because that was what I was there to do. After I had finished, I stared into the lights and held my breath. How many times was I to do this in my career?

John Neville came onto the stage and stood and looked at me. It seemed like for ever.

'Well, young lady, you have talent, that's for sure. I could offer you a job here as an acting assistant stage manager, but you would spend the next year being a general dogsbody and probably get very little opportunity to áct. Much better you go back to Central and try and persuade them to take you on and then, in three years' time, you could come back here as a fully fledged actor.'

Hallelulljah! That was all I needed. I was straight back down the M1 to London.

I DECIDED NOT TO tell a soul what I was up to. Everyone at the jam factory still thought I was going to drama school because I couldn't bring myself to tell them of my rejection. So one Tuesday I called in sick, took the bus from home to town, as usual, and made my way to the station. I arrived at Swiss Cottage in North London around 9 a.m.

The Central School of Speech and Drama was originally a theatre, which is still there today. It is in a lovely leafy street just off the Finchley Road. I sat on a bench outside waiting for one of the teachers I'd met to come past. I watched with envy as students came and went. They all looked so fascinating. Just like real actors!

Finally at about 11, I recognised the lady who took the movement classes. Her name was Barbara Caister. I accosted her, and asked to see the principal, George Hall. She was rather taken aback, but took me to the front office and told me to wait. I waited another half an hour or so until, finally, I was summoned into a studio-type room. There, behind a huge table, sat most of the staff from the drama department.

'What can we do for you, Lynda?' asked George Hall.

You have to appreciate that at this point I was in such a state of panic it could have gone either way. I could have keeled over, and made a fool of myself, or I could have stood up for myself, told them what I wanted and told them what I thought of their cavalier attitude towards my career. I did a bit of both.

When I am nervous or angry, I often get tearful. So I began my plea full of verve and determined self-righteousness, and then halfway through I started to cry. I just needed them to understand how much I wanted this place, and how there was never any thought of ever going anywhere else. That all my friends had come to Central, and that I couldn't understand how, last year, they had all thought I was talented enough to join the school, and so what had happened, since, to change their minds? I told them all about John Neville, and finished up by announcing that if I was talented enough for John Neville, then I should be talented enough for them.

You could cut the silence with a knife. Finally, George Hall took off his glasses and said, 'Well, what can we say? We told you to ring at the beginning of September. Nothing has changed. I'm sorry.'

'But you can't just dismiss me!' I replied. 'Do you realise this is my life we are talking about? It is not as simple as a phone call. This is a matter of life and death to me. How can you treat people like this?'

'I'm sorry,' came back the answer. 'You will have to ring up. Thank you for coming and good luck.'

And that was it. Just like that, these people had destroyed all my hopes and dreams. The journey home was the longest of my life. I sat on the train and howled. I sat on the bus and sobbed. My father opened the front door with a smile on his face. How could he? How could I tell them I was a failure?

'Lynda. Welcome home! We're going to celebrate with my homemade elderflower wine.' Blimey, this *must* be a celebration. Dad's elderflower wine was treated like vintage Dom Perignon.

'What are we celebrating?' I mumbled.

'Your place at the Central School of Speech and Drama.'

'No,' I cried. 'You don't understand. I've failed. I...' Dad cut me off.

'Lynda, they rang while you were out. They've offered you a term's trial. You start on September the twenty-second. Well done, girl!'

In just a few hours, my life had gone from tragedy to triumph – it was always going to be like that for me. But for now it was triumph, and I was over the moon. I was on my way to stardom.

That summer passed in a haze. I triumphed as Puck at the Pendley Shakespeare Festival. I triumphed on the conveyor belt at Moorhouse's jam factory. I was a star in the Dark Lantern. All the lads said I would come back a changed woman, especially as they reckoned I would lose my virginity several times over! Finally, I said goodbye to Karel. He didn't believe I would really go. I think that because he had no ambition himself, he couldn't recognise it in others. He just didn't understand how my love of acting was all-consuming and even made me forget about him (well, sometimes. I had a bit of a plan in the back of my head that I would grow into this amazing, sophisticated woman at college and would come back home and seduce Karel one day).

It was the end of the summer and the end of my childhood. So many people go through this, don't they? It's so bittersweet: the excitement of a new life mixed with the sadness of saying goodbye to all the familiar things around us.

CHAPTER FIVE

LEARNING TO SWING
IN THE SIXTIES

I WALKED UP THE front steps of the Central School of Speech and Drama in September 1966 and it was like my life had finally begun. All around me were fellow students, laughing and shrieking. Energy and hope filled the air. The foyer of the old theatre was full of bright sparkling eyes, animated faces and long hair being tossed flamboyantly. Male and female. This was the sixties. It was just like the musical *Hair*. I expected everyone to burst into song and go into a dance routine. I pushed my way into the girls' cloakroom and was greeted by screams of delight from all the new girls. It smelled of sweat and perfume and talcum powder. Yes, this was it. The smell of the greasepaint and the roar of the crowd. Well, that was to come later but this was where I belonged.

I immediately started into my routine, telling jokes and putting myself down, but it was as though all the last few years had been a rehearsal for this moment. I fitted in here. Yes, I would have to fight my corner to be heard, but I understood all this. I was good at holding court. All those hours in the Dark Lantern were not wasted.

I unpacked my gear. All brand new, of course. My uniform. But unlike my school uniform, which I hated with a passion, this was different. I lovingly placed my black tights and leotard in the locker.

47

I hung up my dark green, full-length practice skirt, and put my dance shoes on the shelf. The tools of my trade. An actor prepares.

I wandered into the coffee bar, got in the queue and waited. The boy next to me was chatting animatedly to all who would listen. Suddenly he turned to me and asked which class I was in. I told him.

'Same as me, that's great. I'm Nik. How do you do.'

'Lynda. Pleased to meet you. Isn't this just great?'

We hit it off immediately and have been best friends ever since. Nickolas Grace has become one of Britain's leading actors, and is probably best known for his role as Anthony Blanche in *Brideshead Revisited*. Nik managed, in that first meeting, to ask me if I was still a virgin. We realised we both were, and made a pact to try and remain so for as long as we could.

We went into assembly together full of hope.

The routine in that first year was pretty easy, really. We had classes every day consisting of movement and dance and voice. Then there was the incredible George Hall, who taught musical theatre. He is the most wonderful teacher and man. So completely talented and inspiring; I just thank God I was lucky enough to work with him.

I asked George, when I left Central, what had persuaded them to take me on that day I came to visit the school. He laughed and said that they had all agreed that even if I was the worst actress in the world, I would always work because I was so pushy.

We used to have tutorials for movement and voice, where we were seen individually by the teacher. Litz Pisk was the movement teacher. She was unique, both as a teacher and as a woman. She was only four foot something tall and had a hunchback, but what she could do with her body you would not believe. She had a mane of pure white hair that she wore up in a bun. She seemed ancient to us but she probably wasn't more than forty. She was from

Austria and had a thick accent. She spoke very fast and often got things in English mixed up. This made her seem very eccentric and sometimes difficult to understand. The boys always used to take the piss out of her because she would wave her arms in the air and tell you to fly.

'Darlinks, you can do it! You can fly!' But, believe me, she was an amazing teacher.

She advised Vanessa Redgrave on her film *Isadora*, and Vanessa would come to some of our classes to work with Litz. She had been to Central a few years before so knew Litz very well. I was completely overwhelmed to find myself standing next to her. She was, and is, a legend to me.

Litz's way of teaching would be to stand you in front of a long mirror and basically pull you apart, physically and verbally. She would say to me, 'Look at you, my darlink. You are like a sack of potatoes and they are all falling out.' Posture was everything to her. I was just not the kind of actress that appealed to her (think of Vanessa and you have the one that does). Short, rather boyish girls who laughed and joked a good deal were not on Litz's radar. But I did so want her approval of me and I worked really hard in her classes.

The most wonderful thing happened years later. When they did my *This Is Your Life* in 1991, Litz was my final surprise guest. She had been retired for years and must have been in her eighties, but she travelled up from Cornwall to London to appear on the show. I could not believe it. It was such an honour. My dear mum knew how much I had adored her at drama school and, all those years later, here she was again. It meant so much to me that she came, particularly because I felt, and still do feel, sometimes, that no one has ever taken me seriously as an actress. To hear Litz announce, on television, that she had followed my career with interest, and that I worked so hard to achieve success meant the world to me. Mind you, she didn't actually say she thought I was a wonderful actress, so maybe I am deluding myself!

By now, I was living in a bedsit quite far from the college. Mum had come up to London with me to find some digs. We had trudged up and down the Finchley Road, and it was dire. Most of the places were uninhabitable: filthy dirty, and depressing.

We finally chose a room, in a huge house in Golders Green. The bus stop was right outside so it was easy to get to the college. It was one big room at the front of a house owned by an old lady. It was very dark inside, with big heavy furniture and all the chairs had antimacassars on the back. She showed us a downstairs loo, with a basin, which was for my use only, she said (but the first time I came home and went to sit on the loo she was on it!)

Thankfully, I only stayed for a couple of weeks because I managed to get a room in a house round the corner from college, where Stephanie Daniel lived. When I moved in, Mum helped me clean it. It took us three days and we both went down with a mystery bug, which I am sure we caught in there, from the filth. I painted everything white and red. I had one gas ring and learned to cook three-course meals on it. I had a white bedspread and red cushions and I painted an old chair red and had red curtains. I was so proud of it. I used to entertain all the waifs and strays. Not with my body, I hasten to say, but with my cooking. I became quite well known for my culinary skills, and for giving out TLC to young men who were too drunk to go home.

Sex was not on the agenda. Nik and I had our pact, as I mentioned, that we were going to keep ourselves pure! But it did not stop me from going out and having a good time. So much so, that by the end of the first term I was admitted to hospital with exhaustion. First they thought it was meningitis, but after tests proved there was nothing wrong with me, they decided I just needed to rest. I never do anything by halves and moderation is not in my vocabulary: I worked hard and played hard.

By the end of the first term I was told I was in for the duration and no longer on trial. I continued to dip in and out of different groups of friends and spent most of my time, as usual, with the guys in the pub. I did have one girlfriend in my class called Carolyn (Carol) von Beckdendorf. She later changed her surname to Seymour.

W HEN I VENTURED out with Carol it was to a different world. She used to frequent a club on the King's Road called the Pheasantry. It was very posh and trendy. I was like the country bumpkin following in her wake of celebrity. It was the combination of theatrical and posh that was so overwhelming to me. I was not sophisticated at all but I learned fast. We drank champagne and vodka in these places – very different from my pint of cider with the lads.

The highlight of this period was Anthony Hopkins. He was going through a very difficult period in his life and drinking heavily. He used to hold court at the Pheasantry doing his impersonation of Richard Burton doing Dylan Thomas. I used to sit on the floor, cross-legged in front of him, just listening. One night he noticed me, and we started talking – and this was the cue for Carol to interrupt and drag me off.

I had started to notice that every time someone showed an interest in me Carol whisked me away. Was it jealousy? Teenage lesbianism? A bit of both, I suspected. Whatever it was, it was very annoying, and I got fed up with it. We would have a huge row and not speak for a week, then make up, and then it would all start again. After we left college, Carol landed a dream job in a series for the BBC called *Take Three Girls*. She became very famous, along with Liza Goddard and Sue Jameson. Some years later, when I was walking along Kensington High Street, a black cab stopped and out jumped Carol. We had a tearful reunion and went and drank copious amounts of champagne in a bar and talked about old times. The whole subject of her feelings for me came up. I tried to make sense of it all.

'Did you fancy me then, Carol?'

'Darling, I adored you. You made my life hell. You were so cruel to me.'

Feeling a bit the worse for drink I decided to test her on this: 'Come on then, let's go back to your flat and make love. If it's what you've always wanted, let's do it for old times' sake.' That shocked her! I never heard another word.

I HAD MANAGED TO hold on to my virginity all through the first year, which was pretty good going, I thought. Especially as I found out that a few of the guys in my year, and some in the second year, had a bet on as to who was going to 'break me in' (a lovely turn of phrase, but one must remember that it was the sixties, and there was no political correctness then).

Towards the end of the first year I started to become aware that, as an actress, it was important to be able to use one's sexuality. Whatever that meant! I was quite self-conscious about my body and had never really thought about it in terms of attracting men. Certainly, I had not realised how important it was to be physically aware of it when performing. Of course, I knew about sex: I had loved my snogging sessions with Karel, but this was a very different ball game; I was beginning to realise there was a hell of a lot more to it than that.

I had been avidly listening to all Carol's tales about her sexual encounters and it all sounded rather distasteful to me. But for all her romantic trysts she did not have a regular boyfriend, and the boys in our class didn't seem to have much respect for her. I had been brought up to believe that respect was paramount – I must save myself for the wedding night. I was also terrified of getting pregnant. I think somewhere deep down inside, I had made a pact with myself never to do what my birth mother had done. Whatever trouble I may get into in life, I did not want to involve anybody else.

But this was the swinging sixties and sex was everywhere. Magazines like *Cosmopolitan* were full of articles telling us how to enjoy multiple orgasms. Whenever I had quizzed my mother about what an orgasm felt like she just smiled rather benignly and said, 'Oh, don't worry, Lynda, you'll just know when you are having one. It is very lovely when you are married.'

Considering that is what she said when we were watching Bill the bull service the heifers, I did not have high hopes for the whole business!

A defining moment for me was during a rehearsal for a play called, ironically, *The Rehearsal* by Jean Anouilh. I was doing a scene with the lovely Robin Nedwell (tragically, he died very young. He had found fame early in the *Doctor* series for ITV but did not follow through, and I think the dreaded drink took over for a while. He did try to make a comeback, only to be struck down). In a particular scene in the play, his character tries to seduce a young woman – me. I had to be vulnerable yet give out a sexual vibe.

Our director was not one of the regular staff. Every now and then, the college would bring in outside directors and tutors to give us a different take on things. This play was being directed by a man called Peter Oyston. He was very intense with long blond hair, and we all thought he was wonderful, especially the girls. Because I wanted to impress him, I found I was very nervous and self-conscious. I felt awkward and clumsy, and anything but sexy.

We had to show the scene in front of the whole class, before we finally performed it for the staff, as part of our end-of-term tests. Peter had made me wear a long Victorian nightie – the kind that is all white and done up to the neck. In front of the whole class, he said, 'Lynda, you're way too stiff and inhibited. I want you to take off your knickers and bra. I want you to feel your nakedness when you kiss Robin.'

Everybody sniggered. I was mortified. I cringed with embarrassment the first time I did the scene. But then when it came to the showing in front of the teachers, I had composed myself a bit and gave the performance of my life. Yes, I did feel naked and uncomfortable, but that was exactly what the scene needed. Well done, Peter Oyston.

This incident made me even more aware of my virginal status. I had been going out from time to time with a guy in the second year called John. He was pushing me to sleep with him but I was just not ready. He was also the guy who told me they all had a bet on as to who would do the dirty deed with me, so that put me right off for a start. Sod the lot of you, I thought – if I'm going to lose my maidenhood, I would choose someone who wouldn't blab. But who? I still loved Karel, really, but he was too far away and, anyway, I reckoned if he hadn't tried already he probably wasn't interested. Maybe now was the time to put into action my plan to gain experience in the bedroom, and then go home and seduce my childhood sweetheart?

At the beginning of the second year I went to live with Nik and his flatmate, Carlos de Carvalho. It was so lovely, and right in the heart of the West End in Marylebone High Street. I loved living there near all the shops, and you could walk to the theatres. It was the best address I ever had.

So here I was, in my new room, in my lovely flat, planning the assault on my virginity. I usually told Nik everything but I had decided to keep this plan to myself. Writing this now, I cannot believe I was so calculating about the whole thing. All I had ever heard from my mother was how wonderful it was to meet a man and fall in love. To discover the trust and confidence in one man and to be able to give yourself to him, completely, and want to bear his children. I still wanted that to happen, and would search for it for years. But at this moment in time it seemed the most important thing I could do was to get the whole sex thing out of the way, so I could get on with my acting. Maybe all the time spent with lads in the pub had given me a warped sense of how romance should be? Perhaps, by osmosis, I had become more like a man in my attitudes. There was sex, and there was love, and maybe the two did not always go together.

I decided who was going to be my seducer. He was called Jay and he was in my class. He was very handsome in a Brad Pitt kind of way, and all the girls fancied him. He was always with impossibly beautiful girls who looked like models. This was another reason to choose him, because it was a challenge. He was also very shy and I knew he would not tell anyone. Looking back now, I just can't believe I had all that confidence.

I got loads of wine in, so the next time he came round to see Nik I would be ready. The dreaded night arrived, and we all had supper, while I poured copious amounts of wine all evening and hovered until, finally, Nik went to bed, and Jay got up to leave. I jumped him. Well, in for a penny... He looked very taken aback and, I have to admit, not that interested, but he was a well-brought-up young man and didn't turn me down.

I would like to have been able to report here that the earth moved, and bells rang out. But sadly, real life isn't like that, is it? I hardly felt a thing. I wasn't even sure if we had done it. Climax, no.

Anti … very much. Jay sloped off into the night and I went to bed feeling decidedly let down. I awoke in the morning not so much feeling like a real woman, as feeling like a complete prat. You know that moment, in books and films, where the heroine rushes to a mirror and looks at herself, long and hard, and then smiles a little enigmatic smile? Well, I rushed to the bathroom, not to use the mirror, but to examine my nether regions. Horror of horrors! I had got crabs. Welcome to the real world, Lynda. *Cosmo* magazine forgot to mention this when it was harping on about orgasms and free love.

So that was my first introduction to sex. Not surprisingly, it took me a while to find Mr Right. Thirty-eight years to be precise. But more on that later.

CHAPTER SIX

A FINE ROMANCE

AFTER MY DISASTROUS introduction to sex, I went on a bit of a mission. I was determined to discover the secret of success in bed. Of course, this was doomed from the start, as experience has shown me that good sex is not necessarily about the mechanics, but very much about the emotional involvement. But the trouble was that I was surrounded by everyone seemingly having a wonderful time, and I wasn't.

I confessed to Nik what I had done and he was appalled. It was worse than telling my parents. He was so censorious about it. Every time I brought a bloke home he would sit and glower at us or look at his watch. One time he actually turned off the electricity. This had the reverse effect, though, as we went to bed that much more quickly! I was really very confused about sex and couldn't distinguish between the guys I liked as friends and the ones I went to bed with. I did make some good friends though, including Michael Elphick, who was in the third year. He was the kindest man, but God did he drink, even in those days. I remember sitting with him in my little bedsit, in the very early days of Central, and trying to get him to eat something. He just laughed.

'Lynda,' he said, 'I drink. I don't eat.'

'But it is so bad for you,' I replied.

'I know, darling, but listen to me, I don't want to grow old. I will be dead by the time I am forty.'

Well, he made it to his fifties and the world is a sadder place without him.

My close mates remained in my own year. The lads consisted of Robin Nedwell, David Robb, Greg Floy and David Nicholas (who is also sadly dead now), who was Robin's oldest friend from school in Wales. He was the first gay man I ever knew. No one really talked about it; David was outrageously camp and it didn't matter, except when they all came to stay for a weekend on the farm. My father took us all out on the tractor and trailer to pitch bales of hay. Nobody wanted to look a cissy, so the boys gave it their all, except David. He took one look, threw his hands up in the air and screamed, 'No, dears! I am *not* doing manual labouring for anybody. Now, where's the gin?' My father's face was a picture. But he took it all in his stride and really got on with David after that.

The other lads would spend all day on our old horse, Shammy. Tiddlywinks was long gone by now, but for some reason we had this old horse still, and the boys used him to practise for the films they were – one day – going to star in. David Robb always made us laugh because he had long blond hair and a beard, and looked like General Custer. He would sit atop the horse raising a stick in the air like a sword and practise his charge. Actors!

The rest of my time was spent with dearest Nickolas. He was the perfect student. He went to see every production in the West end. He would accept any invitations we got as students. He practised his voice exercises religiously and could stand on his head for hours! He is still very fit now, forty years on, unlike the rest of us.

Nik was the one who educated me in all things non-sexual. Although, we did have a 'moment' that I'm sure he won't mind me telling you about. After I had confessed to my escapade with Jay it took a while for us to get back on an even keel. I know he was disappointed with me and felt our friendship might be threatened if I found a boyfriend. But as the weeks went on and he realised I was quite happy with just having the odd fling, we were back to normal. Then, one day, while we were talking, he confessed he was frightened that as he did not seem to get on with girls very well, maybe he was gay. 'Nonsense,' I replied. 'Come on, I'll sleep with you and show you that you're not gay.' It may seem a bit shocking now, but don't forget that we were in the Age of Aquarius. Sex was not a big deal any more and, as Nik was my best friend, it seemed a natural thing to do. So we had a night of passion and as far as I was concerned it was OK. Quite good, in fact. Nik seemed happy enough. However, it was only a few weeks after that that he announced to me he had decided he *was* gay. Well, you can't win them all!

FINALLY, MY QUEST for romance was satisfied. That summer, in 1968, Carol and I decided to hitch to La Baule in Brittany. Carol had told me she had an aunt who lived there, so once we had got ourselves there it would be a cheap holiday. Carol's parents lived on the Isle of Wight so we decided we would take the ferry from there to St Malo, and then hitch down to the coast. I think we had twenty-five pounds each for spending money, and our return ticket on the ferry. Carol's parents were going to meet us at St Malo in two weeks' time. I had never been abroad without my parents before, and despite Carol's tall stories of world travel, I suspect that neither had she.

The crossing on the ferry was a gas. We met a group of yachts-men from New Zealand who were going down to La Baule for a regatta. Carol immediately fell in love with one of the guys and disappeared, leaving me with the rest of team. We drank copious amounts of red wine and I remember I had to leave the table rather abruptly to be sick in the loos. On my return, I didn't let on to the guys because I didn't want to look like a wuss!

By the time we arrived in St Malo, Carol had organised everything. The boys would give us a lift to La Baule, we would find her auntie and then the party would begin. Fair enough. I had started to relax a bit seeing that, actually, Carol wasn't completely useless, and had her upsides. The guys dropped us on the esplanade and went off to find their campsite.

'So, what's your aunt's address?' I asked.

'Um, I am not quite sure, darling. But don't fret, I'll remember it when I see it. Let's just wander up the promenade a bit.' An hour later, we were on our third turn of the promenade and Carol was in tears.

'I just don't know,' she wailed, 'it all looks the same!'

We then tried to find a phone box (these were the dark days without mobile phones) so we could ring her parents and check the address. We finally got through to her mum who announced that, as far as she knew, the aunt had died.

'Didn't you organise all this before we came?' I demanded.

'Oh, darling, I meant to, but you know how it is? I got waylaid.'

'*Laid* being the operative word,' I snapped. 'So, basically, we have nowhere to go and not enough money to stay anywhere?'

Carol burst into tears again. This was to become the pattern of the holiday. When things were going well Carol was the fun-loving temptress who was up for anything. But the minute things went slightly pear-shaped she collapsed in a heap.

At least I discovered I am quite practical and inventive in a crisis: 'Come on,' I said. 'Let's go and get a drink and make a plan.'

As we set off down the bloody promenade again I spotted our New Zealand friends on the beach.

'Rescue ahoy!' I said, pointing them out to Carol. She was off like a greyhound from the traps.

Within thirty minutes we were set up. The boys had an old tent we could use, so as soon as they had organised the yachts, they would take us up to the site and pitch it for us. Carol was back up to speed. She was in her element. She danced round the men like a firefly, teasing and flirting with them all till they were putty in her hands. I was quite happy to let her do all the work if it meant we had a roof over our heads.

Our roof proved somewhat lacking. The tent was very old and tiny and leaked. This we discovered the second night, to our dismay. Someone suggested we rub butter on the holes (don't ask!) So then we had a leaking roof *and* butter in our hair from where we kept hitting the top of the tent, because it was so low. After bursting into tears again, Carol pissed off and slept with her bloke every night, so it was just me who had to endure these trials. Believe me, it was a relief.

We had great fun as the whole yachting thing meant we had access to all the parties. We used to go to the casino every night and spend hours drinking and messing about. Then it was a stagger along a winding road, back up the hill to the campsite.

During the day Carol and I would sunbathe on the beach. One morning, I was lying there and a voice above me remarked, 'You have beautiful breasts.'

I opened my eyes and saw an old man standing there. Very well dressed, and not bad looking, for an old person. Looking back now, he was probably only in his early forties.

'Would you care for a coffee?'

'No thanks, I'm busy,' I snapped.

'But you don't look very busy, Mademoiselle, and I will buy you something lovely.'

'What do you mean?' I asked.

'Well, I am sure a young girl like you would love to have some beautiful clothes to wear.'

'I can buy my own clothes, thank you very much,' I retorted. Despite this, we started a conversation and I realised he thought I was some kind of waif and stray. Maybe he had a Henry Higgins-complex and wanted to turn me into a lady. Who knows? Anyway, we parted with a slight plan that we might bump into each other in the casino that night. We did. He took me to dinner while the rest of the gang looked on, from afar. They were under strict instructions to keep an eye out for me, and to come and drag me away if I gave a signal.

The guy seemed to think that I was some kind of peasant girl. I had proudly told him my dad was a farmer, thinking he would realise I was not destitute, but he must have taken that as a sign that we were mere peasants who tilled the land. All evening he kept telling me how to hold my knife and fork and which glass to use. He also spent a great deal of time trying to get his hand up my dress, under the table. When we had finished dinner, I announced I needed to get back to my friends. He shrugged his shoulders in that wonderful Gallic way and said, '*Alors, mon amie.* I give up. You do not want a present then?'

'What sort of present?'

'Some money, perhaps, to buy some clothes?'

'What do I have to do for this present?' It was slowly beginning to dawn on me exactly what was at stake here.

'Just a little kiss for me.' But where, I thought?

'Sorry,' I replied tartly, 'I don't do anyone favours for money. I am an actress, and an independent woman. Bonsoir, Monsieur,' and I flounced out.

When I told Carol and the gang they all laughed. But later Carol told me I should think about it. Just a kiss or two. What harm was there in that? And I would get some wedge.

'No, Carol. That's like being a prostitute.'

'Well, suit yourself.'

The next day I was sunning myself in my usual spot when I heard the Frenchman's velvet tones again.

'Bonjour. *Comment ça va?*'

'Fine, thank you. What do you want?'

'I have come to apologise for insulting you, Mademoiselle. I realise you are from a good family, and that you are quite correct not to accept gifts, especially money, from men. But I hope you will allow me to make amends with a small gift now. You were charming company last night, and it would give me great pleasure if you would take this money now, and buy yourself something wonderful.'

Well, what was a girl to do? Yes, quite – I took the money and ran! I bought myself some gorgeous pink cord jeans that were all the rage in France at the time, and a rose pink Shetland sweater. I was the bees' knees. Carol couldn't believe her eyes and I don't think she believed I got them for nothing. But I didn't care what she thought, because my street cred had gone up one hundred per cent.

At the end of the week we said our farewells to the yachting brigade. Carol did her *La Dame aux Camélias* act, looking sad and tragic as she waved goodbye. Needless to say, as soon as a fit guy in a car stopped to give us a lift, she was away again giving her *femme fatale* impression. You had to hand it to the girl, she was a good actress.

We arrived in St Malo in the afternoon, in time to meet the early evening ferry bringing her parents to meet us for the next leg of the holiday. We had just enough money left to buy ourselves a drink. So we did, and sat down in a café to wait. No ferry arrived. On inquiry, it was revealed that bad weather meant it had been postponed till the following day. Disaster had struck again. And yes, you guessed it – Carol burst into tears. It was now seven o'clock at night and the owner of the café was giving us funny looks. But at that moment, help arrived.

Into the square roared a red sports car. It screeched to a halt outside the café and out got the most beautiful man I had ever seen. In fact, he was exactly like the hero of a film that I had just seen called *Un Homme et Une Femme*. It was the best film I had seen for ages. Very moody and French and the music was incredible. So evocative. This bloke was *it*. White linen trousers and a white silk shirt, with slightly too-long hair, but clean and shiny and, when he smiled, a row of perfect, white teeth. Both Carol and I stared. He was followed by a rather short, slightly plump man with receding hair. As Carol moved forward to meet the Adonis, my heart sank. Guess who was going to end up with Shorty?

They were absolutely charming when we explained our plight. Well, I explained our plight because I could speak passable French. They invited us to have dinner with them in Shorty's apartment. We had great fun going round the supermarket buying groceries and such, and then we went to a lovely flat and cooked dinner. Alain, the Adonis, suggested we go on to a nightclub. Why not? So we all piled into his car and drove into town. The club was typically continental. Half outside, with lots of soft lighting in the bushes and ridiculous French pop music.

Carol was trying very hard to seduce Alain on the dance floor, while Shorty and I drank a lot. He was quite nice really, and had a good sense of humour, so I reckoned if the worst came to the worst and I had to spend the evening with him, at least it would be a laugh. But suddenly, I found myself on the dance floor in the arms of my hero. He was whispering in my ear that he thought I was very lovely and why didn't we go for a drive?

What, me? I was beside myself. I just couldn't believe my luck. I had pulled Mr Gorgeous. We drove along the coast road with the top down and, on the radio, the music from the film I loved so much was playing. Was this real? Was I in the film? Was this a dream?

We finally pulled up at a block of apartments right on the edge of the sea. I followed him in and found myself in the most exquisite room. Beautifully furnished with white sofas and glass tables. He went round opening the shutters and moonlight flooded in. The sound of the waves breaking outside made the whole thing so romantic. Alain led me upstairs to the bedroom, which contained an enormous bed with crisp white sheets, and cushions and bolsters. Rather like a magazine cover for *Good Housekeeping*. He opened the shutters in the room and the moonlight fell perfectly across the pillows.

I didn't know what to do. I was not on the pill, and my sexual experiences to date had been pretty grim. I also felt completely inadequate as the heroine in this scenario. I hated my body and just felt useless. Alain began to undress and indicated to me to do the same. This would normally be the moment when I cracked a joke. The trouble was, I could speak French OK, but not well enough to make jokes. Instead, I found myself performing an elaborate mime to indicate that the bolster on the bed must go IN the bed between us. Alain laughed and proceeded to arrange the bed as I had requested, which was something. He was a gentleman, at any rate.

I climbed into the bed and lay back on the pillows, feeling very wobbly. The linen smelled of lavender. Alain leaned across and kissed me. A long, lingering kiss. Very gentle. He stroked my face and looked into my eyes and smiled. He was so beautiful. Wasn't this what I had dreamed about? Romance? My whole body was trembling with longing for him. Was this love at first sight? I just couldn't stop kissing him. He touched me in places I didn't know existed. He told me how beautiful I was and I really began to believe I was. Every bone in my body cried out to be touched and stroked. The bolster somehow disappeared and he was making love to me. Very gently at first and then harder and harder. I pulled him into me and was completely lost to the world.

When I woke up a few hours later, I lay for a moment listening to the sea, remembering every detail of our lovemaking. Then I felt Alain stir beside me, and we were once again in each other's arms. I was completely hooked.

In the morning we had coffee and croissants in a little café by the sea, and then we drove back to town. I was dreading having to say goodbye. The tears were pricking the back of my eyes already but I put on a brave face.

We met Carol and Shorty, who seemed very cosy, and drove to the ferry. The weather was a bit grim and my hopes began to rise. Could it be possible there was a delay…? Sure enough, my fairy story continued for two days with the ferry finally arriving on the third day. Three days of love and romance. I was completely besotted. This was what my mother had tried to tell me about. Well, maybe not quite this, but near enough. When it was time to leave I stood on the quay at the end of a perfect holiday and, guess what? I burst into tears!

As we left, I knew I would never see Alain again, but it didn't matter. It had been perfect and would remain perfect in my memory. I now understood what was missing from my life. Romance.

I also understood that if I was to continue my search safely, I needed to go on the pill. When I got home to London, I went straight to the doctor and sorted myself out. I thought I was being very responsible.

So, back to college and the daily grind, and my French fancy was stored away. The final year of drama school was fast approaching and real life beckoned. Would we all be ready to take up the challenge of what lay beyond?

CHAPTER SEVEN

'I LOVE ACTING. IT IS SO MUCH MORE REAL THAN LIFE'

(OSCAR WILDE)

OUR FINAL PRODUCTION at Central was the musical *Guys and Dolls*. I played Sarah Brown, the girl in the Salvation Army. I could sing in those days; quite well, though I say so myself! It was a fantastic production directed by the wonderful George Hall and proved a fitting finale to our three years at drama school. It was so emotional leaving the place. We had all grown up so much and had all our turning points and crises, and now were on our own in the big wide world.

In those days you had to be a member of Equity to be able to work professionally, so we were all keen to get our required forty-two weeks in the theatre out of the way. This then gave us full membership status and allowed us to work in television and film. We all thought we were going to be film stars, me included, so it was a shock to find myself in weekly repertory in Frinton on Sea!

I remember Nik, who had also landed a role at Frinton with me, giving me a list of famous actors who had started their careers there which included Vanessa Redgrave.

It may not have been the Royal Shakespeare, but we did have a laugh. It was crazy trying to learn a new play every week. Especially as we would much rather sit on the beach, and sometimes I would find myself having to sit up all night to learn my lines. Each play morphed into the next and, as they were all very similar, and either a thriller or a farce, by week five I was mixing the lines up from all the bloody plays! One performance, I was sitting downstage on a stool and I felt a tug on my skirt. I looked down to see a little old lady staring up at me. I leaned down and she whispered very loudly, 'I liked you much better last week, dear!'

I had been engaged as an assistant stage manager (or ASM), also playing small parts. So not only was I a general dogsbody and scenery painter, but I was also acting at night. This meant there were some wonderful moments, such as me running on from one side of the stage to do a bit of acting, then running off the other side to bang on a water tank for a sound effect.

Every Wednesday night the set would be changed for the next play, which would open on the Thursday. This meant the scenery had to be painted overnight. Most of the plays were set in either a country cottage or a London living room, so each week we would either be painting wooden beams, à la mock-Tudor style, or wallpapering mock-Regency stripes for a townhouse lounge. It was hysterical.

It was a happy eight weeks and wonderful to be with Nik. It also gave us lots of valuable experience, especially about learning lines quickly, something you have to do in television. I kept my first professional programme in which I was billed as 'ASM: Lyfta Bellingham'! Quite appropriate, really, considering all the scene-shifting work I had had to do.

By the end of the Frinton season, things were looking up for both of us. Nik was off to the prestigious Nottingham Playhouse;

I was off to Crewe. Not so glamorous, but I was going to be playing leading roles.

M Y NINE MONTHS at Crewe were another learning curve. Not so much in terms of my acting experience, but in terms of how to live and work in close proximity with a company when you are away from home and all your creature comforts. This is where actors are like gypsies. We move around from place to place and make our lives around the people and places we find ourselves working with. I think this was the beginning of me always needing a home. A base from which to work, and somewhere to come back to. The idea of a permanent home became very important to me over the years. It was my security blanket.

We did some great stuff, including a production of *Hamlet* starring Richard Beckinsale (made famous by his role as Lennie Godber in *Porridge*, with Ronnie Barker). He was just starting his career. He was wonderful. Very undisciplined, but when he was on form he was magic. It was so very sad that he had to die so young. He was very naughty and had a wicked sense of humour. Then there was a lovely actor called Peter John, who was the longest-serving member of the company, and kept us all up to scratch. When we did musicals we joined forces with a local band, run by Frank Stubbs, who was a coalman. He and his wife, Monica, were wonderful. They would have all the actors round to a Sunday roast dinner, because they knew we never had any money. They were so kind. Frank died a long time ago now, but I still exchange Christmas cards with Monica.

In stark contrast to *Hamlet*, we did the musical *The Boyfriend* and I played Polly Browne, the lead. Unfortunately, the part was vocally too high for me and I strained my voice. One morning, I woke up, cleared my throat and thought, 'I've pulled!' My voice was so low it sounded like a man's. It proved to be a disaster as I had a nodule on my vocal cords. Nodules are caused by straining the voice, which affects the tiny hairs on your vocal cords. This is where the cords swell, and rub together, and form little nodes on the hairs, stopping the air from passing through your throat and nasal passages. This creates the husky sound you hear in some peoples' voices, and is the one thing you are taught to fear at drama school.

All that vocal training, gone to waste. I went to see a specialist who informed me I had two choices. Surgery, which could be dangerous and not completely successful, or silence for three months. Can you imagine what I felt hearing that? I had only just begun my career and now I had to stop speaking for three months. Well, I had no choice. Once again, I had to make the best of things. I went home to my parents and stayed there for the duration. I used to go round with a pad and pencil and write everything down. It was an interesting experience because, when my mother would explain to people that I couldn't speak, nine times out of ten they then shouted things at me. One day, my mum, who was never rude to anyone, turned to a shop assistant who was loudly asking me what it was I wanted and said, 'I told you she can't speak. She is not, however, hard of hearing.' God bless her!

After the three months, my voice was on the mend but it made me very aware of not straining it again, especially if I was going to do a musical. Which, as luck would have it, was something I was about to embark on again.

WEST SIDE STORY is one of the most exciting musicals ever written, in my opinion, and I heard that Coventry Theatre was going to be casting for it very soon.

It was 1971 and I was working as a telephonist at the British Drama League. This was an old and established society for theatrical usage. It combined a reference library, with courses for young people in all aspects of the theatre. It was headed by a real character called Walter Lucas. Nik Grace had made his acquaintance during his school days, and Walter had taken us both under his wing and, in my case, given me the job on the switchboard.

It would be hard for anyone born after 1960 to begin to imagine this contraption. It was a board with rows of sockets, and one sat with a head-set on and plugged connecting wires into the sockets as calls came in. It was ancient. If it was busy, I lost track of who was speaking to whom, on what line, and had to pull them all out and start again!

There was an actress called Fenella Fielding who used to ring quite a lot because she was friends with a man who worked at the British Drama League. I loved her very low, very posh, husky voice, and I could do a mean impersonation of her on the quiet. One day, she called and asked to be put through to this man, and I just couldn't resist responding in her voice. There was a silence on the end of the line, and then she said, 'Are you taking the piss?' I was so surprised I hung up. Then later I plucked up courage to call back and apologise. She was not very amused.

While I was working at my telephonist's job, I would often have to oversee auditions that would be held in the rehearsal room, which was booked by any producers and directors who wanted to use it. I would show people in and make the director and suchlike tea and coffee. I would then wait till the end of the day and, after they had seen everyone, I would burst through the door and try and impress them with my talent: 'Hi! guess what? I'm not really a telephonist. I am a budding actress and I am begging you to please give me an audition!' Amazingly, it worked most of the time.

However, when they were auditioning for *West Side Story*, I was not so lucky. I was told by the assistant director that the director, Roger Redfarn, was only going to be seeing people up in Coventry and I would have to ring up. No problem. I was straight on to the switchboard. I tried every day for a week. The answer was always no. Finally, on the last try he said yes! I have no idea why, but maybe he just wanted to shut me up. I took the train to Coventry and got the part of Rosaria, one of the girls in the Puerto Rican gang who sing '(I want to be in) America' with Anita. Of course, I really wanted to play Anita, but that was pushing my luck. I had so little experience. But I was happy. It was going to be a big production that would attract lots of people from London to come and see it.

With this new role, I was part of a wonderful company made up of many different types of entertainers. Roger Redfarn was fast acquiring a reputation as a great director of musicals and he had hired a choreographer called Sheila O'Neil to handle all the dance routines. There were dancers brought up from London to do the hard bits and we actors were sort of slipped in between. The dancers taught the actors to dance and the actors gave the dancers tuition with their lines. So many people remain locked in my heart from this time: Leo Dolan, who was one of the funniest men I ever knew. We became firm friends, and I introduced him to his wife, Sheila Mackintosh, and am godmother to their daughter, Joanna. They also have a son, Luke, who is now a producer on *The X Factor*.

Leo and I played a husband and wife in a play about Burke and Hare called *The Body Snatchers*. We used to crouch in the dark, supposedly terrified of these two dastardly men and, at one point, I had to scream loudly. As you will recall, I had only just recovered from losing my voice, so this was not a good idea, night after night. But Leo hit on the solution: he would do the screaming for me, then I would run on and say my lines!

We were also sharing our dark corner with the wondrous Carmen Silvera, of *'Allo 'Allo!* fame. We used to spend every night in fits of laughter, because Carmen had a terrible wind problem. She would happily scoff baked beans on toast at tea time and then Leo and I had to suffer the consequences.

Then there was Gareth Hunt, God rest his soul. A beautiful man. He was the leading man at Coventry at the time and did he know it. He was very popular with the ladies. When we did *The Prime of Miss Jean Brodie*, and we were all playing the schoolgirls, he had a full-blown fan club! Leo and he became very good friends, and when times were hard over the years, they used to have a decorating business together. A far cry from Gareth's starring days in *The New Avengers*. Then there was Wally Michaels, a Ukrainian dancer from the wilds of Saskatchewan, Canada. He has become a lifelong friend and now lives in Toronto.

I HAD BY NOW got myself an agent, Peter Campbell, and he had an assistant called Felicity Larner. We had become good friends. She had a flat in Maida Vale and needed a lodger. The timing was perfect. I had left Coventry and got a small part in a television series called *The Misfit*, starring Ronnie Fraser. I had been away from London for the last year and a half. My flat-sharing with Nik had reached a natural conclusion, for many reasons, but mainly because we were both off discovering ourselves and doing what we had to do. We were too close as friends to part company for ever but, at this moment in time, we needed a break from each other.

So here I was in my new flat about to embark on my first television role, with a group of actors who were as famous for their drinking as they were for their TV roles. And these guys were *serious* drinkers. In fact, it seemed to me that most of the drama staff was on the pop. Someone once said to me that going into the bar at ATV was like joining a cocktail party that had been going on for twenty-five years. The rehearsals would start at 11 a.m. and be over by noon so they could all get to the bar! Every day Ronnie would come in and rehearse, holding a large glass of water. Why does he drink so much water, I wondered to myself? The answer became very clear, one day, when I asked him if I could have a sip. It was neat vodka. Help!

I was playing a hippie, with a boy who had a guitar. They had asked me if I could sing. Yes. Play the guitar? No problem (well, I could learn!) I even had the cheek to suggest I could write a song that I could sing, while accompanying myself on the guitar. I only got away with this ridiculous fabrication because I could play the piano a bit. I had a go on the piano in the rehearsal room, and wrote a little ditty which this bloke then transposed for the guitar and taught me the chords. Job done!

All the starring actors were very funny and witty and flirted with me outrageously. I loved it. They would often go out, after we finished, for a long lunch at the local Italian restaurant. One day, they asked me to join them. By the end of the afternoon I didn't know where I was, or what day it was. They poured me into a taxi and sent me home. I rang my mum, in tears, saying I could never be a star, because I could never keep up the drinking.

Then one day, Ronnie Fraser rang my mum and asked her if he could take me to Paris for dinner.

'Don't be ridiculous,' came her reply. 'How will she get home?' Ronnie was very sweet and, in the years to come, I would often bump into him in the Richard Steele pub in Haverstock Hill, Hampstead. I even met up with him, one day, when he was out drinking with his old buddy, Robert Mitchum. Yes, I drank with Robert Mitchum!

The trouble was, I drank with everyone. At this stage in my life it was more a game: if you didn't drink you were out in the cold.

My love of being with the lads was still with me, and to keep that going meant I was entering the ring with the big boys.

My second job on television could not have been more different. I went up to Leeds, to Yorkshire TV, to do two episodes of *Kate*. It was all about an agony aunt played by Phyllis Calvert, who was a very famous and respected star, and also quite old fashioned. At the beginning of rehearsals, I was told by Pieter Rogers, the producer, that I must address her as Miss Calvert, until she told me to do otherwise. This was fine by me, but there was another young actress in the show who was very edgy and rebellious, and she was having none of it. She was downright rude for no reason whatsoever, as far as I could see; she just wouldn't play the game, and she got the sack. That taught me a useful lesson in diplomacy. Showbiz is as much about whom you know as what you know, so it's important always to be good to people on the way up because you may meet them on the way down!

I was very nervous, because although I had just done the other little job in *The Misfit*, it was such a small part it had hardly given me a chance to learn any technique at all. Now that I had a proper role, I had a good deal to learn about lighting and camera angles and all the rest of it. Someone had said to me not to let on it was my first real role on TV, but I took no notice of this advice, thank God, because I told everyone, and they were all so kind and helpful.

Whenever I wasn't needed, I would stand at the side and watch and learn. One day, Phyllis Calvert called me over and invited me to join her and Penelope Keith for a coffee. Well, I was very flattered. They had a special area at the side of the studio where they could sit when they were not wanted. It was like a green room, but for their personal use only. It was like being in a private sitting room, with a sofa and armchairs. There was a coffee table, laid with coffee and biscuits and, as I walked in, Penny was pouring out glasses of sherry!

'Would you like one, Lynda?'

'Um, no, thanks very much.'

I was completely out of my depth as they proceeded to talk about gardening. Not something I was interested in. But at least I had been accepted into the fold. It was a lovely job. Very civilised. I was put up in a wonderful hotel and went out to dinner every night. This is the life, I thought.

I DID VARIOUS BITS of telly over the next year. I spent some time in Manchester doing a series called *A Family At War*. It was a very exciting place to be then, because there were several theatres and a small studio theatre called The Stables. Many careers were started here. I remember seeing a new play by a wonderful writer, Jack Rosenthal, and watching a young actress called Maureen Lipman there. Many of the stars of *Coronation Street*, which was filmed in the studio next door, would take time out to appear in plays at this small theatre. I loved going to Manchester: it was before WAGS were invented, but there were still lots of footballers to watch. It was the Georgie Best era and he was king of the clubs. I saw him surrounded by girls one night. He was very gorgeous but would never have looked twice at someone like me. He did go out with Sinead Cusack for quite a while around this time. She had a lot of class, I must say.

CHAPTER EIGHT

DREAMS, DISCOVERIES AND DISAPPOINTMENTS

Y NEXT BIG job was a tour of *Salad Days* in 1971, produced by Cameron Mackintosh. It was to be his first production as a professional producer. Cameron was an avid fan of Julian Slade who wrote the musical, so it was a fitting debut.

It was wonderful to be back treading the boards. It is such a different kind of acting to TV or films (not that I had any experience of films, yet). It's always a problem for English actors to keep a foot in both these camps. In America, there's New York, which has a theatre history; and then there's LA, which is the land of the movies. Nowadays, television also plays a huge part in terms of entertainment but, twenty-odd years ago, film actors in America never did telly. It was considered very low rent. You were either a theatre actor, in which case Hollywood producers reckoned you were too theatrical to do movies, or you were a child of the film genre, and hardly ever strayed into the theatre. Here in the UK, there were so few films we didn't have the same problem, but there was still a feeling that you were either a theatre actor or you did TV. I was determined not to fall into either category. I was going to do everything. In order to keep my hand in, therefore, it was important to keep going back to live theatre.

Salad Days is classic English theatre at its best. The cast for this production were all quite young and inexperienced and, I suspect, cheap. Always an important criterion for producers. We opened at the Harrogate Theatre in Yorkshire. What a lovely place to be, and it hasn't really changed all that much over the years, apart from the crowds of people who now visit every year. Betty's Tea Shop, where I used to have my poached eggs on toast as regular as clockwork, is still there, just twice the size!

It was a very happy time and I was in my element. I was twenty-three and fancy free. There was still no regular boyfriend in my life, but I had decided there was no place for anyone. I had to concentrate on my career. After three weeks in Harrogate, we were off on our UK tour. It was a hard slog and relentless. Eight shows a week, come rain or shine. Even illness. In Birmingham, I can remember having to go on for the Saturday matinee with the runs and sickness. They gave me a bucket in the wings and, if the need took me, I would dance off into the wings for a few seconds, be sick, then dance back on again!

After about ten weeks, we arrived in Croydon. We could all commute to the venue, which meant we could live at home for a week, which was bliss. By this time the whole tour was a bit of a chore. I was struggling with my voice again because of singing every night. I didn't want to tell anyone because in this business if they think you are not one hundred per cent fit you will not get the job.

Word had gone round that we were getting a new addition to the band, and that he was very hunky. Sure enough, I looked into the orchestra pit during a dress rehearsal one day, and saw this gorgeous guitar player smiling up at me. Things were looking up. Every male member of our cast was gay so there had been no romance for weeks. I, and another girl in the cast, set our caps with a vengeance.

The third night of our gig in Croydon there was a power cut all over London, something you pray for some nights, in a long run, as we had to abandon the show halfway through. As we were walking out of the stage door, I made a beeline for the guitar player.

'Fancy a drink? We're all going to the pub for a few bevvies to celebrate our freedom.'

'Why not?' came his reply, accompanied by a dazzling smile.

We had a lovely evening and got on like a house on fire. As usual, once I had a few drinks inside me I knew no fear, and I was flirting outrageously. I suggested we went and had a curry, on our own. I could see Jeanie, the other actress who fancied him, bearing down on us and I did not want to share him.

'I can do better than a curry,' he said. 'I know a great little restaurant in Mayfair.' Mayfair, eh? That was posh. When we arrived the whole restaurant was candlelit due to the power strike so it was incredibly romantic. I was falling in love already. He told me all about himself. He was Robert Mackintosh, brother of Cameron, and he wanted to be a singer and musician. He was doing this gig while he got his act together. I was completely smitten. We went back to my flat and made use of the darkness.

Robert and I moved in together. I adored him and we had such plans. I don't think his mother was thrilled. Diana Mackintosh was like the Queen Mother. Very impressive. In those days her son, Cameron, was not the King of the West End that he is now but, even so, no one was good enough for her boys. I think his dad liked me a lot, though. Ian was a real character and played the trombone. He liked a tipple and his idea of a good time was to play his trombone into the early hours. When everybody else had gone to bed, I would still be there listening to him.

It was 1972, life was sweet and, to top it all, I got an amazing job. A leading character in a new afternoon soap called *General*

Hospital, with ATV. It was the first daytime soap and everybody was very excited about it. When they were casting it, I went along and was turned away because they wanted a very pretty nurse and a fat nurse, and I didn't fall into either category. So I went away and made a plan. I would turn up again for the part of the fat nurse and persuade the producer to have me. This I did. I wore flat shoes and a dress that cut my legs across the calves, making them look twice their normal size. I put my hair in a bun and rouged my cheeks. I forced my way into the casting office and demanded to see the producer. It was just like my audition for Central all over again as I battered the poor man into submission, telling him that television did not take enough risks with new young talent, and that they were not imaginative with the casting.

To my complete astonishment I got the part. I was going to be a star! I had it all now. A terrific new job and a beautiful man who loved me and had asked me to marry him. Yes, I was sporting a black pearl engagement ring (too late, I discovered that black pearls are considered unlucky).

The pretty nurse was going to be played by an actress called Judy Buxton. We were to be great friends for a year. I remember buying a quarter-bottle of champagne and some orange juice to make Buck's Fizz to celebrate Judy's birthday, and all the older actors shaking their heads and saying we would soon be drinking ourselves to death! Sadly, on this job, the older members of the cast would often cast doom and gloom on us, saying we were getting above ourselves, and that it would all end in tears.

I know that I was always aware of the dangers of my way of life, especially when they sometimes took me over. During the year I spent in *General Hospital* my relationship with Robert was getting rocky. I became insensitive and selfish, and far too full of myself. I was cruel and thoughtless.

Robert was a year younger than I, but he was quite mature, and tried to get me to calm down and take things more seriously. A big bone of contention between us was my smoking. Because I had had all the trouble with my voice, he wanted me to stop, for obvious reasons. I just thought he was being bossy and controlling. I would also stay in the bar at the studios late after the recordings, rather than going home, doing my usual thing of showing off and entertaining everyone. It was never a question of having other men, as such, just other people taking my attention. If I could have an audience I was happy.

During my year at ATV there were all sorts of distractions. The studio made big musical spectaculars for American TV and I was able to sit in the studio and watch people like Barbra Streisand singing live. Tom Jones and Engelbert Humperdinck were there all the time, too. They had massive caravan-dressing rooms in the car park, and there would always be hundreds of screaming girls at the gate. Sometimes there would be screaming mothers asking for their daughters back!

One of my ambitions since childhood was to scat sing with Sammy Davis Jr. For those too young to know who Sammy Davis is, let me enlighten you. During the fifties and sixties there was a group of American singers called the Rat Pack. It consisted of Frank Sinatra, Dean Martin, Joey Bishop, Peter Lawford, and Sammy Davis Jr who was not only famous for being a singer but for being a black, Jewish singer. He was amazing. Really tiny, like a doll, with enormous energy and verve. He used to improvise his songs like they do in jazz; turning his voice into an instrument. It was called scat singing. When I was growing up on the farm I used to hold a ping-pong bat like a microphone and practise scat singing for hour after hour. I had a fantasy that one day Eamonn Andrews would approach me with his big red book and say: 'Lynda, this is your life and the special guest for you today is Sammy Davis Jr!' Sammy would then come on and we would do a duet together. Now, suddenly, here I was in a studio at Elstree and, singing in front of me, live, was the man himself!

He was a guest with Anthony Newley and they were singing 'Gonna Build a Mountain', which was Tony Newley's big hit. Around midday, they broke for lunch and, as the band was packing up, Sammy Davis Jr was chatting to his make-up girl. Before I could stop myself, I was across the floor and tapping him on the shoulder.

'Excuse me, Mr Davis, could I ask you a favour?'

He swung round, looked me up and down and said, 'Who the fuck are you? First aid?' (I was still in costume, of course.)

I explained I was an actress from the studio next door and that I had always wanted to scat sing with him. He waved the band back and handed me a mike.

'Take it away, girl. What do you want to sing?'

'Well, what you were just singing with Mr Newley will do.'

And there I was, singing with the great man, and giving it all I'd got. Suddenly, I felt my feet leave the ground – I was walking on air! No, I was being physically removed from the studio by a big, burly security guard. When I got to the canteen, the crews all gave me a round of applause. Oh, happy day!

ROBERT AND I had a big bust-up at the end of 1971. I had stopped smoking for a while, and then on New Year's Eve, after a few drinks, I had started again. Robert was angry and disappointed with me; we rowed and he packed his things and left.

I threw myself into *General Hospital*. It was hard work, six days a week, but I loved it. There was always so much going on. I had made friends with a make-up girl called Pat Hay. (She is still one of my closest friends today. She is extremely talented and, after she left ATV and went freelance, she did many fantastic films and TV series. I think she is one of the best in the UK. Sadly, she has suffered like the rest of us in this industry because there is so little work and so many talented people available. She's the make-up designer on *New Tricks* at the moment.

Pat I and I formed our friendship for life as we set about enjoying being in regular employment in London. Pat shared a mews flat with her best friend, Anne, from their childhood in Glasgow. I was footloose and fancy-free again, and determined to stay that way until I had made a real name for myself.

It was around this time that I first met Christopher Biggins. He lived on Charing Cross Road, in a little flat above the Phoenix Theatre in London. We gradually began to form a big circle of mates. There was Jack Tinker, the theatre critic; Marilyn Johnson, a casting director; Bryn Lloyd, a wonderful Australian casting director who then formed his own agency for making trailers for films; my flatmate, Flic; and a director on *General Hospital* called Malcolm Taylor, and his wife Annie. Others came and went, but we were all round each other for a few years, and still are.

They were heady days. We were all just starting out in our chosen careers. We didn't have much money but we knew how to enjoy ourselves. We would take turns in giving long Sunday lunches – they started out as dinners, but then we would play poker or silly parlour games and the evening would go on all night. So, we decided to make them at lunchtime, but they *still* went on all night!

Flic and I would have the odd gentleman caller. Poor Flic was desperate to fall in love and find a husband. Her mother's maxim was: 'It is better to have been married and divorced, than never to have been married at all.' I didn't agree and kept trying to persuade Flic that the more she kept looking for Mr Right, the less likely she was to find him. One morning, I wandered into the kitchen to find a gorgeous hunk making a cup of tea. One of Flic's better choices. He was also absolutely charming. After he had left I said to Flic, 'Well he was fab. Will he be coming round again?'

'I don't expect so,' she smiled sadly. 'He's off to LA soon to make his fortune.'

'Well, he should do well, looking like that. What's his name?'

'Pierce Brosnan,' came the reply. Enough said!

One evening, Flic had a dinner party. I arrived halfway through because I had been working. Flic had told me that she had met a young, struggling film producer called Greg Smith. She thought he was very nice and she wanted my opinion. Plus she reckoned it would be good for me for future work prospects.

I can't remember who else was there, but as soon as I sat down, this Greg Smith character started to have a go at me. Not in a horrible way, just a lot of teasing. He was very cocky and thought he knew it all. I was also a Miss Know It All at this point, as I considered myself well on the way to fame and fortune – not like this young upstart who was still struggling to put a film together. Right from the start we were bandying words about and challenging each other.

Finally, I made my excuses and went to bed to let Flic get on with it. Greg was exactly who I would have expected my flatmate to fancy: he was flash and cocky and obviously had an eye for the ladies. Which didn't bode well for a long relationship.

About half an hour later there was a knock on my bedroom door. It was Greg, asking me if he could see me tomorrow.

'No, you're here to see Flic,' I replied indignantly.

'Look, I'm sorry, but Flic is just a friend. Please meet me tomorrow. I'm going away the day after on holiday to Malta.'

'I don't know. I'll think about it. Now go away.' I shut the door in his face. I think I was a bit flattered that I had made such an impression on him but I decided not to say anything to Flic at that point. The next day, Greg called me.

'Does Flic know you are ringing me?' I asked.

'Yes, I told her I was going to ask you out.'

'What did she say?'

'She was fine about it. I told you, we're just friends, that's all.' I was not convinced that that was exactly what Flic had thought. Anyway.

'Please will you have dinner with me tonight?'

'I can't,' I replied. 'I'm already seeing my friend Leo and his girlfriend.'

'All right, I'll take you all out.'

Well, that did it. None of us had two shillings to rub together and this was a free meal.

'OK. Fine.'

I rang Leo (Dolan) and Sheila, full of it. I told them we were going to dinner with a film producer who fancied me, and they could have a look and tell me what they thought.

Greg took us to a very nice Indian restaurant on the Edgware Road, near where he lived. He was good company and full of stories. He had been an agent before, and now was trying to produce films. He obviously loved the industry and was very animated and upbeat.

Like a lot of men who are or become successful, Greg had an aura about him. Although he was a bit on the flash side, he was charming and bright. I really warmed to him, and Leo and Sheila gave me the thumbs-up sign when they left. I walked back to Greg's flat and he asked me up for a brandy. I was curious to see where he lived and he had also told me about his dog, a red setter called

Zackary. We talked for a long time and drank a lot of brandy. Greg told me he was separated from his wife, Cheryl. He was so sensitive about her and their relationship, I thought what a decent man he was and began to think there may be something between us. This was the usual pattern for me. I drink for Dutch courage and end up losing all my inhibitions. Once again I fell into bed without a thought.

In the morning I left very swiftly. I was disappointed with myself. I hadn't found Greg *that* attractive, and I had no intention of seeing him again. So why had I behaved like a slut?

He rang me later from the airport and was very keen to meet up when he returned from his holiday. I wasn't so sure. I told Flic about it, and apologised for nicking her potential bloke.

'He's much more your type anyway,' I said.

'Oh, he didn't fancy me at all. And he was besotted with you! Don't worry, Lynda. I'll get my own back one day and pinch one of yours!' She is a lovely woman.

Life went on and I forgot all about him. Three weeks later, I got a call. He was back. When could he see me? I was away that weekend to stay with my old pal, Nik Grace, who was at the Royal Shakespeare in Stratford upon Avon. Since we had parted company, Nik had progressed through the ranks of legitimate theatre and was earning a reputation for himself as a serious actor. Greg offered to drive me. What could I say?

We spent the weekend with Nik and had a good time. It was so good to see my dearest friend. As in the old days, I don't think he was very impressed with Greg, but then it was always difficult with him because we were so close.

From then on, Greg pursued me with a vengeance. I can honestly say I really wasn't that interested, but he drew me into his life. He was trying to set up a film called *Confessions of a Window*

Cleaner – hardly intellectual stuff – from a series of books written by a man called Christopher Wood.

As time went on, I realised Greg had no money at all. Not a bean. This was the story of my life: there has not been one serious relationship – until now – with a man where I did not have to keep him.

Greg finally got the money together to begin casting on his film. I suggested my friend, Marilyn Johnson, to cast it. So far, she had not done any films so it was a useful notch on her belt, although I'm not sure it would have been her first choice of film, but there you go. The most vital role in the film was the window cleaner. Because there was a good deal of sexual activity in the script, it had to be someone who had oodles of charm and could take the edge off the sexual content and make it fun.

Previously to this, the only slightly risqué films were the *Carry On* series starring Sid James, Barbara Windsor and the gang. What Greg hoped to do with the *Confessions* films was make them sexier, and grab a more adult audience. Not overtly pornographic or anything, just naughtier. These were still early days as far as censorship was concerned and were the days of 'X'-rated as the top of the range for the over-eighteens. None of this 12- or 15-certificate stuff. The films look so tame compared to what is on offer nowadays, but at the time, when the first *Confessions* film came out, it caused quite a stir because of the nudity and sexual content.

I had recently seen an advert for Kit Kat on the TV, starring a bloke as a window cleaner. I recognised him as an actor who had been in quite a lot of TV and films. His name was Robin Askwith; I suggested him to Greg, and a star was born.

Dear Robin was a one-off. Completely mad. He still is. He had a mop of blond hair, a cheeky grin and a wicked sense of humour. He was perfect for the part. He was also very professional and very good at his job, something I don't think he got enough credit for, as the focus, as far as the critics of the film were concerned, was always on the girls and the nudity. Of course, the script was incredibly sexist and very un-PC. But this was 1974!

My relationship with Greg, meanwhile, had developed into a full-blown affair. Well, of sorts. We didn't live together and I was still very much into doing my own thing and getting on with my master plan to become a star. There was also a problem in the physical side of our relationship. During the first six months all was reasonably OK, but I have to say that our sex life wasn't the best, and not very frequent.

I can't remember exactly when I suddenly realised we had not made love for weeks, but I talked to my mother about it and she suggested it was simply pressure of work. Maybe. I mentioned it to Greg and he agreed he was working very hard and he did find it difficult to turn his attention to me sometimes.

But Greg was always on the phone to me, two or three times a day, and we were always out and about with Robin, and then later Linda Hayden, who was cast to play his girlfriend in the film. She was young and gorgeous, and she and Robin soon became an item. Greg was outnumbered by the actors, but he loved holding court, as a producer, and putting us in our place. Or so he thought.

I loved the camaraderie. We were all very excited about the film: Greg's oldest friend, Norman Cohen, was going to direct it, so it was very much a case of the gang makes good.

It was around this time that I began to notice some of the photos that were being sent to Greg. These were photos and CVs of 'supposed' actresses who were looking for work. Lots of them were nude! I even read one letter that stated: 'All producer's requirements would be met.' Oh, really, and what were they?! I quizzed Greg about this, and he just laughed and said some of the applicants were, indeed, old slappers and, of course, he just threw their stuff in the bin. When I told my parents about this, my mum said she thought I should consider the possibility that Greg had another woman. I laughed. Not because I was particularly confident about myself and our relationship, but because he was never off the phone to me. He always wanted to know what I was up to when he was not around. If he was so concerned about me, how could he be unfaithful elsewhere?

How naive can you be? How stupid was I? It all came to a head one evening when I was having a drink with my old mates Gareth Hunt and Leo Dolan. Gareth let slip he had been seeing an actress called Olivia, and she had suddenly given him the elbow because she was going to marry a film producer called Greg Smith.

My stomach lurched to my mouth and then plummeted to my toes. Married? I was in shock. Both the guys realised that something was wrong, and once I had explained, Gareth kept apologising and saying he was sure he had made a mistake. But I knew, the way you just do. Everything fell into place. How could I not have suspected? Even my mother had connected with the possibility that he was straying.

I drove to Greg's flat, completely numb but somehow very calm. It was as if I had been let off the hook. I knew the relationship was not right and I knew also that I didn't really want to get too involved because of my career. But why did it have to be like this? I felt so humiliated and betrayed by his disloyalty, not least after all the support I had given him, both emotional and financial, to make the film a success.

When I confronted him, Greg embarked on a tirade of attack. Well, it is the best means of defence. He denied it all and said I was mad. The girl was a fantasist. He had cast her in the film but that was all. I was to stop worrying. For my own good I had to trust him, because there were always going to be women throwing themselves at him. It was the nature of the job. But what about our sex life? He just said again it was pressure of work. Then he took me in his arms and told me how much he loved me, and needed me, and that nothing could break us up as a team.

I should have followed my instinct and left then and there.

CHAPTER NINE

'WE MAY GIVE WITHOUT LOVING, BUT WE CANNOT LOVE WITHOUT GIVING'

(BERNARD MELTZER)

THE NEXT TWO years were a rollercoaster ride. God knows why I stayed with Greg. Once the trust was gone it was impossible to regain and, anyway, the house of cards was falling down round my ears at every turn. Girls, like the one I had found out about, were not only ruthless in their pursuit of Greg; they were jealous of me as an actress. I was doing OK, and I did not have to send photos of myself, nude or otherwise, to producers to get work.

While they were filming at Elstree Studios, I would receive God knows how many calls from different women. Always in the same vein. The worst call I ever received went something like this:

'Hi, how are you? Do you know where Greg is? I'm waiting for him to arrive.' A pause, then, 'Don't you mind him screwing me?'

At first I tried to laugh it off with my best line: 'Well, tell Greg his dinner is in the dog, then.'

The response to this was, 'Tell the dog that Greg is in me.'

It was so horrible and I did not know how to handle it.

Greg just lied, barefaced, to me, that it was all my imagination.

My parents were very supportive and I could talk to them about everything. My father just couldn't understand how Greg could not fancy me. What was the point of having the relationship? The more I tried to understand, the more I found myself being pulled back into the problem. Greg insisted I could help him through it. That it was just a phase. He did fancy me, and he did love me, but he needed help. OK.

I thought I was strong enough to give him that help.

Things, however, were going on in my life, too. I had been to a party at my agent's office and met a beautiful man called Norman Eshley. I had been standing in the midst of a crowd of people, all talking at the top of their voices, and had looked across the room and noticed an amazing-looking man in a white suit, towering above the heads of everyone. It was like a sequence in a film: suddenly, there was silence and, as our eyes met, everything faded into the background. He had given me a dazzling smile, but then the moment had been broken by a shift in the crowd.

All night we kept catching each other's eye. It was a game. We were introduced, and discovered we were both actors, and both Geminis. There was an instant attraction, not just physically; we both recognised something in each other. Just as I was about to leave, Norman caught my eye and mouthed, 'I suppose a fuck is out of the question?'

My knees buckled. It was so blatant. And so exciting!

The next day I got a call from Norman and met him for a drink. He was doing something at the BBC. I learned he was married, and separated, from Millicent Martin, the very famous and wonderful singer and actress who used to appear in *That Was The Week That Was*, hosted by David Frost. He was hurting very badly and was obviously still in love with her. I poured out my story about Greg.

We were so alike. Male and female versions of each other. We were both complete romantics underneath, but terrible slappers at the same time.

I felt I had known Norman all my life, and that he completely understood where I was coming from. We were also both drinkers who drank for courage. We fell into bed together.

Fortune smiled on us, as the next morning there was a strike, and no one could go to work. So Norman stayed. We went out for suitable groceries (wine and a bit of cheese, that sort of thing) and just laughed and talked and made love. We gave each other confidence and a shoulder to cry on.

Over the next couple of years we would meet up, in between going back to our partners, and remind ourselves that we were nice people, and we were attractive, even if the object of our desire did not desire us. I loved Norman a good deal, in my way. Of course, he was always letting me down as well. There were always other women, but I didn't mind so much with him because I understood him. The need for the attention. The feel-good factor of the chase and being wanted. I recognised it in myself.

It's interesting that I should call myself a slapper from this episode. As ever, it was much more difficult for a woman to live like that in society, because she was labelled a slut or promiscuous. Considering we had been through the sixties, and women had burned their bras for equality, it would appear, even those days, to have been in vain. But don't judge me: I had many more mistakes to make before I found the true me.

Greg and I continued to stumble on. He was on his way up and did have the grace to recognise my part in it, to an extent, but I was becoming more and more unhappy when I was in his company. Dear Robin Askwith tried so hard to keep us all together as a group. We had some very happy times and the first film was a huge success. I did meet some lovely people, like Linda Agran, who went on to become one of the most successful women in television. I would take refuge in her friendship. She was working for David Niven Jr at the time. I also had another dear friend called Jennie Carr, who died tragically of a brain tumour. These women were my saviours because I felt so isolated much of the time.

The next film in the series that was set up was *Confessions of a Pop Performer*, in 1975. Greg was on a roll, and roll he did, with every actress who would have him.

There is a horrible thing that men like Greg do to their women, which makes them think they are really going crazy. He would always make me think I was imagining everything. The phone would ring and he would answer it, then glance at me, and I would know he was talking to a woman, but if I tried to grab the phone, he would hang up, or a couple of times he actually pulled the phone cable out of the wall. Then he ranted at me that I was impossible and neurotic and imagining things.

I was becoming more and more obsessed with trying to catch him out, and I decided to catch him 'at it'; an evening that was to prove the nadir of my relationship with him.

As far as I knew, Greg was in his flat with a girl, and I waited outside, thinking she would be leaving at some point, because Bill Maynard was staying with him, and he would be home later. I waited and waited. Hours and hours. To the point where I was desperate to go to the loo.

I didn't want to leave my post because I had waited so long. I had a blanket on the back seat of the car so I reached back for it, folded it up, sat on it, and peed. I couldn't believe I had reached so low a point in my self-esteem. I was at my wits' end. I couldn't sit there like that, so I drove home and just cried myself to sleep.

NONE OF MY successes had made me feel any better about myself, or helped me deal with my wayward man. I felt that as long as I did not have to know about all the shenanigans, I could cope. But it was impossible to ignore them when I was confronted by some of the women in public. Wherever I went with Greg, there would be a girl hovering at his elbow, trying to catch his eye. I knew there was all sorts going on and used to quiz Linda Hayden and Robin but they were very loyal to Greg. It must have been awful for them really, because who wants to get involved in stuff like that between a couple? They had to work with him.

Finally, I decided enough was enough. I told Greg it was over.

My guardian angel was on my side, because at this point I got a commercial that was filming in the Caribbean. I could fly away, out of reach.

It was a commercial for Dry Cane rum, to be shown in cinemas. Normally, these adverts for drinks were full of gorgeous girls, and when I told a couple of people about the job they looked amazed that I was going to be in one. But in this particular commercial there was a lot of comedy. I was playing a very English, rather upper-class girl in a boat with her young man, played by Royce Mills. Royce was a very funny actor who did a lot of farce with Ray Cooney.

As usual, the production company seemed to want to spend as much money as possible, so we were all going to be flown to St Lucia for two weeks. Why two weeks to film a sixty-second commercial? Because it was cheaper to book flights on a fortnightly basis. Oh, dear, what a shame!

It was one of the most wonderful jobs I have ever had. We were staying in a five-star hotel, and I will never forget when we arrived, quite late at night, the sight of the luxurious surroundings. They were overwhelming. We walked into the bar that was right at the water's edge, the sea lapping at the legs of the bar stools. We had been on an airplane for eight hours, and then had an hour in a coach from the airport, but the management of the hotel had laid on a feast, with huge cocktails lined up for us. We had arrived in paradise. I was shown to my cabana on the beach. There was a huge bed, soft white linen, and an enormous bathroom with walk-in shower. I had never seen anything like it in my life.

The crew were all very blasé. They were used to this kind of treatment. When the make-up girl caught me washing my smalls in the sink one morning, she was highly amused at my frugality. She explained that all my laundry bills would be picked up by the production company, and even my calls home, up to a point. I just couldn't believe the lifestyle.

So there we were, two weeks in the Caribbean, and we only had to film for three days. Because I was supposed to be very English, the make-up girl had dyed the front of my hair blonde, where it showed, and then put me in a big floppy summer hat. I was instructed not to go in the sun because I had to look quite fair. I am very olive skinned at the best of times, and I only have to look at the sun to go brown. I never quite knew why they cast me in the first place, but I wasn't going to argue. I sunbathed with a huge hat on, and the top half of my body under an umbrella.

We filmed on a yacht, in the middle of a lagoon, on the other side of the island. The whole thing was crazy. There was a bay, with a jetty reaching into the sea, and the deserted ruin of a once very grand hotel. It was like the set for an Ernest Hemingway novel. Every evening, when we had finished filming and before we were driven back to the hotel, the entire crew would sit on the jetty and watch the sun go down. As the red fiery orb disappeared into the sea, there would be flashes of phosphorescence in the water. A natural firework display. It was truly unbelievable in its beauty. Someone had a tape machine, and we would all smoke a joint, listening to Elton John singing: 'Don't Let The Sun Go Down On Me.' It was a bit of magic and I will never forget it.

In the midst of all this beauty I was trying to get over Greg. It had to be done. Not just because he had made me so unhappy, but because the whole lifestyle I had led with him went against everything I had been brought up to believe in. I started an affair with the producer of the commercial. His name was Mike Stone and he was a lovely, gentle guy, unlike a lot of the people in the advertising world, who can be very brash. He and the writer/director, John Webster, were very well respected and had made lots of very successful commercials. John Webster was a brilliant writer. Sadly, he is dead now.

Mike and I got on really well. It wasn't difficult though, considering the circumstances! It was like having a holiday romance and I expected it to end. But on the flight back we decided to try and make a go of it and, as we landed at Heathrow, I began to feel hopeful for the future. I said goodbye to Mike at the terminal and got into a taxi. We had agreed to meet up the next day and review our plans.

Back in London, I walked into the flat and dumped my bag on the bed. I felt a bit flat, the way you do when you get back from a holiday. Everything looked dull and grey. Then the phone rang and brought me back to reality. It was Greg. He wanted to see me. It was really important. I tried to refuse but he insisted. He would come to the flat right away. I sat and waited for him to arrive, trying to put my thoughts in order. What did I really want? Someone kind like Mike? Or the insecurity of life with a womaniser?

Greg arrived and we sat in the lounge and I waited to hear what he had to say. More excuses, more lies? None of these things. He proposed to me.

Very calmly and quietly, Greg explained that he couldn't live without me. He realised he had a problem, and he was prepared to go into therapy to get help. He had spoken to my parents and promised them he would always take care of me, and he had bought a house in West Hampstead. A Victorian terraced house that he knew I would love. He also wanted me to star opposite Robin in the next *Confessions* film. We would work together and be together.

I was flabbergasted. He had caught me completely off-guard. Greg needed me and he was prepared to make it official. I hardly paused to think before I accepted, and then, to top it all, he made love to me. Right there on the living-room floor. I was stunned. It was the first time we had made love for months and months. I was so shocked and happy and flattered and confused. I was going to be Mrs Greg Smith for better or worse. And, yes, you guessed it. It was worse...

CHAPTER TEN

TRYING HARD, COULD DO BETTER

GREG WAS ON a mission to make me feel secure, and we made an appointment to see a therapist. The first time we went together, which was just as well, because when Greg was talking about our difficulties, he was in complete denial. It was down to me to point out to the therapist just how bad things were. It was not just the lack of intimacy in our relationship that was the problem. It was all the other women, and also the pornography that I had found in his flat. His whole attitude to women and sex had to be addressed.

After a few sessions the therapist asked to see me alone. He explained that Greg's problem was very common and that quite a lot of men have difficulty seeing the woman they are in love with as a sexual object. They could have casual sex – one-night stands with the kind of woman they had no regard or respect for in any way – but as soon as they became emotionally involved the problems began. He said he was very sorry to have to tell me but he didn't hold out much hope for any improvement in Greg's position, as he was thirty-five and set in his ways.

I was very disappointed and upset. I discussed everything with my parents. My sisters were busy with their own lives and I really didn't see them very much. Mum was worried for me because she reckoned it meant it would be more difficult for me to have any children. At this point in time, that didn't really bother me. I was not remotely maternal, and wanted to concentrate on my career. As long as Greg was loyal to me and looked after me, I thought I could help him with his career and he would help me. I could cope without the sex, I thought. I hoped.

Looking back it is so easy to see how naive I was. One could say my parents should have tried harder to dissuade me, but that was not their style. Quite rightly, they did not interfere in their children's decisions and Greg was adamant that things would improve; now we were going to be married and in our own home, things would be different.

The date for the wedding was set for 7th November, 1975. I was twenty-seven. We were to be married in Marylebone registry office because Greg had been married before, but we also decided to drive to my local village church in Aston Abbotts to be blessed. We would then come back up to London for a reception at the Metropole hotel on the Edgware Road, then fly to Paris that same night for two nights' honeymoon at the famous Georges V Hotel.

Greg could only spare two days because we were about to start filming *Confessions of a Driving Instructor*. He had a meeting with the writer, Chris Wood, in Paris, hence the venue for our honeymoon. I was not really consulted on this part of the arrangements. With Greg business always came first, and I accepted that as part of my life as Mrs Smith. It was also Greg's decision to throw a huge party when we returned. It was ostensibly to celebrate our union, but it was a double celebration. Our nuptials and the start of the film.

The wedding turned into a press junket for *Confessions of a Driving Instructor*. Warning bells should have been clanging in my ears even then. But I was too swept away by the whole circus. The attention of the press and that sort of thing. I sometimes wonder now why my friends didn't try and stop me. They must have guessed it was going to be a disaster. My dear friend, Pat Hay, did my make-up for the day. We sat in my kitchen at the flat drinking vodka at 7 o'clock in the morning, and she may have tried to suggest to me that there were problems. I know my dad came and said to me that I didn't have to go through with it if I didn't want to.

'But Dad, I do,' I'd replied. 'You don't understand. If I don't try and give this one hundred per cent I will always wonder if it would have worked out or not. I know there are problems, and it is not a normal marriage, but I am not a normal girl. I'm strong, and I can help Greg, and in a way, if we are only just good friends, that is all I need in my life. Because the most important thing in my life is my career.'

What was I thinking? How warped was my view of life?

The day went to plan but it was exhausting. The press turned up on the steps of the registry office and it was like a photo call for *Confessions*, and when one of the photographers encouraged Robin Askwith to pull my skirt up higher, he did! I hardly remember the blessing in the village church. It was all like a film. I was watching myself from above. I remember seeing Karel in the congregation as I walked down the aisle, and having a flashback to him and me in the bus shelter. It was like another life. Dear Nik Grace was unable to come to the wedding because he was working, but whenever we have talked about it since we decided it was just as well he wasn't there because he never trusted Greg and would probably have said something he regretted.

The reception was a melee of noise and flash bulbs and faces. I just wanted to kick my shoes off, tear off the false eyelashes, and plonk down in front of the telly. When I look at the photos from that day, I just do not look like me. I have blonde hair, dyed from the commercial, and then dyed even more for the film. Masses of make-up and long red false nails. And I was really thin because I had lost so much weight due to stress. I also look middle-aged. I have on a naff silk suit and a mink stole. What was I thinking!

I was trying to be what Greg might fancy. I had chosen a load of Janet Reger underwear in preparation for the honeymoon: uplift bra, lacy knickers and suspenders. Silk stockings and impossibly high heels. It was like a costume for a part I was playing.

When we arrived in Paris, we went straight to our room. I unpacked while Greg was straight on the phone to Chris Wood to talk about the film. I turned the TV on. It was *Match of the Day* so I knew Greg would be pleased. I put on my negligee that matched the rest of the outfit, and draped myself seductively across the bed. Greg took one look and said, 'Oh, Bellie, love, not tonight. I'm knackered. Tell you what though, you can give me a blow job while I watch the football...' That was the first and last time in my marriage I had any physical contact with my husband.

We returned home to our wedding celebration at EMI Studios. Greg had organised it from the office, so it was full of people I had never met and who were only there to do with the business, and then there were my friends and family. We stood in the line-up greeting people, and there was an endless stream of faces I did not know, mixed with blonde girls with big tits, who smiled at me knowingly. One actress, who shall remain nameless, shook my hand and then moved on to my mum, who was standing next to me, and whispered to her, 'Well, I only hope he's made the right decision.'

It was a nightmare. The only good bit was when Windsor Davies and Don Estelle came out of a big cake singing 'Whispering Grass', which was their big hit single of the day.

We spent the first three months of married life in Greg's old flat because the house he had bought for us was being done up. I was allowed to oversee the decoration and furnishing elements.

My parents gave us the most beautiful Wedgwood dinner service as a wedding present. I tried so hard in those next few months to make everything perfect and make it feel like a real home. We had dinner parties from time to time but slowly I found myself more and more alone.

We started filming almost immediately so there was no time to brood. I was playing a wonderful character in *Driving Instructor*, who was the daughter of the owner of the local driving school. My character's father was played by Windsor Davies, a brilliant actor and friend. George Layton was playing my fiancé; again, a friend and terrific actor. Avril Angers played my mother, Irene Handl was playing a small part and Bill Maynard and Doris Speed headed Robin's family. It was a lovely, talented cast. It was a pity that a few of the so-called actresses who had to take their clothes off were not up to speed, but I guess Greg had cast them for their other talents...

The moment we started filming, Greg gave me some feeble excuse about having to work late every night and getting too tired to do the drive home from the studio. But I was doing it, so why couldn't he? Silly question, Lynda. He moved into the hotel at Elstree.

I was beside myself. Now I not only had to act on screen, I had to act that all was well in front of the cast and crew. I had only been married a few weeks and my husband, the Big Producer, was screwing his way through all the female artists. Just not me. Very nice.

Thank God for my mates. Pat and Flic were there for me. One night, Pat was round for supper to my marital nest. Prison more like: I hated being in Greg's flat. It was full of him and his sordid lifestyle. There was nothing of me. The only good thing was his faithful dog. Zackary used to look at me with his soulful eyes as if to say, I am so sorry about my master, Lynda, but I could have told you that the only thing he really loves is me.

Pat and I were eating and the phone rang. It was one of the slappers ringing to give me a hard time. I just burst into tears. Seeing I was unable to cope at all, Pat grabbed the phone from me and shouted down the phone, 'Why don't you just fuck off, you old tart. You're only jealous because Lynda is a successful actress. Now piss off.'

She was wonderful and made me laugh. Another glimmer of humour was when my mother came to stay around this time, and asked me how things were going. I told her they weren't, adding that, 'One blow job does not a marriage make.' I hadn't meant it to slip out.

Mum had looked at me for a moment and then said, 'What's a blow job, dear?' I couldn't bring myself to explain so I showed her some of Greg's porn mags. I stood guard at the door, in case he came back, while she trawled through the pages of horror and depravity. She was there for ages! I had to drag her away.

'Well,' she finally announced, 'your father and I have had sex practically every night since we were married, and I've never had to do that.'

Way to go, Mother!

It just got worse and worse. One day, I came home to find the door was locked. I called through the letter box to Greg to open the door and waited and waited until finally he came to the door. I marched into the front room to find an actress standing there, dressed but with no tights on, looking very uncomfortable.

'Do you know—?' said Greg blithely.

'Not as well as you, obviously.'

I joke now but it really was humiliating. I was slowly dying inside. Every time we went anywhere I dreaded some woman coming up to me and saying, 'Hi, I'm having an affair with your husband.'

Apart from my close friends I couldn't tell anyone there were problems. In that business no one would have sympathised with me, anyway. All the men were at it. I remember the producer's wife, Lilly Klinger, trying to give me some advice. I had hinted that I couldn't cope very well with all the women and the late nights. She just smiled and said, 'Lynda, dear, don't let it get to you. He's *your* husband. He won't leave you and when he can afford to buy you mink and diamonds, you will be able to say to everyone, "Look what he gives me!"' I tried to explain to Lilly that I would buy my own mink and diamonds, and that it didn't compensate for being treated like shit. But she was old school and didn't want to know.

I began to retreat into the bottle. Every time we had to go to a do I would have a little nip before we went out. This just meant I got drunk quicker and annoyed Greg.

A̲T THE END of filming there is always a party for the cast and crew. The first assistant on *Driving Instructor*, Billy Westley, was one of the old school. He was brilliant at his job and knew everything that was going on. He was completely loyal to Greg, who was his boss, but he knew the pain I was going through as he had seen it many times during the filming.

In one incident, Greg came in to watch Robin and me filming a scene in the back of a car. We were supposed to be snogging passionately, and Robin's character was trying very hard to get into my knickers. Norman Cohen was directing, and he was being very sensitive about making sure I did not flash any parts of my anatomy too much. Suddenly, Greg stopped the filming.

'I think we should see a bit of Lynda's tits, Norman. What do you think, Bellie? Just because you are the producer's wife doesn't mean to say you shouldn't get your tits out.'

I thought he was joking. We all thought he was joking. There was a ripple of laughter from the crew and then a pregnant pause.

'But, Greg, you said I wouldn't have to take my clothes off,' I said.

'I am not asking you to take your clothes off, just flash your tits,' came his charming reply.

Robin grabbed my hand and squeezed it hard. 'Don't worry, Bellie,' he whispered, 'we'll work something out.'

He was so kind. We managed to work it so that although my left boob was on show for a millisecond, the next shot made much of me exaggeratedly scooping it back into my bra and laughing in my character's horsey, upper-class way. (It came back to haunt me though, because when I got the Oxo commercials, there was loads of press coverage, and either the *Sun* or the *Sport* – I can't remember which – printed a blow-up of the scene. My left tit was all over the front page with the headline: LYNDA PUTS THE X IN OXO.)

Just another humiliation heaped on my head.

I was at my lowest ebb and something had to be done. My life was a mess. I was drinking heavily and my husband of three months was staying in an hotel five miles up the road without me.

My friend Lynda La Plante's husband, Richard, was training to be a therapist. He introduced me to a man called Joshua Bierer who was doing very interesting sessions with couples with various problems in their relationships. Richard suggested I talk to him to see if there was some way he could advise me on how to deal with the difficulties in my marriage.

I went to see Joshua at his house in Golders Green. It was rather out of the ordinary, I must say: people just seemed to wander in off the streets. Joshua was quite elderly, at least in his late sixties, but his wife could not have been more than thirty and had a new baby.

I was in a dreadful state. I poured out my story and he was very charming, listened very attentively and seemed to understand the situation perfectly. He would be able to help me, he said, but not for several weeks, as he was going to Israel to visit family and the Kibbutz he had founded just outside Netanya. But I was desperate now. Could he do nothing for me? Just speak to Greg, at least? He agreed and did so. Then he told me that in cases like ours, he advised the couple to separate for a while and not have any contact with each other.

Joshua then suggested I come to Israel with him and his brother, who was a doctor and also founder member of the Kibbutz, and he would take me through things, away from Greg. I had no money to go trolling off to Israel, and told him so. Joshua suggested that that was not a problem; Greg would pay. I was doubtful about that but agreed in principle.

I went to see my parents, who were very upset to see me so distressed. My dad thought Joshua sounded like a complete fraudster and I should leave well alone. I remember going into the pantry at the farm and taking a bottle of sherry, which was about all my parents drank in those days. I put it in my handbag and set off to drive back to London, despite the fact I had already drunk quite a lot already.

I arrived home to an empty flat and opened the sherry. I was in despair but really too drunk to care. Then Greg rang to say he was paying for me to go to Israel with Joshua.

Now he had money, he could afford to be magnanimous. The caring husband helping his wife out in her hour of need (all the support she had given him was not mentioned). He was probably delighted to get rid of me for two weeks, so he could romp away to his heart's delight.

The plan was that I would fly out with Joshua and his brother, and his nineteen-year-old daughter and her friend would be joining us later on. I was concerned that his daughter could be discreet because I did not want the press getting hold of all my private details. Joshua said she was used to her dad having patients to stay, and all would be fine. I asked if I would have my own room. Naturally, was the reply. So, I packed a case, and also all my diaries that I had been keeping, detailing my ups and downs.

It was crazy travelling with these two old boys. They were both as deaf as doorposts. It was a long and tiring trip. I kept up the drinking and everything was in a haze. Looking back on parts of my life, I am ashamed to admit that there were quite a few times when I was functioning well enough to fool the outside world, but I really wasn't sober. The drinking went with a kind of relentless energy that just took me over. The adrenaline enabled me to grit my teeth and keep going, but it was like hanging over a cliff by my fingernails.

When we finally arrived in Israel, Joshua informed me that I was sleeping on the sofa.

'But you told me I was to have my own room,' I wailed. 'Please, I must have my own space.'

'Now, my dear, calm down,' soothed Joshua. 'You are irate and disorientated. Tomorrow you will feel better and we can make a plan. There is not enough space for you to have your own room now because my daughter is bringing her friend and they will have to sleep in that room.'

I was actually too tired to argue with him. He went off into the other room to join his brother and I shut the door and fell asleep on the sofa, in my clothes.

I was awoken in the middle of the night by the sound of a door knob being turned and I looked up to see a shape moving behind the glass door of the living room. I was terrified. I hardly knew where I was, as I was still half asleep and the drink had made my brain fuzzy. Before I could get myself up and off the sofa, there was

Joshua, stark bollock naked, coming towards me with his arms outstretched, sporting an enormous hard-on. Clasping me in his arms, he tried to kiss me while I shrank away, screaming at him to get off me. He tried to quieten me, and when I wouldn't shut up, he grabbed me again, not quite so pleasantly this time, and pushed me more deeply into the sofa.

'Get off me, you dirty old man!' I was sobbing now. 'Let go of me or I'll wake your brother.'

Joshua went into full manipulation mode: 'Now, now, my dear, calm down. What are you saying? You're hysterical. You're just having a bad dream. Go to sleep now and we'll talk in the morning.' All this while he was sitting on the edge of the sofa, stark naked with an erection. It was, indeed, a nightmare!

I lay awake for the rest of the night trying to decide what to do. Just leave, I reckoned. Over breakfast, the crafty old sod made a suggestion. If I kept quiet about last night he would leave me alone.

'But I want to go home,' I said.

'That is not possible,' came the reply. 'There are no flights this weekend because it is Independence weekend. You will have to stay until Monday, at least, by which time my daughter will be here and you will have calmed down.'

Thanks to the airplane schedules I had no choice but to stay; besides which, Joshua had taken my passport and locked it in his safe.

I went out for a walk and to buy some wine. I sat on the beach and tried to assess my situation. However, within minutes, I was surrounded by young Israeli men all trying to vie for my attention. Normally this would have been a dream come true, but I was in no fit state and just got hysterical. I tried to run away but they were all round me, hemming me in.

Suddenly, the crowd parted and walking towards me was an angel. Tall, athletic, with a brown body topped by a mop of long shaggy hair. He pushed the boys aside, took my hand and led me away down the beach.

We walked for a long time, in silence, until finally I begged him to stop and let me rest. He hardly spoke a word of English but he could see I was very upset and just held me. I calmed down and tried to explain that I had to return to the apartment. He walked me to the front door and we managed to agree that I would be there tomorrow at ten.

Joshua was waiting for me. Unbelievably, all he said was, 'You didn't waste any time, did you? I wonder what you husband will say, if I tell him you are picking up young men on the beach.'

'I wonder what he would say,' I replied, 'if he knew the man whom he had trusted with his wife had tried to rape her.' Touché! From then on he left me well alone.

The next day I met Davide again. We went to a café and sat and tried to understand each other. He was gorgeous but very arrogant. He suggested we went to a hotel. Did I have money? Hang on a minute, this was all happening a bit fast! But I was extremely unhappy and didn't want to be alone with Joshua. I would do anything not to go back.

I did have some money but now I was frightened Davide was going to rob me. I must have looked a sorry sight because the next thing I knew he was walking me up the road, saying something about mother. His mother? I followed helplessly, with no other choice, really, except to run. But run where? It was the first time I had been in a country where I not only didn't speak the language, but the alphabet was different as well.

Davide took me to a shack halfway up a hill, where a family was just sitting down to eat. I have no idea who they all were. But they were friendly and one lady could have been his mum. She pointed at my wedding ring and I nodded. Yes, I was married. She said something to her son, who looked glum.

They gave me a glass of something disgusting to drink, but it was alcoholic so I threw it down. By now I was becoming quietly hysterical again and just wanted to go home. What the hell was going on here? Davide got me a chair and we sat and had something to eat. As the alcohol took over I perked up a bit, and even managed to make myself understood a bit, with some French and lots of gesturing. Afterwards, Davide walked me back to the apartment, and we parted with a long kiss. He was delicious but very overpowering.

When I went into the flat, I was greeted by Joshua and his daughter. She was a big Jewish princess, full of confidence and wise-cracking humour. Her friend was a timid little girl from Wales. We all went out for a meal and got on well.

When we got back, the two old boys went to bed and the other two girls and I stayed up drinking wine. I was trying to fathom what Joshua's daughter was all about. She was very open and suddenly said, 'So, my dad's sorting you out, is he?'

I was a bit taken aback that she knew about me at all.

'Well, yes, in a way, but I hope you'll be discreet.'

'Ha, there's nothing discreet about Dad,' came her reply, which really worried me as he had all my diaries about me and Greg. 'Has he tried to rape you yet?'

It was surreal. A nineteen-year-old girl asking me if her father had tried to molest me. I told her what had happened. She found it all very amusing and explained to her friend that she should be careful to make sure she was never alone with Joshua for the same reason.

'Don't worry, I won't tell anyone,' this gob-smacking girl continued. 'So what are you going to do?'

'I want to leave here as soon as I can,' I said, 'but your father has my passport, and there are no flights for another two days.'

'Don't fret,' she replied. 'We're all going to the Kibbutz tomorrow and will be away for a week. I'll get your passport for you and you can leave as soon as there's a flight.'

I heard her go into her father's room and start screaming at him. She must have woken him up. Five minutes later she reappeared with my passport.

The next day they all left, and I was free. I met up with Davide and he took me to the airport to sort out my flight. I had to stay one more night. I spent it with him. He was kind and aggressive in equal measure, but I was beyond logic or fear or anything. I just wanted to get home.

At the airport the next day, Davide presented me with a Star of David with a tiny diamond in it. He explained that one of his family, who worked in a diamond mine, had got it for him to give to me. I was touched and felt quite guilty that I had his motives wrong until, just as I was leaving, he pointed to the gold chain round my neck and gestured that he would like it. I tried to explain it was a present from my parents, and that's when he got very grumpy with me. I just saw red. So that was it. All this was about trying to get something out of me. The Star of David was probably a fake. I had been conned again. I was a very stupid woman who had learned nothing about life. I deserved to be unhappy. I pulled the gold chain from my neck and hurled it at him, turned and ran to the plane.

There, I was greeted by a lovely English air stewardess who recognised me, and upgraded me to Club class. As the plane took off, I sank back in my comfy seat, clutching a glass of champagne, and looked down on Tel Aviv with tears coursing down my cheeks. I wanted to go home so badly. But where was home, and what awaited me?

CHAPTER ELEVEN

DIVORCE, AND THE KINDNESS OF STRANGERS

WHEN I GOT home Greg seemed genuinely pleased to see me. I told him everything, including sleeping with the Israeli. He had the nerve to judge me, and give me a hard time. I couldn't believe it. He was so pompous about it. We had a big row and I told him that it was pointless our going on like this, and maybe we should call it day. He then went into classic male-under-pressure mode, threatening to throw me out without a penny.

'What happened to the promise you made my parents to look after me?' I asked.

I went down to see my parents, and told them everything that had gone on. My father was livid about Joshua and threatened to go round and deal with him. I persuaded him there was no point. I really wanted to get my diaries back, but I could get Richard La Plante to do that for me. I just wanted to forget the whole thing.

I felt so ashamed of myself. Let Greg break our marriage vows, ten times over, but I should not have done so. I was as bad as him. My confidence in my abilities to make decisions was so shattered that I basically asked my parents' permission to leave the marriage. Of course, they gave it to me.

But even then, I didn't leave straight away because I was still trying not to accept defeat. I was so low, though, and thought I was the ugliest woman in Christendom.

The problem with sex is that if it is right one takes it for granted, but if there is a problem it takes over your every waking thought. Once I had stared failure in the face, it was so hard to carry on with my life with Greg. To lie in bed with someone who cannot bear to touch you is a nightmare. He couldn't even give me a hug or any kind of affection. He wouldn't talk about it and sometimes I would have a stomach ache I wanted him so much. If he had even kept the problem between us, it might have been a little more bearable. But to see him go off at night, knowing he was going to screw another woman, was torment.

THERE ARE MOMENTOUS decisions in your life that have to be taken and, once I had made up my mind, I became quite cool and collected. I had my parents' support, and I finally told Greg I was leaving him. His initial reaction was typical, and the same as last time: 'Don't think you are going to get a penny from me. And if you try and take me to court I will destroy you. Remember I have the might of Columbia Pictures behind me.'

I told him I wanted nothing, but I did remind him that he had made a promise to my parents that he would never see me homeless. Eventually, he agreed to give me £2,500 as a deposit on a flat. Which was very generous of him considering he was now a millionaire, and that I had kept him for three years.

Mum came to help me move my stuff and pack up. I was all for leaving everything, but good old Mum was not going to let him have anything more than she could help. We even took the Wedgwood dinner service that my parents had given us for a wedding present.

'He'll never use it,' she scoffed. 'What does he know about giving dinner parties? You were the class in the relationship.'

I WENT TO STAY with Lynda La Plante, and hid away in her flat for a couple of months until the press interest had died down. Greg was already seeing an actress called Mary Tamm, so any doubts I may have had were confirmed. It's strange, isn't it, how when we don't want to see the obvious, we don't? In my case I had always seen the obvious but just did not want to admit defeat.

My dear mum had always said, 'If you give a person enough love, they will return it.' That thought has haunted me all my life, as I just wish someone else had pointed out that sometimes you also have just to learn to let things go, and that some people will never be able to respond to you, even if they want to. Everyone has to go their own way in the end.

I felt a complete failure. I thought the problems in my marriage were all down to me, that I wasn't pretty or sexy enough … the list just went on and on. But enough was enough. I was going to take myself off and lick my wounds, and find out who I wanted to be in the future.

ONE OF THE things that came out of this disastrous liaison was that I confronted another major issue in my life – my nose.

Since day one of leaving drama school, all I had heard was, 'You must be Jewish with that nose.' A casting director, very early on, looked at my profile, and pronounced that I would never work until I was forty. When I had photos done, the photographer would try and get me to stand at certain angles so that my nose didn't look so big.

I decided that if I was going to start a new life, the nose had to go. I could not risk becoming known as Cyrano de Bellingham.

When I had been working on *General Hospital*, I had met an actress called Anna Barry. She had told me her amazing story about how she had been in a car accident and lost an eye. Her surgeon, Roy Sanders, had reconstructed the side of her face and that no one was aware she had a glass eye. It was a fantastic piece of work. After the operation, she had moved in with Roy, and they were still very happy.

Roy's main area of expertise in plastic surgery was with his work on burn victims and harelips and such like, but he was not averse to performing the odd bit of cosmetic surgery. I gave Anna a call saying that I'd like to see him as I wanted his professional opinion about my nose. I told her I was embarrassed to ask Roy because it seemed so petty compared to the kind of work he did normally, but she was great about it, and said he loved doing stuff like that because it meant he could practise!

I made an appointment and went to see him. I started to explain that as an actress I was very conscious, on camera, that my nose was too big. Not so bad on the stage, but on camera I felt it was the difference between playing just character parts, and getting the chance to play the leading role.

I was under no illusions about my looks. I was attractive, but not pretty, and my nose was definitely a problem. Roy listened to my spiel, took loads of photos and measured my nose. I told him I didn't want him to think it was just vanity. I realised there were people with terrible problems, and that I shouldn't really be making a fuss, but my career was everything to me. As I started to talk about these more personal things, I found myself starting to sob, and it all came out. Poor Roy had to listen to a crazy woman blubbing on about her troubles!

He let me finish and then he said, 'Lynda, first of all, you have every right to get your nose made smaller. It is, indeed, too big for the proportions of your face. And as a man who lives with an actress, I can completely understand where you are coming from. The other problem you have is much more complex, but I feel honour-bound to tell you that having a nose job is not going to help your marriage.'

'Oh, don't worry, I know that,' I replied. 'But it will sure as hell make me feel better about myself as an actress, and that is the first step to getting my act together and surviving this mess.'

That must have been the answer he was looking for, because he agreed to do the operation. It was going to cost me £1,000 for his contribution and then there would be the anaesthetist's fee of £50, and two nights in a clinic, another £50 (this was 1976). I agreed.

A few days later I went in for the operation. I had just been offered a lovely part on TV in a play called *Cottage to Let* starring opposite Timothy West. I told Roy I had to be on camera in three weeks, and would there be a problem with bruising? None whatsoever, he informed me, as he would insist that, after the operation, I would have to sit up all night to ensure there was only minimal bruising.

And he was right. I turned up for the rehearsal, on camera, a changed woman. No one noticed except the director, the lovely John Sickle, who looked at me very carefully for a full five minutes and then announced, 'Lynda Bellingham, you've had a nose job, and it looks great!' I was so thrilled. I really did feel like a new woman. I was going to go forward with my life. Sod Greg Smith. I would show the bastard.

Over the next couple of weeks, I waited for Roy's bill to arrive. I had saved the money, and put it to one side specially. Finally, when nothing came, I rang Anna and explained that maybe the bill had got lost in the post and I was embarrassed, because I didn't want Roy to think I was dragging my heels over paying it.

'Please don't worry, Lynda,' came the reply. 'Roy felt that you might need that money if you were leaving your husband.'

How wonderful, and how kind. I have been eternally grateful to him. He has played a major role in my life in more ways than one.

I N THE LAST two years I had been working steadily, despite all my unhappiness. My friend Marilyn was now the casting director for *The Sweeney*. It was a brilliant show about the Flying Squad, starring John Thaw and Dennis Waterman. I appeared as the girl-friend of Patrick Mower, and he was playing a conman with his partner, played by George Layton. It was a very male-dominated crew and they were all big drinkers.

John and Dennis were a great team and filming was fast and fun. They didn't hang about and didn't suffer fools. John Thaw was always a gentleman but sometimes I found Dennis difficult. I had first met him when he was going out with my friend Pat Maynard when we were doing *General Hospital*. In fact they got married. He was very much a man's man, although he got a reputation as a bit of a lad with the ladies. In fact, the ladies were a side issue compared to the camaraderie of drinking with the lads down the pub. Robin Askwith knew him very well and they were all very similar. Women were either mates or slags! I tried hard to be a mate but I felt that he thought I was snotty and when he had had a few, he would always have a go at me. He could be very harsh, and once at a dinner party at Pat's house, reduced me to tears. Pat made him send me flowers to apologise! He was OK after that, but I kept my distance.

But when we were filming *The Sweeney*, there was no time for tantrums and tears. It was just get on and film as quickly as possible. Time was money. But it worked because John and Dennis were so professional, and people were cast for their ability and experience.

A family portrait: Dad with Barbara,
Mum with Jean, and me to the side, 1953

My little pony, Tiddlywinks, 1958

Jean, me and Barbara, bathing belles, 1957

First professional role as Puck in *A Midsummer Night's Dream*, 1966

As fat nurse Hilda Price in *General Hospital* in 1972 (I was wearing padding)

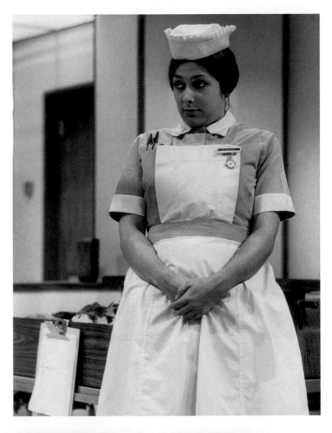

Confessions of a Driving Instructor with Robin Askwith, 1975 – love the big hair

My first wedding,
to Greg Smith,
November 1975

In *The Sweeney* – Oh,
the innocence of youth!

India 1977, with
Jean and Barbara

I loved the period costumes
in *Funny Man*, 1981

Definitely a passing
resemblance to
Joan Collins in
Doctor Who, 1984

One of my many families, *All Creatures Great and Small*, 1988

My famous Oxo family

My second wedding
day, July 1981, with
Lynda La Plante,
Mum and Biggins
(nice to see he dressed
up for the occasion)

Out on the town
with Nunzio

Ladies who lunch, with
Princess Diana and
Annie Nightingale, 1987

What a star! Michael Peluso, 1983

What a cutie! Robert Peluso, 1988

The producer was a lovely man called Ted Childs. He had the most incredible sense of humour. Very wry. He and his wife Kate are still friends today. He happened to direct the episode I was in, and we had a laugh.

So I was doing well in my chosen career. I made appearances in *Z Cars* and *Billy Liar*, and *Within These Walls* which starred a wonderful actress called Googie Withers. It was the seventies version of *Bad Girls*! I also did an episode of *The Professionals* starring Martin Shaw and Lewis Collins. I have to say this was not such fun. Lewis thought he was a sex god and Martin took himself way too seriously. There were not many jokes during the job. The only person who was worth talking to was Gordon Jackson. He was a true professional and so charming.

On the back of the part I had in *The Sweeney*, one job I really enjoyed was the film of the TV series, where I played a high-class hooker. There were only two female roles in the film and the lead went to Diane Keen. The ridiculous thing was that when I went to meet the director, David Wickes, he gave me an elaborate spiel about my part; how important it was to the plot, how he must have a good actress even though the role was very small.

And then came the rub. The scene required the actress to be totally naked. Great! She was murdered and then left on a bed. I reckoned it would be OK to be naked as I was not moving (a bit like the girls at the Windmill Theatre, in the forties and fifties, when, to get past the censorship laws, the girls were allowed to be nude as long as they did not move!)

I had to accept the part as there were so few films being made. one had no choice. So there I was, back with the lads and standing in a towelling robe waiting to strip off and lie dead on the bed. The wonderful Billy Westley was the first assistant so he took care of me. He cleared the studio for me before the scene started, and when the director shouted 'Cut!', he made sure the dresser would rush to my side and gave me my robe. But by the third take no one was interested, and when they finally called, 'It's a wrap!' (technical speak for the scene is over), there was no wrap for me. I had to walk out and find it on a chair somewhere!

The worst moment was my actual murder. The villains were to give me a lethal injection of something. Normally, this would involve a retractable syringe being used, often on a stand-in. (This is because the insurance for an actor doing anything remotely dodgy is very high, so it's cheaper to pay a daily rate to a stand-in.)

The budget on the *Sweeney* film could not have been any lower. We came to film, and they had no retractable syringe and no stand-in, just an extra, who was supposedly a trained nurse. It was the end of the day and everyone was panicking about finishing on time because if they didn't, I would have to come back tomorrow, and that would mean another day's wages. So, trying to be helpful, I said it was fine for them to inject me if they wanted a good close-up of the needle going in. Apparently, if the needle went just under the skin and not into a vein, that was not dangerous.

The only problem was the supposed nurse doing the injecting. Her hands were shaking so badly! The shot was set up for a close-up of my arm being injected. I had to look away because I hate needles. Everyone held their breath. The nurse had been told she must get it right the first time. Bless her cotton socks, she did the business. 'Cut!' cried the director. All done, phew. But, as I looked down, I was shocked to see my arm had swollen and all round the injection site was a bubble under the skin.

The crew all looked rather shocked then, suddenly, a buzz of activity. Someone sat me down and brought me a brandy and everyone was very solicitous. It was only later I learned that things could have been very different – if the nurse had hit a vein, the air bubble would have killed me. Talk about dying for one's art!

When the film came out, I went to see it in my local cinema in Kilburn. I was staying with Lynda La Plante at this time. There were only about three people in the audience and two of them were a couple in front of me. When the shot of my arm came on, the man turned to his wife and whispered, 'That's not real, you know. They use a special needle and a dummy arm.'

MY NEXT JOB in the theatre was *Bordello*, a musical about the life and loves of Toulouse Lautrec. It starred Henry Woolf as Lautrec and ten assorted actresses as his various muses and models. It was terrible and only lasted forty-one performances! But it did give me the chance to be the first nude on stage at the Queen's Theatre in Shaftesbury Avenue.

I was playing, among other characters, the role of Suzanne Valadon, a mistress of Lautrec's who liked to embarrass him. In the play, when his mother comes for tea, Suzanne walks into the room stark naked and proceeds to lift the cups off the table, looking for the coasters. She announces she is going to wear them to a fancy-dress party as she is going as Eve.

When I auditioned and was asked if I minded taking my clothes off in front of an audience, I had airily replied, 'Not at all!' When it came to it, however, and we were rehearsing in a cold and drafty disused cinema in Brixton, I wished I had kept my mouth shut! The producer and owner of the theatre, Anthony Chadet, was very concerned for the reputation of his company and insisted on seeing the scene in rehearsal before deciding whether it could be included in the show. I went to the pub with the girls at lunchtime and had a few glasses of wine for Dutch courage. The scene ended up being a great success and very funny, and everyone agreed it must stay in.

During the show we had loads of quick changes as we were all playing so many different characters. They had rigged up a huge mirror backstage in the wings, so we could all check ourselves for correct costuming before we rushed on to do another scene. It was hysterical – we would all be queuing up and, just as most of the girls were throwing clothes on, I would be throwing mine off. When it got to my turn to use the mirror, I would check my hair, then look at my pubes and give them a quick ruffle!

On the first night, it took the audience a good few seconds to register I was completely nude. Then you could hear the whispers begin, running round the theatre: 'Oh my God! She's naked!' My father was there for the opening night. Poor man, he was so embarrassed. Mum said he just sat there, staring into his lap, until she gave him the all-clear.

One evening, after the show, there was a call for me to go to the stage door. Standing there was an elderly gentleman dressed from head to toe in tweed, with a deerstalker hat on, and an ivory-tipped walking stick. He raised his hat and said, 'Good evening, Miss Bellingham. I just had to come and congratulate you on your performance. I would also like to ask you a personal question, if you don't mind.' I told him to go ahead.

'Well, um ... do you have help from a wig specialist?'

Can you believe it?!

'No, I just ruffle it a bit,' was my reply.

It may only have lasted forty-one performances but it was a classic, believe me.

CHAPTER TWELVE

PICKING MYSELF UP, DUSTING MYSELF DOWN AND STARTING ALL OVER AGAIN

I HAD FIRST MET Lynda La Plante in 1974 on a tour we did together for the Oxford Playhouse. She was then known as Lynda Marchal. The play was called *Diet for Women*, written by Aristophanes, who is most famous for his play *Lysistrata*.

In those days, Lynda was a fantastic actress and comedienne. She was never really appreciated and because she was so good at comedy it went against her. As I have said before, comedy is not respected. Then she started writing and has never looked back. She married Richard La Plante in the early eighties and took his name. She's always been a good friend to me.

Diet for Women was directed by a mad Greek called Minos Volanakis. It was a great cast of women including Lynda and me, Lesley Joseph and Jenny Logan. I have never laughed so much as we did during that play. It was all about women withholding their sexual favours to stop their men from going to war. Minos had us appearing in the first scene in blankets with wooden sticks in our hands and big beards on our faces. You couldn't hear a word we were singing, which was probably just as well as they were rubbish lyrics: 'Up with women and down with men…' or something like that.

It definitely lost something in the translation. Minos used to ramble on in his broken English and none of us could understand a word he was saying. And when the day came for the dress rehearsal and we finally saw what he wanted us to wear, we all burst into tears. We had big rubber tits to strap on, plus he then proceeded to have them painted blue. We had rubber bottoms to match. It was horrendous. While we were weeping and wailing, Jenny Logan took charge and tried to cheer us up. She was being very positive and encouraging until she saw her own costume. She had a horse head to wear, and a row of rubber tits all down her front. She collapsed in a heap. Now, that did cheer us up! We were hysterical. We toured all over the UK to empty theatres. In Liverpool, we got abusive letters and three men in the front row every night with raincoats on… Happy days!

MY DAD'S BROTHER, dear Uncle Percy, had died and left me and my sisters £12,000 each, God bless him! It saved my life. With the £2,500 Greg had given me, I was able to put down a considerable deposit. I had spent many hours wandering round West Hampstead and Maida Vale: the latter was way out of my price range but one day, as I was walking down a road off West End Lane, I spotted some builders working on a conversion in a Victorian house very much like the one Greg and I had lived in. I found out who the estate agents were who were dealing with the development and put in my offer. It was accepted. I was going to be a home owner!

I was so proud and excited, although I had no idea how I was going to pay the mortgage each month. I moved in after Christmas, and it was sod's law that I was then booked to go on tour again, with the Oxford Playhouse. This time it was *The Norman Conquests* directed by Gordon McDougall and starring David Jason. David was an up-and-coming actor then and we hit it off straight away. This particular play of Alan Ayckbourn's is extremely clever and hysterically funny – it's of three separate plays within a play, where the action runs simultaneously in different rooms. We had a ball. We packed out the theatre wherever we went.

Gordon appeared one night, and was telling us how thrilled he was that because we had made so much money for the Oxford Playhouse, they could now afford to do some 'real theatre' and produce a drama like *The Cherry Orchard*. Yet another example of people's attitude to comedy. It drives me mad.

M Y LIFE WAS back on track. I was working a lot and seeing all my friends; dipping in and out as usual. Flic was still a constant, although she went off to California eventually to seek her fortune. Biggins and Marilyn and Company were a great source of joy. We were still having our Sunday lunches. I had missed all that when I was married to Greg, but now I had my flat, I could return the hospitality. Leo and Sheila were married and had two children, and I was really enjoying being godmother to Jo. They used to have us all round on Saturday nights because they couldn't go out with small children. They were good times. I realised I had so many really good friends, they were like family. Who needed a husband?

Greg was still in the background, though. He would often ring for a chat. I tried hard to be mature about it all but it hurt. My confidence had taken a real beating and even my wonderful new nose did not make me feel attractive to the opposite sex.

Around this time, I did a play with Liza Goddard, Simon Williams and Colin Baker. We went on a short tour and I got very close to Liza. She was married to Colin at the time and things were not good. I poured my heart out to her about what had happened with Greg and me, and she was very sympathetic.

We had lots of fun on that tour. Michael Cochrane took over from Simon Williams, and he was a terrible giggler. He would make me laugh so much and one evening actually left me on the stage on my own because he couldn't stop laughing. I wandered around aimlessly for some moments, and finally I went off after him! He had to go back on. Actors can be a pain in the arse I know, but we are also wonderful company!

When we finished the play and got back to London, I stayed in touch with Liza. Her marriage ended, and she was on her own. I decided to invite her to a dinner party I was giving. Then I had a call from Greg who sounded very down, and invited him along at the last minute. I have no idea why I did that, except that maybe I was determined to show Greg what he was missing – I had a lovely home and lovely friends and he was on his own. I don't know. Anyway, they all tipped up and the evening was a great success. Liza was staying with me and after they had all gone home we sat and chatted. She asked me loads of questions about Greg.

'Do you fancy him?' I asked.

'No, of course not,' came her reply.

Then Greg rang me and asked me for Liza's phone number.

'Do you fancy her?' My heart sank.

'Well, you don't mind if I ask her out, do you, Bellie?'

'Yes, I do as a matter of fact. She's a friend of mine, Greg. There are plenty of women out there, why pick her? She won't go, anyway; she doesn't fancy you.'

I was really upset with him. Why did he still have to hurt me?

The next day Liza rang: 'Hi Bellie. Guess what? Greg's asked me out.'

My heart stopped. 'I know,' I rallied. 'I gave him your number.

Told him you didn't fancy him though. Isn't he a bastard, Liza, asking you out?'

There was a terrible silence at the other end of the phone.

'You're not going, are you?'

'Oh, Bellie, I didn't think you'd mind.'

'Actually, I do,' I replied, suddenly furious. 'But if having a fuck is more important than our friendship, you go ahead.' I slammed down the phone.

I was so upset. I felt betrayed by my friend and humiliated yet again by my ex-husband. Why were people so selfish? They went out together for about a month, and I didn't speak to Liza again for several years.

This incident was the beginning of a downward spiral for me. Once again, I had lost my way and had to crawl back out of the pit. The next few months were very up and down. I was doing well professionally, with guest appearances in *Yes, Honestly* and *Doctor on the Go*. I had made the *Sweeney* film and even made a series called *The Fuzz*, which was pretty dire but it paid the mortgage. I was going out a good deal and putting on a brave face but I was still hurting from Greg's betrayal. I was lucky to have good friends around me but I was lonely. I loved my flat but it was empty when I came home. I had been out a couple of times with guys but nobody seemed to find me in the least bit attractive. Because I was still doing my comedy parts, I was inevitably doing the kind of sexy type of character I hated – tits and arse. I hated it. I hated myself. I wanted to be taken seriously as an actress. I was also drinking all the time.

It was also around this time, in 1977, that I found I was very often picking up the bill for nights out. My self-confidence was so low that it was as though I was trying to buy friendship.

I also made a complete fool of myself at one point with Paul Smith. Paul was a director I worked with at London Weekend

Television. He was a great guy and had a smashing girlfriend called Sarah, who was a PA at LWT. Paul has gone on to become incredibly successful. He is, or was until recently, a director of Celador, which created *Who Wants To Be A Millionaire?*, and is now a fully fledged producer of films like *Gosford Park* and *Slumdog Millionaire*. He married Sarah and they had two lovely children who are now grown up.

However, my behaviour then meant I was about to ruin my friendship with Paul. I cringe when I write about this now – I'm so ashamed – but I really was struggling to keep a hold of my life at the time.

I was spending the day with Linda Hayden and we had had a right old time of it. We were drinking all day and then in the evening, I was going to have dinner with Paul. I could hardly speak I was so drunk, and really made a fool of myself by trying to get him into bed. He was the last person I should have been doing this to. I loved him and Sarah. Normally, I would never have thought of him in that way. He was a mate.

Poor Paul, he coped very well. He got me home and put me to bed and tried to explain to me that he loved me as a friend and that I was not to worry so much. Things would work out. After he left I tried to sleep, but the drink was just making my brain whirl and buzz: all my troubles and insecurities had crowded in to take me over. But I had to sleep. If I went to sleep everything would be OK in the morning: my mother always told us, when things get you down, go to sleep and wake up to another day. But how was I going to get to sleep? I was too overwrought. I had a terrible headache so I found a bottle of paracetamol and tried to get two out. A whole load tipped out on to the kitchen counter.

Everything seemed to stop. I stared at them. Those little white pills could put a stop to all this pain, and not just in my head. If I could just sleep for a long, long time… I felt so weary. If I could just make everything go away. I had had enough.

I took a lot of pills, panicked and picked up the phone to ring Mum. I didn't – why put her through all that worry? I rang Lynda La Plante. Her husband, Richard, answered. We talked for a bit and he must have realised something was seriously wrong. He said he would come round and that I should go and open the front door in case I fell asleep before he got there. I stumbled across the room and out into the hallway to the front door. That is the last thing I remember until I woke up in a hospital bed.

Richard told me later that when he got to my flat, the front door was open and I was lying in the hall. I had on a pink towelling robe with my name embroidered on it, and he had the presence of mind not to take me to hospital with an overdose while I was wearing it. He called the ambulance and dressed me in something else while he waited for them to arrive. They took me to St Mary's, Paddington and pumped my stomach. Richard also called my poor parents and told them I was going to be fine, so not to try and come up in the middle of the night, but to wait until the morning.

So there I was, in a hospital bed, slowly becoming aware of what I had done. I couldn't speak, my throat was so sore from the tube they had shoved down it. The nurse gave me some water. I couldn't bring myself to look her in the eye, I was so ashamed.

I was taken to see the resident psychiatrist for evaluation. I blabbed on about knowing how stupid I was, but things had got on top of me, and now I would take stock, and I had a wonderful family who loved me, and so on. He signed my release form. Looking back, it seems very strange he didn't recommend I had some counselling. I mean here was a young woman of twenty-nine who had tried to commit suicide. Surely this was the perfect time to offer her some help?

I went back to my bed and waited for Mum and Dad to come and pick me up. As I saw them coming down the ward I just let the tears flow. My darling parents, who had done so much for me. How could I have let them down like this? They both gave me a big hug and hardly said a word. They took me back to my flat and put me to bed. My dear friend Libby had agreed to come round and look after me. I had first made friends with her when she shared a flat with Sheila Mackintosh before she married Leo Dolan. Libby was David Frost's PA and we all became great friends. There was a lot of champagne consumed over the years and when Libby went to live and work in New York I spent a fantastic two weeks there being shown the high life. Mum and Dad left and Libby fussed round me. She had brought beautiful flowers and pink champagne! We cleared up the mess in my living room where I had knocked things over in my drunken stupor, and then sat down and talked. She was very kind and understanding but, as I was talking to her, it was slowly beginning to dawn on me that no one could really help me except me.

The doorbell rang and it was Greg, who had come to see if I was OK. At some point the night before, I had rung him, and delivered a drunken tirade about how it was all his fault because he had made me feel so worthless. He stood in my living room looking sheepish and then said, 'Well, I'm sorry, Bellie, but really, I can't be held responsible for this sort of behaviour.' And then he left.

I didn't speak to him again for twenty years.

I knew I had to sink or swim. Thank God, my guardian angel had not deserted me, and threw me a lifeline in the shape of a trip to India with my parents and sisters. When my father had been a pilot we always got discounted travel. We hadn't been away as a family for many years and this suggested holiday would turn out to be the last one we would ever have *en famille*. Dad had always wanted to go to India so we all sat down one Sunday and made our plans. Happily, we all agreed we wanted to go to Agra and Kashmir. We would fly into Calcutta, spend a day there, go on to Agra and then to Kashmir, then back to Delhi and home.

I was feeling very fragile and was quite happy to return to my childhood and let my family take over. Calcutta was a complete culture shock. The poverty was overwhelming. The dirt and grime, noise and crowds. Just so many people everywhere. Children ran under our feet like beetles. None of us could take it in. We had been told not to give money to anyone but it was so hard not to. One morning, my father went out for a walk and when he returned, he was being followed by a line of children. He looked like the Pied Piper.

We had all decided to take turns to pay the restaurant bills, and this caused great amusement wherever we went, because my dad was the only man with four women, who were all paying for him. He was treated like a king! We were forced to stay in Calcutta for four days as there was a cock-up with the internal flights so we had to forfeit our trip to Kashmir. Not a good exchange. It was extremely hot, but the hotel swimming pool was full of dark green algae so there was no swimming. Anyway, we survived. We visited the Ganges and had to distract my mother's attention away from the dead body floating past the boat. It really was an extraordinary place. When the sun rose, huge and burning red to orange, hundreds of people gathered at the water's edge, either praying or washing their smalls, or cleaning their teeth. It was bizarre and awesome in equal measures. We went to see a Hindu temple that was incredible. It was full of carvings, all of them pornographic. The guide was showing my mum the detail, which she really couldn't see without her glasses, and when I went across to look at what he was point-ing to I realised it was filthy: a row of soldiers being buggered by their horses. And there was my spectacle-less mum trying to be polite and saying, 'Yes, I see, how lovely. Lovely!'

We eventually arrived at the high point of our trip: the Taj Mahal, Agra. I knew it was one of the wonders of the world and was sceptical as to just how wondrous it would be. I can only say that if you ever get the chance to go and see it, grab the opportunity with both hands. It is a spectacular sight.

We arrived in the early morning, just as the sun was beginning to get warm. Outside, the entrance was like a market. Just a noise of men and women, and children running round like ants. Then we were through the arches and, suddenly, all was quiet. All the noise and the voices seemed to melt away into the far distance and we found ourselves walking up that long drive one sees in the photos. Halfway down is the marble seat made famous by the photos of Princess Diana taken there. As you walk into the main temple, you take off your shoes, and feel the cool marble under your feet. It was strange, because outside was so hot, yet suddenly your senses are assailed by this cool marble. It was like all the walls were full of sounds from years gone by. They almost vibrated. It was so wonderful. So majestic. I was lost in wonder, and my imagination ran riot. All the things that must have happened in this place.

I loved it there, but we had to move on, back to Delhi. We nearly had a disaster at the airport because we were staff and had to travel standby. There appeared to be only four seats. So one of us would have to stay another night. It was manic trying to sort anything out. The Tannoy system did not seem to work, and if a plane was arriving, it was Chinese whispers. Someone told someone, who passed the news to someone else, and before you knew it there was a queue at the gate! I will never forget when a sweet Indian gentleman, in a panama and carrying a rolled-up umbrella, who was standing next to us, said with a smile, 'It's bloody awful, isn't it?'

The holiday had been a success for all of us. It was great to feel part of the family again, and I realised how important it was for me to keep close to home in times of stress. It grounded me and kept me in touch with reality. My sisters were so good to me: I sometimes thought they must have got so fed up with me and all my dramas. Being the eldest tended to mean our parents had to pay more attention to me because I found the trouble first. Barbara and Jean learned to miss the same mistakes I made, but sometimes found new ones of their own! But we were all very lucky to have a mum and a dad we could talk to about everything. Back in London, very much refreshed, I was ready to pick up the pieces and get on with my life.

CHAPTER THIRTEEN

FALLING IN
LOVE AGAIN

I LANDED A FANTASTIC job in a series called *Funny Man*, starring Jimmy Jewel. After my years trying to crack comedy, I had realised that I had got myself up a blind alley. It was just not possible for directors and casting agents to understand that, as an actress, one could be funny *and* attractive and intelligent. The attitude was still that comedy meant tits and arse and seaside postcard humour.

I had done away with the big blonde hair, which I had never really intended to keep. None of that was the real me, I knew that now. So I cut my hair short and went back to my natural dark brown.

In the series, I was playing a very tragic character called Gwen, who ends up committing suicide. The story was based on the real-life career of Jimmy Jewel, who had started in Variety, and toured all over the country with his family from a very early age.

Jimmy was a real character. He had found fame on TV in a comedy series called *Nearest and Dearest* with Hylda Baker. Apparently, they couldn't stand each other! When we first started filming he was quite prickly with us girls in the chorus. Pamela Stephenson was one of us. She and I had worked together on Greg's film *Stand Up Virgin Soldiers* and, when the cast first all met, I started to explain that we had worked together on the film.

She kicked me under the table to stop. Afterwards, when we were alone, she said to me, 'Don't you ever mention that film again. Do you hear me? Never.'

I knew the film wasn't great but I thought this was a bit of an overreaction. It seemed she had bigger fish to fry, though, as she spent the time toting a big envelope around and telling everyone she was writing a film script. She was also playing the juvenile lead in the series and had lots of nude love scenes to do. The director was quite unkind to her, and to be fair to her she handled it all very well. But she always kept herself at a distance from the rest of us girls. Years later, I bumped into her when she was pregnant with her first baby. I went round to see her and we discussed the whole process of breastfeeding, because I had had my first son by then. I must say she was so much nicer. Obviously being married to the Big Yin (Billy Connolly) had changed her for the better!

I loved doing *Funny Man* and my co-star, David Schofield, was a joy to work with. He has gone on to achieve a fantastic career in the theatre, films and TV. I had high hopes that my career would change direction in much the same way, but it was not to be. I left the series halfway through, having been killed off by the writer. Jimmy and I had formed a real friendship and it was very sad saying goodbye.

In 1978 I got a really fun job for London Weekend Television called *The Pink Medicine Show*. It was directed by my friend, Paul Smith, and had been written by two doctors called Chris Beetles and Rob Buckman. It also starred them both as a variety of characters, but mostly as doctors. There's a surprise! It was very zany and pre-empted the shows like *Not the Nine O'Clock News*. In fact, it turned out to be too ahead of the times.

We made the first series and, although it was a great success with the audience, it was cancelled because the TV executives of the day did not understand the humour (I have often wondered if TV executives have any humour). But we had a fantastic time making it. The cast was made up of me; a lovely girl called Georgina Melville, who became a real friend over the coming years, who died tragically, very young, with multiple sclerosis (in fact, she was diagnosed while we were making the show); my great mate, Nik Grace; and a wonderful actor called Peter John, who had been the leading actor at Crewe theatre years before.

It's always so lovely to work again with actors one knows and likes. So often, it is the ones that you get on with the least that tend to appear like bad pennies. Although I had tried to steer away from comedy for a while, it was lovely to be performing with such a bunch of professionals. Unfortunately, the mainstay of the female contribution was still tits and arse, but being medical made it more bearable. Just. Chris and Rob were outrageous, though, and abused their position as doctors. They would do appallingly rude things to me and then say, 'It's OK, Lynda, we're doctors!'

I had a good year from the end of 1978 to 1979. There were different guest appearances in *Hazell*, starring Nicholas Ball, and *Shoestring*, with Trevor Eve. I also made a short film called *Waterloo Bridge Handicap* starring Leonard Rossiter. My life was good. I had a group of friends I loved to be with, and I had also become friends with Richard Polo, the owner of Joe Allen restaurant. He was a great theatre-goer, and we would often spend an evening together. We all loved Joe's; it became our second home and we had many parties and gatherings there for every occasion.

I now had a wonderful agent called Sara Randall. Over the last few years I had changed agents a couple of times for different reasons. Now I had found Sara who, with her assistant Bryn, was not just in charge of my career, but became a good friend. I had fallen quite happily into my niche as a character actress who was not unattractive. The point was, in no way was I a sex symbol, except when I was doing comedy where I would adopt the tits and arse pose which, sadly, was still the way women were viewed comedically. It probably did me no good at all in my bid to be seen as a more serious actress, but it kept me in work.

This has always been the dilemma for an actor. Being choosy often means being out of work. It's all very well saving yourself for the big Shakespearean role and practising in the privacy of your room, but if no one ever sees you then no one knows you exist. I believed you had to get out there in the marketplace. What I continued to secretly crave, though, was to be taken seriously as an actress, and the only way that was going to happen was to be in a drama.

My guardian angel answered my silent pleas and in 1979 I landed the role of Ruth Isaacs in *Mackenzie* by Andrea Newman. This was to be her big follow-up series after *Bouquet of Barbed Wire*. My time had come. Now, finally, I was starring in a major television series for the BBC.

Filming *Mackenzie* was hard graft, but I loved every minute of it. There was a wonderful cast headed by Jack Galloway, Sheila Ruskin and Kara Wilson. And me! The action spanned twenty years, starting in the sixties, so we all had to 'age up'. I was playing a woman who was married to a lawyer, and had a daughter, a very young Tracey Ullman, but was also in a long-term affair with an older man, played by Richard Marner. Richard went on to find fame as a German SS officer in the BBC series *'Allo 'Allo!* In classic Andrea Newman style, all the women had an affair with Jack's character, the leading man, who is a young property tycoon, and all the characters' lives become intertwined. It had a great plot, with lots of sex!

Sadly, the BBC, in its wisdom, chose not to publicise it very much, and as it was up against *Minder* on ITV, it took several episodes before the public knew it was on. Once they did, however, the ratings soared. But it was too late. What should have happened is that the show should have got repeated, but no such luck. So my dreams of being discovered in a big hit series evaporated (although Graham Benson, a very successful producer at that time, told a friend of mine that my performance in one episode where I had to burst into tears was the best he had ever seen on TV. So someone appreciated me!)

I was not too disappointed in the lack of interest from the business because, in 1980, Nunzio Peluso walked into my life, and took over every thought in my head.

I was still filming *Mackenzie* when we met. He was a waiter at the very trendy restaurant, La Famiglia, in the King's Road. It was a lovely place, and very popular with film stars and the Chelsea set. It was miles away from me, in North London, but sometimes I would travel across town to join friends there.

This particular night we had gathered for a birthday celebration for Liza Goddard (we had made up by this time). I think Christopher Biggins had organised it, and there was quite a big group of us, including me and Richard Polo. We were all a bit pissed and discussing a very handsome waiter there – Biggins was being outrageous and kept calling him over. He was called Nunzio, he told us, and he was from Naples. He took all the ribbing in good humour and impressed us all with his wit, as well as his looks.

I was in the restaurant again a few days later. Again with Biggins, and Max, who was the maître d' of Joe Allen at the time, and his girlfriend. We had all had way too much champagne before we arrived. To my delight, Nunzio was serving us again. We were making a bit of eye contact through the lunch and I remarked to Chris that I fancied him (the waiter, not Chris). Big mistake! Chris called Nunzio over and proceeded to wind both of us up:

'My friend fancies you, Nunzio.' No response.

'Come on, Lynda, tell him you fancy him.' I smiled pathetically and murmured I was sorry: never show your weakness when Biggins has got you in his sights; he is ruthless.

'Lynda, now come on, why don't you ask this nice young man if he is free? I'm sure a fuck isn't out of the question!'

No! Wrong!

Nunzio gave us all a look that would have wiped out an army and stormed off. Well, I wanted to leave, then and there, but Chris was having none of it. He thought it was all very amusing. When we did leave I tried to catch Nunzio's eye to apologise, but he resolutely avoided my gaze, and disappeared into the back of the restaurant. I kept thinking about it afterwards, and decided I had to go back and apologise.

As luck would have it, a few days later, I was going to meet Sarah Smith (now married to Paul). I told her about the incident at La Famiglia with Nunzio, and we arranged to go there for dinner, so that I could make my peace and she could have a look at this gorgeous waiter who seemed to have stolen my heart.

When we arrived I made sure Nunzio was serving our table. He nodded in recognition, but there were no smiles or greetings. Sarah and I had a lovely dinner and, as we were waiting for the bill, I made an excuse to go to the loo. I found Nunzio and accosted him: 'I am so sorry about the other night. I would not have offended you in any way. I hope you don't think too badly of me.'

He studied me intently for a few moments. It made my heart pound. He smiled (he had the most amazing smile, which one rarely ever saw, so it made it even more special): 'I forgive you, signorina. Let me bring you a glass of wine before you go.'

But before I could stop myself, I heard myself say, 'Why don't you come to my flat when you've finished work, and I'll give you a glass of wine?'

I could not believe I had been so bold.

He stared at me for a long moment and then took my number. I was feeling very wobbly when I went back to the table and Sarah and I left. I dared not tell her what I was up to. I had shocked myself with my cheek, and I did not want to advertise it.

I drove home in a complete panic. 'Nunzio must think I am a complete slapper,' I thought. He could be a nutter. I could be inviting a murderer into my flat. Well, he probably wouldn't ring anyway. Why would he want to come and see me? He was so handsome, he must have thousands of girls after him.

When I got home I paced about for ages. Then the phone rang and it was him. Oh my God! I gave him directions from Chelsea. It was miles away and he would take for ever to get to my flat. I rang my friend, Flic, in LA, in a panic and told her what I had done. She immediately forecast that it would be a disaster, because he would turn out to be a serial rapist. Very helpful, Flic. We chatted for a bit and then, suddenly, there was a ring at the door. He had arrived already. I hung up from Flic, promising to be careful, and went to the door and let him in. I was quite sober by this time and really regretting my impetuosity.

Nunzio was very shy, which made me feel a bit better. If he had been arrogant, and swaggered in, I would have felt very nervous. He had brought a bottle of red wine from the restaurant, and we sat down to drink it. We talked and talked all night. He was so interesting about his life. He had travelled the world since he was a young man. His family was all in Naples, and he obviously missed them all very much. He spoke really good English and had a wicked sense of humour. And he was so handsome. I was in love. I was buzzing and had only had a couple of glasses of wine. We watched the sun come up and, as the early morning light streamed into the flat, Nunzio suddenly took me in his arms and said, 'May I kiss you?'

'I thought you'd never ask,' was my reply.

We went to bed and did not surface until the afternoon. I was completely smitten. I just couldn't get enough of him. Over the next few days we barricaded ourselves in my flat, making love and drinking champagne. Nunzio was everything I had ever wanted. He seemed to feel the same.

He had to go to work, but every chance I had, I would go and pick him up and we would go out. I was still doing *Mackenzie*, so there were many early mornings when I had hardly been to bed. But I thrived on it. I felt so alive: my nerve endings were tingling and I was on a constant high.

I wanted to show him my life. I think I wanted to impress him a little bit as well. Here I was, the famous actress, living *la dolce vita*. Nunzio was very proud and insisted on paying his way. We went to all the places I loved, and some he knew as well. I took him round to meet barmen and maître d's in places like The White Elephant and Langan's. I wanted everyone to meet him and see how happy we were.

We did have one or two hiccups, however. Unbeknown to me, Nunzio had a girlfriend. Nothing important, he said, but he would have to end it with her. It made me feel sick, the idea he had someone else, and I begged him to end it quickly. He played me a bit, enjoying his power, and I had no shame or pride. I was completely under his spell. I just didn't seem to be able to impress him. He didn't know my work and that made me feel really insecure, so I hid behind my persona as an actress, protecting myself behind the image I gave out to everyone as the tough actor who knows it all, who is in control. Nothing could have been further from the truth.

I felt completely out of my depth, both physically and mentally. Nunzio had talked a little about all the women who approached him. How, when he worked on cruise ships, there were dozens of rich women after him. He also told me how much he hated being used by such women. He promised me that he loved me because I took him for what he was and liked his personality. I wasn't just with him for sex. But as the first waves of passion subsided, I felt so inadequate. I could see how girls looked at him when we were out together. The kind of people who ate in La Famiglia were the crème de la crème. All the women were gorgeous and beautifully dressed. How could I compete? I felt full of anguish and insecurity. But whenever it threatened to engulf me, Nunzio would make love to me and I would forget everything. It was just me and him against the world. Within the month he had moved in with me. My life was perfect.

CHAPTER FOURTEEN

LA DOLCE VITA

I SPENT THE WEEKS after Nunzio had moved in, in a constant state of euphoria. I could do nothing but eat, sleep and live Nunzio. When I wasn't working we were out and about. But there were still little warning signs. It was Pat Hay's birthday, and I gave her a party at my flat. As usual everyone got very drunk. So much so that at one point I had to retrieve my new man from on my bed, where he was being seduced by two ladies. I was not amused.

I took him to meet my parents and I think they were pleased I had found someone not in the business. There was one awkward moment over lunch when Nunzio was waxing lyrical about Naples, saying how beautiful it was. Dad was nodding in agreement and then said, 'Oh, yes, you're right. Naples is very lovely. I bombed it during the war, you know.' Whoops.

We went to see Nunzio's family for a week's holiday. His father was dead, but I met his mother and two sisters, and his younger brother, Michele, and his nephew, Gennarro. He was the son of his younger sister, Rosaria. I was so nervous about meeting his mum, but she was lovely. Very gentle and quiet. Not at all like the loud, Neapolitan housewife I had imagined.

They lived in a big old apartment with shutters on the windows and tiled floors. The front room was only used for weddings and funerals, and all the furniture still had the plastic covers over it.

The kitchen was the hub of the family: his sisters Anna and Rosaria never seemed to stop cooking. I loved the lifestyle. It was so different from my own. Everything went so slowly. We would all stroll down to the market to buy the day's food. No frozen food here. Everything was fresh on the day. If we had fish we went to the market, and spent a good hour studying the catch of the day. Then it was on to the fruit and vegetable stalls. Everything was poked and plumped and sniffed for freshness.

Through all this the sisters would carry on a constant stream of conversation, none of which I could understand. But that didn't matter; I followed on behind with bags of groceries in each hand, drinking it all in. I was astonished at how many men there were everywhere. I guessed it was because there was not much work. Many of the men join as crew the ships that sail out of Naples; either the cruise ships like Nunzio did, or the tankers like Anna's husband, Franco. He was away a good deal. In the early evenings, as one walked around, it was nearly all men who were chatting at the tops of their voices over a coffee or a beer. The women were all indoors cooking the dinner or getting dressed for the daily *passagiato*.

The continentals love this time of the day. The whole family puts on their gladrags and walk through the town meeting and greeting. I fell into the routine easily. Maybe because I am an actress, I can pick up things and take them on as my own? Everybody remarked on how Italian I looked and how well I fitted in.

I was a little overwhelmed by the amount of housework involved in this lifestyle. It never ended, and when everyone else fell asleep after lunch I would be toiling over the washing-up. But I was desperate to create a good impression. Nunzio was very attentive and explained everything to me. As these were the early days, he didn't revert to his Italian culture and join the other guys and his friends in the coffee bar without me.

However, I felt very strange when we did go out, because I felt like a pet on a lead. I would stand around while the men all talked, without joining in or saying a word. Even if I had spoken the language, it's unlikely any of the men would have included me in the conversation. That was not how it worked. It was all so different from home. But I loved it. Nunzio would borrow a scooter and we would zoom round the crowded streets, weaving in and out of the traffic and the pedestrians. I often had to beg him to stop at a café so I could have a large brandy to fortify my nerves! It was very scary, and of course we weren't wearing helmets. But I was so happy, and all thoughts of work and London left me cold. I was going to live here, and learn Italian, and have babies...

When we got back to London, though, we both had to find work. There was no money and I needed to pay the mortgage. In fact, I was still contracted to the BBC and filming *Mackenzie*. Nunzio was still working at La Famiglia but he was not happy there. He felt he wasn't appreciated. I wonder now whether the owner, Alvaro, was getting a bit fed up with Nunzio not always being there, and maybe throwing his weight around now that he was living with me. I was to learn to my cost that Nunzio was never happy with his lot, and that he always blamed other people. Things were never his fault.

He was also beginning to dislike it when I had to work long hours. It is difficult enough explaining our working hours to someone English who is not in the business, but to someone Italian it was impossible. He started to make demands. Just little things like I must ring him when I was at work. He would come and pick me up (when I was working I would leave him my car sometimes) and he wanted to know what my relationship was with all the male actors and crew. It was not a big problem, but I wasn't used to sharing my life with anyone, and certainly had never had to account for my time.

Nunzio also started to display signs of jealousy about my past. It's always difficult in a new relationship, because we all have baggage. Guys would call me at home, and Nunzio wanted to know all about them. I was so open, I would always tell him if they were old lovers. Actually they were mostly friends, as I tended to lose contact with anyone I had been out with. Sometimes the phone would ring and then go dead. Nunzio would always make a bit of a fuss and suggest it was someone who knew he was there and didn't want him to know anything. It all got very complicated to me. I didn't have any problems with the way things were. As far as I was concerned, I was with Nunzio, and people knew that.

Greg was a big problem for Nunzio. He did not like me talking to my ex-husband. Not that Greg and I talked that much, but every now and then he would call. In fact it gave me great pleasure to let Greg know I had finally found someone again.

But all these little niggles were forgotten when we were together, on our own. How different it all was from my life with Greg, when I was lucky to get a peck on the cheek. Now I had a man who regarded sex like food and drink, as part of his existence. Nunzio used to say that the English talked about sex too much and never did it enough.

However, Nunzio's problems were never far away. When we had nights with my friends we all drank copious amounts of wine and loved nothing better than to talk about everything from sex to fashion to gossip. Nunzio would sit and take it all in, then when we got home, would offer me his opinions on everybody. It wasn't always positive and I would spend a good deal of time defending my mates.

Nunzio's jealousy started to get the better of him. When we were round at Marilyn's, for instance, there was a guy there with whom I had been at drama school. He was being very flirty and insinuating all sorts of things about me. In actuality, I didn't know him that well as he had been in the year below me and so we didn't mix. But he obviously felt the need to make people think he knew me very well. Nunzio got really beady with him and that just made things worse. There was quite an atmosphere when we left. When we got home, Nunzio went on and on at me, trying to find out if I had slept with the guy. I explained that if I had I would have told him. It got quite heated and I was very upset. And on another occasion, one morning Nunzio went off to work and left me doing the ironing. A perfectly innocent task. About half an hour later the front door burst open and in rushed Nunzio, shouting at me to own up, as he knew I had someone in the flat. It was so ridiculous, besides which it was such a small flat that had I been hiding someone he could have seen immediately. I just couldn't understand what was the matter with him.

It is so easy, in hindsight, to see the beginnings of the problems. I should have seen the cracks but like most people in this situation, I ignored the signs.

I WAS BEGINNING TO feel uncomfortable and tried to talk to Nunzio about his behaviour. The trouble was that he was not only jealous of me in our relationship, but he was jealous of my past, about which I could do nothing.

There was a sense in which he realised he had a problem but just did not know how to control the misgivings he had when he felt them. I tried to make him feel secure at all times but it was very difficult because I couldn't anticipate all of the problems all of the time. I would tell friends not to mention anything about my past or past boyfriends that might set Nunzio off and I made sure he knew where I was at all times. But more often than not my plans were foiled somehow by circumstances beyond my control.

After about two months Nunzio and I had a row, and I told him we couldn't go on like this and that I thought it was better if he moved out for a while. He told me that if he left that would be it; he would not come back at all. He went off to work and I spent the day in turmoil. I just didn't know what to do, but my work was suffering. I felt so hemmed in. Instead of going to work and feeling secure in my relationship so that I could concentrate on the job, I was beset with niggles and worries about Nunzio. I had to be strong and tell him to leave.

That evening when I got back, Nunzio showed me a contract with a cruise ship. He had signed up to go to work on a ship that sailed out of Miami. I was devastated. Why did he have to be so extreme? I think we were both testing the water and neither of us would back down. So after a night of tears and lovemaking, Nunzio left.

I thought it was all a bit of a game and that he would come round eventually, but as I waved him off at the door I did feel a sense of relief: it was as if a great weight had been lifted from me. There was calm again in my little home. I had it to myself again. Yes, I was upset, because I did love Nunzio; there was no doubt about that. But time would heal my heart. How wrong could I be?

From the moment Nunzio was gone I felt bereft. My life was empty. I missed him so much. I physically missed him with every bone in my body. It was like having flu. I ached for him. I couldn't concentrate on anything at all. I rang him and he was very cool. I asked him if he was missing me but he was very noncommittal.

After a couple of weeks I was a wreck. I had a gap in my filming and I decided to fly to Miami and see Nunzio. I rang him with the news, and he agreed he would be there to meet me. He was working with another young Italian called Ciro, and he and his new wife had a small flat in Miami where Nunzio stayed when his ship was docked. I was so nervous about the whole deal. I had had a long talk to Lynda La Plante who had told me that when she had her ups and downs with her husband, and they split for a while, she had had to make a decision about what she wanted from life. If I missed Nunzio so much I should go and tell him. I could overcome the problems if I wanted him that much.

I arrived in Miami and was overwhelmed by the whole place. It was such a different environment from what I was used to in London. I felt very vulnerable, but Nunzio was wonderful. He seemed really happy to see me and I was welcomed by Ciro and his wife into their home. For the next week, it was as if Nunzio and I had never been apart. We were like any young couple on holiday. The four of us had a ball, going out to bars and restaurants. The beach was amazing. Just miles of white sand. Everyone was so beautiful in Miami, it was like being on a film set.

We went to Disneyland for the day and laughed and laughed. I began to relax. My Italian hadn't improved, so sometimes it was hard when the other three all chatted amongst themselves, but I made an effort to get on with Ciro's wife. Sadly, I can't remember her name. She was very sweet and I could see it was very hard on her because she was on her own a good deal when Ciro was on the ship.

One morning, Nunzio and I were in the tiny bathroom together, getting ready to go out. I was in my bra and pants by the door. Ciro knocked and half opened the door to say something to Nunzio, not realising I was in there too. I laughed and told him not to worry and peered round the door to speak to him. Nunzio went crazy. What was I doing showing myself to his friend? I was a slut! I was stunned. I was hardly naked – a bikini would have shown the same thing. What was the problem? He wouldn't speak to me all day; then, when we went out in the evening, he watched me like a hawk. I felt so uncomfortable. For the rest of my stay he would keep on about that incident. Did I fancy Ciro? Why did I show him my body? I was completely taken aback. Why would I come all this way to see him if I wanted anyone else, for God's sake? I longed to talk it over with Ciro's wife because she was Italian, and maybe she could help me understand the mentality. But I just did not speak the language well enough. All we could do was smile at each other, and she gave me a hug when she saw I was down.

Nunzio had to leave on his ship the same morning I was to get my flight home. However, he had to leave really early so he had arranged for Ciro to take me to the airport. We said our goodbyes on the dock and I begged him again to forgive me if I had in any way behaved badly. He just shrugged and said to forget it. He promised to ring, and so did I, and we kissed each other, and he left. I had such mixed feelings. I still loved him so much but it just seemed impossible for us to find a level playing field for our relationship. Ciro took me to the airport and I flew home.

For the next three or four months, Nunzio and I spoke regularly on the phone. My bill was huge! But our phone calls were not the loving billing and cooing of lovers apart. It was mostly Nunzio ringing me and accusing me of having men next to me in my bed. It was ridiculous. We wasted so much time and money on the phone having massive rows. I would bore my friends about it, but most of them just thought it was sweet that Nunzio cared so much to be that jealous. My parents felt differently and I knew they were not happy about things, but what could they do?

Nunzio finally responded to my pleadings to come back to London and appeared on my birthday in 1981, when I was thirty-three. We talked and talked about all the problems and recriminations. He still went on a great deal about Ciro, and kept asking me if I had slept with him after he left. I begged him to ask Ciro. I had tried to explain to Ciro and his wife at the time that I was worried about what Nunzio thought, and would they please explain to him and put his mind at rest. But as I was to learn over the years, whatever went on in Nunzio's head was impossible to change.

Nunzio's mother became very ill and he was going to go to Italy to see her. I wanted to go with him. I wanted her to know I was there for Nunzio. He went on his own first and when he came back he was very upset because he knew she didn't have long to live. We were very close now and I really felt that he needed me. So I proposed to him. Yes, I did. I wanted him to know he was loved and that I would always be there for him. We decided his mother would be happy if she could see us married, so we set a date for July that year. We would get married in London and then try and go and visit her afterwards. In fact, all our friends clubbed together and bought us tickets to go to Naples for a long weekend as a wedding present.

We had very little time to prepare, but in any event we wanted a low-key affair. After the circus of my wedding to Greg I did not want the press to find out. Because I had been married before we had to have a civil ceremony at Camden registry office. But then I wanted a blessing. Nunzio's family were Catholic and I wanted his mother to know I was taking this marriage very seriously. I had a dear friend called Peter Delaney, whom I had met through Chris Biggins, who was the vicar at All Hallows by the Tower, a very old church next to the Tower of London. He was someone that Nunzio liked very much, so it was appropriate he should perform the blessing. Peter was to become a very important influence in my life.

The other person that Nunzio had formed a close friendship with was Jack Tinker, the *Daily Mail* theatre critic. Jack was an extraordinary figure in the theatre world. He was tiny in stature but huge in personality. He had such style, which Nunzio loved because he was always saying the British have no style. Jack was to prove a dear and trusted friend over the coming years. He was the only person Nunzio would ever listen to, and when times were desperate, I would turn to Jack. He died very suddenly in 1997 from an asthma attack. It was such a shock and a devastating blow to everyone who knew and loved him. He left a partner, Adrian, and two lovely daughters. He was a one-off and I still miss him now.

Jack was to be the best man at the wedding and Lynda La Plante was my bridesmaid. We were to have the reception at my flat, and Mum and I were going to do the catering. Richard Polo, the owner of Joe Allen restaurant, very generously gave us crates of champagne, which we put in the bath with tons of ice. On the morning of the wedding, Mum and I were up at five making smoked salmon sandwiches. I had gone to bed quite late because Jack and I had both been appearing on a quiz show at London Weekend Television called *Tell The Truth*. Everyone had been sworn to secrecy about the up and coming event, because of the press, but suddenly, on camera, Jack let slip he was off to my wedding the next day. Never trust a journalist! Thankfully no one picked up on the information and we were left in peace.

It poured with rain all morning but Nunzio assured me that was regarded as good luck in Italy. I wanted to believe him. I had spent rather a lot of money on my wedding outfit, which was peach silk and lace. Hand-made, it was the nearest thing I could find that looked like a wedding dress for someone who had been married before. It was so important to me that when Nunzio's mother saw me, she knew I was serious about my intentions towards her son. I did not want her to think I was some flighty actress. The venerable Peter Delaney performed the blessing with all the right mixture of seriousness and joy. Then it was back to our place for a knees-up.

The next morning Nunzio and I flew to Naples. We wore our wedding outfits and when we got to Naples we drove round Torre del Greco, the town on the outskirts of Naples where he lived, on a scooter. People threw flowers at us and shouted their congratulations. His mum had made a huge cake and her living room was packed with friends and family, most of whom I had never met. In the manner of the wedding culture in Italy, people pinned money on us; Nunzio actually gave it all to his brother who was hard up at the time: I had no say in the matter. It was family! But it did not spoil a perfect day.

We rode to the hotel up the road to spend our wedding night in splendour. Our room had a balcony from where we could look up at Vesuvius towering above us. The volcano was like a giant shadow over the town. It had last erupted in 1948, the year I was born, and was still active. To understand the power of the devastation it could wreak you only had to visit Pompeii up the road. It is amazing to me how people ignore Nature when it suits them. The people of Naples and the surrounding towns all know the dangers of living in the foothills of a live volcano, yet buildings are still built illegally – then abandoned when the council find out – and all along the road that climbs and winds its way to the top of Vesuvius one can see the ruins of half-built houses. I have been to the top a couple of times and stared down into the vast crater with its hot steaming geezers. It is wondrous. The enormity of its power is thrilling. At New Year the Neapolitans go crazy. They love fireworks and, unlike the UK, they do not seem to have any qualms about the danger of fireworks. They even make their own! It is a seriously dangerous night in the town. I used to stand on the balcony of Nunzio's sister's flat and watch it all kick off at midnight. Hundreds and thousands of fireworks going off all over the city. The noise was deafening but I always enjoyed the irony that the biggest bloody firework of all was right there, above us in the darkness. Just waiting.

On our wedding night in Italy, another shadow fell on us. Nunzio's temper. I do not even remember what set him off, but he had a go at me, and stormed out of the hotel and left me for most of the night. I was confused and tired and bewildered – no change there then, but this was my wedding night. I should be in the arms of my husband. I could feel the knot of uncertainty growing in my stomach. Please, not again! But the next day we made up and I forgot about it as we were feted like heroes by all and sundry.

We returned to the UK high on our love. But it was not to last; all too quickly my dream was shattered. Within six weeks my nose was broken.

CHAPTER FIFTEEN

'TO KNOW THINGS AS THEY ARE IS BETTER THAN TO BELIEVE THINGS AS THEY SEEM'

(TOM WICKER)

THE SILENCE WAS absolute. Like the first few seconds after a car crash. Complete shock. Complete panic. How had this happened? How could this have happened to me? I felt no pain, just the numbness of disbelief. I felt like I was caught in a bubble of stillness, an aching silence that seemed to stretch out forever. Neither of us moved. Neither of us said a word. My breath had literally gone from me.

The bubble broke only when I became aware of blood dripping on to my skirt. Droplets of pain, puncturing the silence.

My marriage was only six weeks old and my nose was halfway across my face. My beautiful nose, which had been created for me five years ago, in another life. A nose that had played such a significant role in my life and in shaping my identity. Now it was broken and my future in tatters. The enormity of what had happened just did not sink in. I just felt numb physically and emotionally.

Nunzio drove me to the nearest A&E, which was at Great Ormond Street. It was after closing time in the pubs and all the usual suspects were lined up in the waiting room. Anyone who has found themselves sitting under the harsh, cold lights of Accident and Emergency will know that feeling of unreality. The screaming of a child and the outbursts of a drunk all seem to come from a long way away. It echoes all around you and rings in your ears.

I was finally put in a cubicle, and a young doctor came and examined my nose and took my details. I tried to explain that I needed to be sorted out pretty quickly as I was due to film on Monday and I was worried about losing my contract with the TV company. This just seemed to irritate him and he dismissed me, saying there was nothing they could do for me until the swelling went down. I spent a long weekend with a throbbing face. It hurt too much to cry, so I just sat and fretted. I decided the only person who could help me was Roy Sanders, the wonderful surgeon who had done my original nose job.

On Monday morning I rang his secretary and, by a stroke of luck, he was able to see me that afternoon. Nunzio drove me to Roy's consulting rooms in Portland Place. We sat in silence in front of the surgeon as he scribbled his notes down. I can still hear the scratching of his pen across the paper as we waited for him to finish writing. Finally he sat back and studied me.

'How did you break your nose, Lynda?' There was a pause and I glanced at Nunzio.

'On the steering wheel of my car,' I replied.

'What make of car do you drive?' Roy continued.

'A VW Beetle,' I said.

'And you're sure you broke your nose on that steering wheel?'

'Yes,' I whispered.

'Because you see, Lynda,' he looked at me carefully, 'whatever

I write down now cannot be changed at a later date. Do you understand?'

'Yes.'

Roy was still looking at me, his gaze unwavering. After another pause, he continued: 'OK, fine. If that's what you're saying. You can come into hospital tonight and I will operate tomorrow morning. You should be back on camera by Friday.'

Twenty or so years later, in February 2000, Nunzio told Lester Middlehurst in the *Daily Mail*:

> I have heard that I am supposed to have broken her nose a few weeks after we were married. What actually happened was that Lynda had gone to a function at about 10 a.m. in the morning and had said she would be coming home at 4 p.m. By the time I went to work at 6 p.m. she still hadn't come home. I was quite worried about her. Then, at 11 p.m. she came to pick me up at the restaurant where I was working and she was fairly drunk. We rowed in the car going home and when we got back I called her a bitch and a slut. She was furious and jumped on top of me and I had to push her back on the bed. That was when she broke her nose. I certainly didn't punch her.

My version of that night varies somewhat from that. Yes, I did leave in the morning to drive up north to a gig for charity. It was at lunchtime, and other celebrities involved included Bernie Winters and Gareth Hunt, both guys I had worked with before. We didn't finish up in Leicester until about 4 p.m. and then we had a two-hour journey back to London. I rang Nunzio when we stopped on the way home because I would be later than I thought. When we got to London the driver was going to drop me off at home but I decided to come into the West End with Gareth, who was sharing the car with me, and have a drink with him and then go and meet Nunzio from work.

We went to a club/restaurant called Legends, where the manager was a friend of ours and where Nunzio had previously worked (he'd left under a bit of a cloud). I was pleased to be able to see Paul, and spent some time talking to him. I then left and went to meet Nunzio. Yes, I had had a few drinks too many but I was happy to be meeting my hubby, pleased with the outcome of my chat with Paul, and was looking forward to sharing all this with Nunzio over a late supper. How naive of me to imagine Nunzio would greet me with open arms. Instead, I was met by a torrent of abuse and accusations. Apparently I had been out with all and sundry. Screwing Gareth Hunt and probably Bernie Winters and the whole club (fortunately not Paul Macbeth, who was gay).

As Nunzio drove us home we rowed all the way. He called me all sorts of horrid names and I ended up with a broken nose. But as it went on to say in the *Daily Mail* article, who knows what goes on between a husband and wife? Only Nunzio and I know the truth. I will leave you to reach your own conclusions.

It's so hard looking back now to understand my actions. Why did I just not leave then and there? Nunzio is quoted in the same article as saying he never loved me. That he only married me because he was in an emotional state about his mother dying and because I offered him a house. I have no idea how much truth there is in that, but if it is true, I really wish we had never wed. We could have saved ourselves years of pain and grief. All I knew at the time was that my entire life had changed overnight, and I just wasn't sure what to do next, or how to get my thoughts in order.

At the time, I was in the middle of filming a children's series called *Murphy's Mob*. This had come with its own set of problems.

I was playing the wife of a man who ran a football club for kids. The main character was played by Ken Hutchison, who was not easy to work with at all and was known to be a notorious drunk and womaniser. Actually he was a lovely man, I discovered, as long as the lines were clearly drawn. When we first started the job I knew I would have to decide whether I would drink with Ken, ignore him, or sleep with him. The third option was not even on the table because I had just got married to Nunzio, but if I ignored him I set myself up for weeks of grief.

Ken was a bit like Dennis Waterman, in that he was one of the lads. You went to the pub and held your own and bought the drinks and took the schtick or they would crucify you. But here was the problem. I couldn't drink with them because Nunzio would go mad if I stayed late in the bar after work. I completely understand that a newly wedded bride does not go to the pub after work with her mates every night, but this was once a week, after the recording, and all the cast and crew were expected to stay behind, even for a quick drink. Not me. I tried to keep it all sweet, but I would get grief from the other actors, especially Ken, and so I would try and stay for a quick one without Nunzio finding out, arriving back at home just before he left the restaurant. Of course, it was not an ideal situation, but I didn't want anybody to know that I had a husband who was a bit difficult.

Of course, it was bound to go wrong and one time, when I had rung Nunzio and said I was on my way home, I stayed in the bar too long so that when he rang home to check I had got back, I wasn't there. By the time I got home, Nunzio had left goodness knows how many messages, screaming at me down the phone. I was so frightened that I left and went to see my friend, Catharine. Her brother, John Hales, had been in the year below me at drama school and we had been friends ever since. He lived with Catharine, who worked in the City, and they were both part of the Marilyn Johnson gang. I arrived at their house in a terrible state and they were just tremendous. John went off to my flat to meet Nunzio and try and calm him down. He succeeded, to the extent that I was able to go back home, but he couldn't save me from the barrage of abuse I got all that night.

I had to face this kind of behaviour on an almost daily basis and it became the norm in my marriage. But in between the bouts, I had a husband who loved me passionately, or so I thought. I would discuss the problem with close girlfriends like Pat and Catharine and, in the early days, we all came to the same conclusion: that Nunzio was very insecure and I would have to work very hard to make him feel secure. All very well in theory, but I was not a therapist and I had issues of my own to deal with in respect of insecurity. Unfortunately, I still needed the approval and praise of my colleagues. And I was still suffering from the effects of my last marriage. I needed Nunzio to show me love and security, not mistrust and jealousy.

I WAS ALSO QUESTIONING my heritage. As I had grown older, I would often talk to my parents about my background. Did they think my mother was still alive? All my faults, I attributed to my birth mother. It had become a sort of family joke with me and Mum that my drinking and carrying-on must come from my genes. My real mother must have been a drunken nymphomaniac! We laughed about it but Mum would always defend my birth mother and say she was sure she must have been a lovely woman who had to give me up for many other reasons besides not wanting me in her life. I used to try and talk to Nunzio about all these issues because, by coincidence, his mother had been adopted, too.

I honestly think that although Nunzio was not stupid by any means, he was not used to discussing things from an intellectual standpoint. I love talking things out till the cows came home, but for Nunzio, it was all much more black and white: your wife stayed at home and looked after you, and the husband went to work. Respect was the byword. Do not *dis*respect me or else. But respect is earned, on both sides. Of course, he accepted we did not live in Naples and I went to work. The problem for him was that my work was, and still is, more than a job. It reflected my whole attitude to life. It had been my life up until now. It had saved me from going under. My work was people, and that involved dealing with men.

Men. God Almighty, men, especially Italian men, do have a problem with their egos. It's all about them. The number of plays and films that are based on men being cuckolded or deceived... 'Cuckolded' is a word you don't hear a lot, nowadays, except in southern Italy, and there I heard it all the time. I was forever being accused of making Nunzio a cuckold: a *'cornu'* in Italian. I would try sometimes to explain to his sister Anna the problems we had but I just did not speak Italian well enough to make myself understood. She was such a lovely woman and I am sure she knew the kind of problems I was having, but her loyalty to Nunzio made our friendship impossible. But it seemed to me that he was not upset at the thought that I might be unfaithful because I no longer cared for him, but because another man may have got one over on him.

While things had been going well between us in the early days my drinking had just about stopped. Now, I began to deal with Nunzio's obsession of my being unfaithful by drinking too much. Things then got even worse because Nunzio joined me. One incident that sticks in my mind around this time was the death of Nunzio's mother. We were arguing a good deal and I was still doing the children's series and having to deal with Nunzio accusing me of having it off with Ken Hutchison every five minutes. I used to get away and go and see my uncle Row (the uncle who loved to tease

161

me when I was young, and the father of my cousin Gillian). Over the years I had grown very close to him. He had made a mess of his marriage to Gillian's mother, my Auntie Joy, and Gillian had had a tough childhood because she was sent to boarding school and Row was away a good deal on business.

Around the time that Nunzio and I were having our problems, Uncle Row had to have several operations on his foot. He had to stay in a nursing home and he was a very bad patient. He drank too much, which had given him gout, and he was under strict instructions from the nursing staff not to drink. I would visit him and sit for hours pouring out my woes, and Uncle Row would see it as a wonderful opportunity to pour me glass after glass of Scotch (which I didn't really like), in order to have some himself. Anyway, the day Nunzio's mum died I was with Uncle Row getting sozzled. Nunzio didn't know where I was or he had forgotten. By the time I got home he was bouncing off the walls. But he didn't know whether to shout at me or cry. He blamed me for everything, which didn't make sense, but I could handle that because he wasn't attacking my behaviour as such; just the fact that I made his life a misery. That day we did talk, in between the shouting and accusations. Nunzio broke down and admitted he was frightened I would leave him. That women always treated him badly and that his ex-girlfriend had gone behind his back and been unfaithful. I could handle all this. I felt needed. I would spend my life making Nunzio feel secure, then he would see how much I loved him and he wouldn't attack me any more. We could move forward.

Nunzio went off to work the next morning as usual. I was sitting on the carpet in the front room of my little flat trying to get myself together. There was a knock on the door and a neighbour was standing there, waving a finger in my face and berating me for all the noise last night. His mouth was moving but I couldn't hear him. I just broke down and sobbed, 'Please, please, don't shout at me. I can't take any more. Don't you realise how unhappy people can be, sometimes? They don't mean to make a noise. I'm sorry, but please don't shout at me.' He looked so shocked; he just stopped and turned and walked away.

From this incident came the idea we should start a family. The trouble was I didn't really want children yet. I still had so much to do in my career. I remember we had a terrible row and Nunzio was leaning into me against the wall and screaming into my face that if I really loved him I would want his children. There comes a point in these situations where there is no logic or refinement in the exchanges; it is fight or just give in, and, for me, it had come to the point where it was easier to just shut up and give in.

The honeymoon was well and truly over – if it ever began. We all make decisions that have far-reaching effects, and we only have ourselves to blame. I knew that, but I don't think Nunzio ever did, or does, to this day.

CHAPTER SIXTEEN

THE JOY OF MOTHERHOOD IN A SEA OF DESPAIR

I N 1982, we bought our first house. It was from a secret auction held by Islington Council, who wanted to get rid of a lot of derelict property. My friend Catharine had got to know about it and we took her very sound advice and put in a bid for a lovely Victorian terraced house in Holloway. Through Catharine we also got a fantastic builder called Eddie Moir. He and his wife, Kath, were wonderful people; sadly, Eddie is dead now but Kath and I still exchange cards at Christmas. They also introduced me to Hetty, who became my cleaner for fifteen years.

Eddie sorted us out in time for the arrival of baby Michael. I was up ladders and scrubbing floors right up to the last minute. I would like to be able to say that my husband was supportive but that would be a lie. He had recently lost his job, and he was very down until well after our son was born. But we were so busy trying to set up our life together that I really had no time to ponder my fate. At least the black moods that descended on Nunzio were more of a general nature than solely aimed at me, so I could pretend to myself that things would improve when our baby was born.

I was having my baby at University College Hospital. I was having an elected Caesarean because the baby was breach. I had been going to private ante-natal classes because although I wasn't a household name as such, people did tend to recognise me and I felt more comfortable practising my breathing exercises in a more secluded environment. I made a friend for life in these classes, called Anna Ferrante. She was a dentist at the time and married to a GP called Albert. They lived in East Finchley, and her daughter, Alice, was born a day or so after Michael. We had such a laugh and, as both of us had husbands who were not very hands-on in the baby stakes, we teamed up at the back of the hall and had a ball. In the event, it turned out my breathing exercises were not required. I had an epidural Caesarean (that enabled me to be awake), having been taken into hospital two days before and then induced.

I lay in my ward for two days wondering if I was in a kindergarten – the expectant mothers were all so young. They were all unmarried and two of them used to go out and get cans of lager to while away the time. One night, one of them insisted to the nurse that her waters had broken, but the nurse just replied that when one had drunk as much lager as she had that night, she was bound to pee it all out. Charming. They used to love coming to look at me: 'that woman off the telly'. I felt like a stuffed dummy on show in Madame Tussauds.

When it was time for the Caesarean, I was wheeled down to the operating theatre with Nunzio at my side, doing his best to be supportive. He was in such a state that I completely forgot what was happening to me and was busy talking him through the procedure. So I suppose in a strange way he did help! With the epidural all I could feel was a bit of pressure, but it seemed to take for ever to find the bloody baby. The doctor was such an age feeling around inside me, I was half expecting him to produce a pork pie and a hat.

Towards the end of the operation, Nunzio decided to lean over and look past the screen they had put up, and take a peek. It was a big mistake and he had to leave the room very swiftly. When I quizzed him afterwards about what he had seen, he said, '*Dio mio* [my God], Lynda, I saw everything. They take out everything to find the baby. I could see your liver. I know it was your liver, because I recognised it from the restaurant!'

Michael Peluso was finally lifted out triumphantly at 11 a.m., 13th April, 1983, weighing 6lbs 12ozs. As they laid him on the scales, he peed in a wonderful arc, much to the amusement of his father. He was then whisked away from me and I was sewn up and taken back to the ward. I fell asleep, only to be awoken by excruciating pain in my abdomen. I couldn't even call out. As I lay there waiting for someone to come, I honestly thought I was dying. Finally, a nurse came and explained that it was because the painkilling drugs had worn off. Well, give me some more then! She refused saying that the epidural should be enough. I just lay there, whimpering, for what seemed like for ever, waiting to die.

In the morning, the gynaecologist came to see me and I asked why I had to endure this pain. He was so embarrassed and apologetic. There was nothing on my notes to explain to the staff that after my epidural I should have had painkillers once it wore off, otherwise I would go into postnatal contractions because my womb thought it needed to expel the afterbirth (or something like that – I couldn't fully concentrate on what he was saying, for obvious reasons). Well, thanks a lot, guys!

Unfortunately, I also got the ward sister from hell, who recognised me from my *General Hospital* days, and who decided she was going to make damn sure I didn't get above myself. Everyone was treated the same in her ward, thank you very much... She would force me out of bed, as I clutched my stomach – which I really felt was going to deposit its contents on the ward floor – and shushed me down the ward to the toilet. I won't go into details but suffice it to say that week was horrendous.

And on top of all the female stuff one has to endure, one then has the visiting to contend with. Every time I managed to shuffle down to the toilet, I would hear shrieks and inevitably it would be a guest of mine, arriving with wonderful flowers and a five-minute monologue to amuse the entire ward. Biggins won that competition, needless to say. Women were clutching their stitches, helpless with laughter. By the time everyone had left I was exhausted. There was little time for bonding with the baby; it was all about nappy changing and wheeling the trolley and learning to breastfeed. I could hardly hold Michael I was so sore, but I was determined, and I was very lucky I had no problems whatsoever feeding him – I had so much milk I was in danger of drowning the poor little mite.

To be honest, I had been so worried that I would not like the baby when it arrived and not be a good mother, I was almost in denial about the whole thing. You're so tired, it's like being in a pit with high walls where, every time you manage to get near the top, you slip and fall back down. I even thought I might hate the baby or it might hate me from all the rows it had heard in my womb. Silly me.

I remember one night, going in to feed Michael. Everyone else in the ward was asleep and for once it was quite quiet. There was just the sound that babies make when they are sleeping; little snuffles and whines. I was still having trouble standing upright but I got Michael in my arms and put him to my breast. His little fingers were trying to grasp my skin, feather light. He sort of opened his eyes and squinted up at me. He really seemed to be trying to catch my eye and hold my gaze, and tears just welled up from deep within me. I had no idea I had this store of emotion inside me. It felt so raw, this love I had for him. It was like electric energy sparking inside every bone in my body and I wanted to scream with this pain of love I felt for this little animal at my breast. The world stood still. I was inside the bubble that all women experience, I believe, where they connect with their child for the first time. The bond is snapped round your heart and can only be removed by your death. I am sorry to be so dramatic but that is how it felt to me. Whatever else happened to me in my life, I knew I would never forget that moment.

So now we were a family. Nunzio's sister, Rosaria, had come to stay so that she could help me in the early days, as after a Caesarean one is supposed to rest for six weeks. Her experience of children was giving birth at fifteen to Gennarro, who was then cared for by her mother and sister. Bless her heart, she meant well, but Rosaria was a bag of nerves. She had no patience and would grab Michael from me and pace up and down the kitchen shaking him in her arms and rocking madly from foot to foot trying to get him to go to sleep. From day one we fell out because she wanted to give him a dummy. No way. Not my baby.

I had also got a deadline to meet as far as my recovery was concerned because I was booked to do an episode of *The Gentle Touch* starring Jill Gascoine. The plan was that I would express my milk into little bottles, which could then be kept in the fridge and substituted for my breast when I was out during the day, filming. I had spent hours getting Michael to take the bottle. He was not keen and had to be coaxed. Patience was paramount.

Two days with his Auntie Rosaria and all my hard work was out the window. He would scream if the bottle came near him. So now I had to go to work knowing that he was crying his eyes out and Rosaria would be in the kitchen, getting her knickers in a twist. And where was Nunzio in all this? Sitting at the kitchen table, day in, day out. On returning home, exhausted from filming on some godforsaken housing estate in east London, my breasts full to bursting, I would be greeted by a screaming baby and two adults sitting at the kitchen table, smoking. I ended up in the bedroom crying down the phone to my mother, who finally said, 'For goodness' sake, Lynda, get a grip. It's your baby, do what you think is best and send Rosaria home.'

Isn't your mum's advice always the best? I found a nanny who would come filming with me so I could feed Michael as we went along. Needless to say, we had a couple of disasters. The first girl was caught, by Nunzio, shaking poor Michael. The second girl was very efficient but I just couldn't stand her.

Anyone who has gone through these early days will share with me the torment of trying to get it all right. I had to work because we needed the money, so I just had to get on with it and improvise where necessary.

Day relentlessly followed day; there was no respite. Nunzio finally got a job so at least I didn't have to worry about him, and I could have some time alone just to be with my baby.

Then, just as I was coming out of that early fog of breast milk and hormonal emotion, we moved on to the next challenge.

CHAPTER SEVENTEEN

A COMMERCIAL BREAK

As if MICHAEL'S birth was not enough to change my life, my agent rang one morning and suggested I go along and meet the director of a new campaign for Unilever, starring as the mum of a family that used Oxo gravy.

I was very snooty about the whole thing and, at first, I declined. Back then, doing commercials could be very dodgy for the serious career. I was still having problems being taken seriously as an actress because of all the comedy I had done, so being in a series of adverts would just about finish off any credibility I might have achieved. But Nunzio and my agent persuaded me to go along and meet Derek Coutts, the director.

Derek was very well known in the advertising business. He was a fantastic director and not only created our campaign but also the Gold Blend coffee adverts with Anthony Head and Sharon Maughan. I was asked to do a test with another actor called Michael Redfern, and an assortment of different children.

It was quite fun and I thought no more about it. Then, a couple of days later my agent called to say they wanted to see me again. So I tested with a different husband and another set of children. I went home and heard no more. I was asked back about three or four more times, at which point I decided I was bloody well going to get this job just to prove I could! And I did!

It was like landing the leading role in *Gone with the Wind*, there was so much hoo-ha about it. The money was fantastic and everybody was thrilled for me. I still felt a bit of a niggle; being a mum making gravy for my family was not quite how I had seen my career advancing. But Nunzio was thrilled, and it would mean we had some financial security for the next three years.

Michael Redfern had been cast as the husband, and we had three children: Nick, Alison and Jason. We all used our own names. Our first Jason lasted a few years and then he was replaced by Colin. It is amazing, looking back, how over the years the children grew up. By the time we were doing the last commercials in 1999, Colin was married with two children! He worked for the Ministry of Food, I think, by then. The eldest boy, Nick, also changed. When we started, the first Nick was a very intense young man, who later became a vegan, and had to give up his role in the adverts because of his beliefs. He wouldn't touch the meat. I bumped into him years later and I think he was working for television in the costume department. He was a very gentle soul. He was replaced by Nick McKechnie – his sister, Donna, is an actress and comedienne, and Nick now has a very successful band. He was very clever and full of energy. Alison, my character's daughter, was a bit of a lost soul. She was a sweet girl and desperately wanted to be an actress. Her father was an actor and started a drama school with Alison's mother. I think they worked very hard when Alison was growing up. Over the years she struggled with her weight. When you're growing up, it is difficult enough dealing with all the usual sorts of issues; all the more so if you are in the public eye. It's also not easy to sit round a table all day staring at piles of food and not eat! Mind you, after staring at a roast chicken that had sat under the heat of the studio lights all day, eating was the last thing I wanted to do. But Alison would pick at the food all day, while still having the odd packet of crisps and her lunch and dinner. I became like her nagging mother, constantly telling her to stop nibbling. Poor girl!

It was particularly fascinating watching the home economist, Sue, cook all day and managing to make things look fresh and inviting. She used to brush the roast with olive oil just before a take to make it look succulent. Another trick, which was revolting, was to blow cigarette smoke under the lid of the serving dish so that when I lifted the lid it looked like steam. We never actually ate anything that was on the table – Sue would serve something separately for us, thank goodness Our house was not real. It was a set built in the studio based on a real house somewhere. Sue would have this oven and little kitchen set up at the side and cook all day.

Michael Redfern was the perfect foil for my character. Stoic and strong, and always there for his wife and family. He used to complain that all he ever did was smile benignly into the camera. He was an amazing joke teller and had a vast repertoire of terrible jokes. We would have to sit for hours round the kitchen table while the lights were adjusted and other bits of equipment tweaked, and he would entertain us all nonstop. Some days, I would have to leave before his close-ups because I was often working in the theatre, and so I was unable to feed him his lines or give him a reaction to his. The poor man had to act to an empty chair at the end of the table! He was brilliant. We laughed so much.

It was actually very tiring to film the adverts as the days were very long. We were in for make-up at 7 a.m. and often we would work until ten at night. There is a saying in the business that the 'pack shot' is the most important thing in a commercial which, as the name suggests, is the close-up of the product being advertised. In this case it was the famous little red cube. Sometimes they would use a hand artist to hold the Oxo cube in close-up, but more often than not it would be me. It could take hours to film the all-important moment when I unwrapped the cube and sprinkled it into the stew. Thankfully, there was a lovely props man who had a big bowl of the stuff and he had a special little gadget that made the dried stock into a square that was then easier to break with my fingers. There was also a special way of pulling off the foil and I had to do this over and over again. It would get really hot under the lights and the smell of the powdered stock would get to me in the end. I would have to go home and have a bath to get rid of the smell.

A very unique kind of acting is required for this sort of commercial, and not everyone can do it. I was very proud of the fact that in forty or sixty seconds we managed to tell a story, with real emotions portrayed. They were like mini soaps and the public really enjoyed the on-going saga of the family. We would all throw in our ideas for the script and often when we were all round the kitchen table, we would ad lib. Some of the improvised dialogue got very raunchy, and I often wished we could have made an X-rated Oxo commercial!

When we first started filming, the Powers That Be had decided I did not look old enough to have three children, so my make-up and hair were designed to make me look more mumsy. Then, over time, as women, in general, got much trendier, I was allowed to look less middle aged – they even had me doing aerobics in one advert. And I was always very miffed I was not allowed to benefit from the lighting cameraman's amazing talent. Gerry Dunkley was very talented and did all the Gold Blend commercials, as well as our Oxo ones. Sadly, he died very young from cancer. He was always allowed to go to town on Sharon and Anthony and they looked gorgeous, but he had to tone his skill down for me and used to apologise that he could not make me look more glamorous as that was not in the remit. Just my luck! I also had a wonderful man to do my hair, called

Pedro. He is still working in TV and film and we often bump into each other. He used to keep me in stitches, and whenever I complained that I looked too dowdy he would scream, 'Don't be so silly!' in his Spanish accent, and threaten me with the hairspray. Sue and Mary, make-up and costume respectively, had the same problem. I had to look ordinary. So I had very little make-up and nice, sensible clothes. Mary was the most incredible costume designer and sometimes she would take me shopping if I had to go to a premiere or something. We would go to town and she would introduce me to all her contacts and find me the most beautiful evening dresses.

The Oxo series of ads started in a very low-key way. They were very realistic and, at first, I don't think people quite knew what to make of them. But as each story unfolded and the audience got to know the characters, they gained in popularity. We won Best Commercial three years in a row in the *TV Times* awards and, in the end, they changed the category to Best Character in a Commercial so other people got a chance. Over the sixteen years it ran, the adverts were incredibly successful and won all kinds of industry awards.

I still have mixed feelings about being involved. In many ways I was very proud of what we did, but there is no doubt that my credibility as an actress was knocked. Certain people in the industry would never employ me as a serious actress after it. On the other hand, it gave me the financial security to go off and work in theatre for very little money, and I was able to be around for my Michael, and help Nunzio financially. Maybe if my private life had been happier I would have enjoyed the whole thing much more. As it was, I felt I was living a lie. Playing the nation's favourite mum on screen and going home to an unhappy and abusive relationship was extremely stressful.

Nowadays, the attitude to commercials is completely different, of course. It is all about profile now, and most actors do adverts or sponsor campaigns. So now I can look back fondly on my days as the Oxo mum and even feel a twinge of regret that the company did not consider bringing us back as a family of the new millennium. I could have been divorced, with a toy boy, of course, and Michael could have a younger model in tow and be ringing me for hints on how to cook a good casserole!

CHAPTER EIGHTEEN

KEEPING ALL THE BALLS IN THE AIR

WE HAD BEEN in our house in Holloway for three years and had been thinking about moving up to Muswell Hill. We found the perfect house there in Woodberry Crescent, just as Nunzio found a restaurant he wanted to buy.

We needed lots of dough, of course, and good old Mr Wyatt – the bank manager of the Aylesbury branch of Lloyds TSB – had been supporting me for years! I can't remember all the figures but we managed to raise the money, with a loan for the restaurant from my dear old dad. Suddenly, Nunzio was a different man. He was all up and at 'em, and for the next three or four years we really were a team. I had a new home to furnish and run, and a restaurant to get shipshape. God, we worked hard.

I was also about to do nine months in the West End in Michael Frayn's *Noises Off*. A brilliantly funny play, but unbelievably hard work. I needed a hand to help me cope, so I advertised for live-in help. I had now experienced the good, the bad and the ugly as far as home help and nannies were concerned, and I realised that even if I paid for a proper nannie it did not mean I was going to get the right sort of support. I still wanted to be a hands-on mum, but with

Michael being so young I needed someone with experience, or at least someone I could trust.

The trouble was that life in our household was never easy. There was a lot of shouting and I needed a girl with a bit of life experience and a healthy dose of commonsense. Cue Alena Steele. She had no experience whatsoever with babies, but after spending an hour or so with her, I knew she was the one. She was so calm and practical. She loved Michael straight away. We had a lovely room to give her in our new house, right at the top under the eaves, with Michael in his room next door. Perfect. I have to say that although I was lucky to be able to afford to have Alena, I did all the night shifts myself and the early-morning feeds. This was quite tough when you remember I was doing a show in the West End every night, going to bed at past midnight and then getting up at five to feed Michael. I tried to have a sleep sometimes in the afternoon but it was not always possible. I was completely exhausted for two years.

I was also helping Nunzio in the restaurant. We had a good deal to do before we could open. I scrubbed floors and cleaned toilets and ran around like a blue-arsed fly. The opening day finally arrived. Nunzio had invited all his old friends from Torre del Greco. They had all done well and were quite wealthy. Nunzio said that when he had been a young lad he had always been made to feel inferior to them all, so this was his chance to show them he could be a success as well. There was more hard work for me, though, because there were two couples staying with us, so I had all that to deal with, plus cleaning the restaurant. Typically, his friends' wives were immaculately dressed women who did not do much housework. So when they arrived at the restaurant there I was, on my hands and knees, with my head down the toilet trying to clean it. Whatever they thought about actresses, they did not expect this! Actually, I knew what they thought about actresses. They had about as much respect for my profession as my husband had. For them, actresses were second only to sluts – how many times was I told this during my sixteen-year marriage? Anyway, I think they were pleasantly surprised by my industriousness and quite impressed.

We opened to a packed restaurant. It was exciting but scary. So many things went wrong. There was a waiter's station with a little sink where glasses could be washed and bottles of wine and stuff was kept. It had a glass screen so the diners were able to see the waiters at work. I spent most of the night and subsequent nights in there washing glasses furiously, while Nunzio passed through and complained to me and at me, and generally took his bad temper out on me. I was pathetic. A dogsbody. But I was too tired to fight back. I would just cry. Somebody once said to me later that they came for dinner to try the food and get a glimpse of me; they were amazed and dismayed to see Mrs Oxo crying in the corner.

But I have to say Nunzio was brilliant at his job. He really knew how to make people feel at ease. He was flirty with the female customers without being threatening to their partners and he was also quite eccentric, which people liked. He loved to tell people what to eat and educate them. Never mind Gordon Ramsay; Nunzio was much scarier. He would go to take an order and some poor woman would order a starter and then her main course. If Nunzio didn't think they should be eaten together he would go off on one, telling her what she should have. Woe betide you if you did not do as you were told. At other times, too, customers would try it on, as in, 'My-wife-can't-possibly-eat-this-rubbish-I-think-you-had-better-give-us-a-bottle-of-wine-on-the-house,' sort of thing. One man tried it on even though his wife's plate was empty. He was very loudly asked to leave and then Nunzio addressed the rest of the diners with, 'This restaurant is like my house. If you behave badly, I will throw you out. You don't like my food or my service? Then you can fuck off!' Everyone applauded!

I always helped when I could. My sister, Jean, and I would make trays of chocolate mousse for desserts. At Christmas I went to town and did table decorations for each table and put fairy lights up, with a white Christmas tree in the centre of the room. I had to put the decorations up in the afternoon, as it was the only time I was free. As some regulars often liked to sit all afternoon drinking, I had to work round them and listen to all the jokes about gravy and stock cubes. People always think they are being so original, but I've heard them all before.

Over the first three years the menu changed dramatically. We started out with the classic, rather old-fashioned Italian cuisine of prawn cocktails and pasta, but then we had a chef who was so useless, Nunzio had to take over the cooking himself, and he became very good. It was kind of international cuisine; mostly Italian-based, but more subtle. Nunzio then tried an up-and-coming chef called Anthony Tobin but they fell out. It was really popular and every Saturday night we did over a hundred covers and the diners always wanted it fast and furious, even though to cook fresh food takes a little time. It was not a fast-food diner, as Nunzio never tired of telling people.

For the time being, things were going relatively well from the business side of things and this should have helped Nunzio's and my emotional relationship. Unfortunately, the relentless stream of put-downs and bad temper were beginning to take effect, after three years of marriage. As long as I did not step out of line all was well. And what constituted stepping out of line? Well, that was the trouble. I never knew until it was too late. The problem was that because I had been made afraid of Nunzio so early on in our marriage, I could never get past that fear. He wasn't an on-going bastard, by any means. He could be wonderful sometimes, and I would look at him and think how much I loved him. But when he turned, and shouted and screamed, I just withdrew into myself.

All through these times I kept most of the goings-on to myself. Pat and Catharine knew because I had to talk to someone, and dear Alena was always there for me. In order to keep working I had to compromise a good deal. Maybe I could, and should, have stood up for myself more, and then the pattern would not have been set. But it was so hard to keep strong. I so wanted to be the perfect housewife and mother, but I just wasn't tough enough to take the bad tempers and the criticism. Then when I turned to my own profession for support or comfort, Nunzio felt threatened and would make it impossible for me to work.

It is easy now to look back and say, 'Oh well, it was all about control.' Yes, of course it was, I knew that. But it was also about trying to survive and keep my children happy and my family together. We all fall back on what we know under pressure. Nunzio became more and more a victim of his own culture and wanted me to fall into line with this. But much as I wanted to keep him happy that was not how I saw my life progressing. I needed to work, to be out there. He could understand that because he loved the attention as well, believe me. All our friends had told him what a star he was and how brilliant he was at his job. And he was, but it did not stop him accusing me endlessly of being a slut and wanting to screw people behind his back. It is exhausting, believe me, to live your life defending every move you make. Every innocent comment, even made when watching TV, was a minefield. If I remarked on an actor, for example, it would be: 'Do you fancy him, then? God, Lynda, you're sex mad!'

There was rarely any let-up, and never any humour. Everything I did, I had to think first, or pay the price. Even our sex life, which had always been so wonderful and spontaneous, was now tarred by his suspicious mind. If I tried to be inventive in bed, he would now hold me at arm's length, stare into my eyes, and then suggest I had got the idea from someone else. This, in turn, made me very inhibited about our lovemaking. I would never have dared to refuse his advances. If I even hinted that maybe I wasn't in the mood, it would produce a list of accusations about how I must be getting it elsewhere. Threats of violence are as bad as actual violence, and plain old-fashioned bullying was my daily deal. I tried to talk to him but was brushed aside. I tried to ignore it, and concentrate on Michael, but even with our child he managed to make me feel I was somehow leaving him out. That I was ganging up on him.

I also avoided any kind of major confrontation because I was so worried that the press would get hold of a story from it. My contract with Oxo stated that I must never act in a way that would bring the brand into disrepute, and if the press found out that my own life was as diametrically opposed to my image as the lovely Mum with her happy Oxo family, they would have a field day. I used to dread doing interviews because I felt such a fraud. I always had to talk about being a mum, and family life, and me and Nunzio in our restaurant, living the dream. The irony was horrific. Here I was, the nation's favourite mum, hiding behind closed doors and becoming more and more isolated from her friends and family.

CHAPTER NINETEEN

ALL THINGS BRIGHT AND BEAUTIFUL

I N 1984, I began a one-woman show called *Catherine of Sienna*. Catherine had lived about fifty years before St Joan and been involved in much the same sort of problems with the Church and the Pope. She was an amazing woman and died in her thirties of cancer. I performed the play at The King's Head, a famous small theatre in Islington run by Dan Crawford, who sadly is no longer with us.

It is quite a feat to be onstage alone for an hour and a half. The challenge for me was to convince a modern audience that someone could believe so strongly in God without looking like a complete nutter. Our society is so often without any spiritual guidelines, let alone religious convictions, that many people have no time for a woman who heard voices. I got wonderful reviews.

The director was a lady called Joan Kemp-Welch, who was a very successful TV and theatre director. While I was doing the play, her husband, Peter Moffat, another well-known TV director, suggested me to take over the role of Helen Herriot in *All Creatures Great and Small*. The producer, Bill Sellars, wasn't keen due to my role as the Oxo mum. However, he saw me and we got on especially well when he asked me about myself and I explained I was a farmer's daughter and had probably had my arm up more sheep's arses than James Herriot. To my amazement I got the job.

It was fantastic because it was the perfect foil to the commercials. I would be on ITV making gravy, and on BBC1 pouring it over the Sunday roast for the famous vet! The only obstacle in my way was my husband. Would he let me go up to Yorkshire for filming? Thankfully, I had a trump card I could play.

A few weeks earlier I had been asked to take over for a week at GMTV from Jeni Barnett. It was all signed and sealed, and the Friday before I started I had been sent a list of guests that I would be interviewing, which included Eddie Kidd, the stunt rider. In the late seventies, before I met Nunzio, I had made a film with Eddie called *Riding High*. It was pretty awful but it was a film. Eddie Kidd and his mates asked me out with them a few times, and we had had a good time. I never heard from them again until just after I had met Nunzio. Typical of my luck, Eddie must have been going through his old numbers and rang me. Nunzio answered and … need I say more? We had a terrible row about it. So, here we were, six years later, and I was faced with the prospect of telling Nunzio that I was going to have to do an interview with Eddie Kidd. He went ballistic and refused, point blank, to let me go to work. I can remember standing by the phone in the hall, begging and pleading with him on the morning I was due to go to work at GMTV. I had to ring Sara Randall, my agent, and ask her to somehow get me out of my contract. Thank God, she knew all about my domestic problems and worked a miracle and got me off.

After he had calmed down Nunzio was very ashamed. He knew he had crossed the line. Work was work. He was also very aware that other people, like my agent, knew about his controlling nature and temper tantrums, which was not a good thing for someone who needed to isolate their loved ones in order to wield their control. So now there was a chance for him to make amends – to let me take the *All Creatures* job and go to Yorkshire. He also knew it was a fantastic opportunity for me, and I would be earning good money. Nunzio did not like to turn down money. So he agreed. I was back up to speed. I had a fantastic job to go to and my career looked like it could move forward again.

All Creatures Great and Small was a phenomenon. A vet called Alf Wight had written a book about his experiences as a vet up in the dales of Yorkshire and spawned an industry. A series of books, several television series and a film. The original Helen Herriot, wife of James, had been played by Carol Drinkwater. Christopher Timothy played James; Robert Hardy, Siegfried; and Peter Davison was Tristan. There had been a gap of a few years before the BBC decided to do a new series, and Carol was off doing other things so they had to recast.

I had the most wonderful time filming those three series. My son, Michael, would always come with me up to Yorkshire, partly to keep Nunzio happy but mainly for me and Michael, because he just loved it out on the moors. We shot all the interior scenes at the studio in Birmingham and then went filming for six weeks up in Leyburn, in Yorkshire.

Sadly, Helen was not often out of the kitchen. For some reason, the writers always put her making bread or doing the washing-up when things were hotting up in the cowshed! So usually we were not away for long.

I relished those few days away from Nunzio's critical gaze. I had found the most perfect place to stay in a village called Middleham. It was an old miller's house that had been turned into a small B&B. They didn't normally take small children but they made an exception in Michael's case and, bless him, he never let me down. We had a beautiful double room that looked out on to the small village green. At the end of each long and happy day, Michael and I would sit in the dining room at the old miller's house and eat an enormous dinner of fresh homemade soup, a roast and piles of homegrown vegetables. Followed by a big pudding. The lady who cooked made a soup called Wensleydale cheese soup. It was delicious; I got the recipe and we still make it today.

There was nothing to Middleham except several pubs and three or four racing stables. Michael and I would be up at five to go filming, and we would stand on the side of the green in the early morning mist and watch the horses and their riders file past. It was magic, listening to their hooves on the road and their snorting, and the whinnying and the jingling of reins, and the laughter of the jockeys disappearing over the hill. There was also a blacksmith, and Michael would watch him for hours.

While I was filming, Michael would stay with the costume van and our lovely dresser, called Ray, would keep an eye on him. The great thing about a film set for small children is the discipline. They learn to do as they are told because everyone on the set has to abide by the rules. When the first assistant shouts 'Quiet!', we are all quiet. Michael also used to wander round the fields and bring back lovely knick-knacks like bits of old wool and a sheep's skull. Don't you love little boys?!

While we were up there we also acquired our dog, Star. There was a scene to be shot involving a bitch giving birth and she has eclampsia (don't ask me to explain it, I'm only an actress). The vet had found a lovely Collie bitch who was about to give birth so we settled down to film with her. The farmer who owned the dog was telling us that he would keep one of the puppies as a working dog and sell the rest. From that moment Michael didn't stop asking me for a puppy. 'But we can't have a sheepdog in London, Michael,' I'd reply. The farmer's wife heard and insisted that the dog would adapt to its surroundings. That was it; we were hooked. Michael chose a puppy with a star on its forehead, and because it was appearing on TV we called it Star. We couldn't take him straight away as he was too small, so we agreed to wait till the next time we came up to film.

When we returned, our dog was waiting. The farmer's wife had knitted Michael a red and white jumper with rows of collie dogs on it and he was so chuffed. Star travelled back on the train with us and made himself completely at home in north London. Because of his herding instinct, he used to give other dogs in the park rather a hard time, but he became a brilliant goalkeeper and was the perfect children's dog. He lived to a ripe old age, and is buried in the garden of my friend Catharine's house in Worcestershire.

I was so happy to be away. It became more and more the pattern. My work was a haven to me. I was with people who liked me and thought I was talented. There was no shouting or ugly scenes, and I was reminded that life did not have to be a battle. I could relax and be myself and, most importantly, being me did not mean I was behaving like a 'slut'. I could go and have a drink or a meal with the cast.

Actually, this was not quite true, because Nunzio was always on the end of the phone. When I got back to the hotel in Birmingham at night, I would always have to phone him, or take calls through my meal. I started inviting people to the hotel so we could have dinner. Lovely actors like Wanda Ventham would join me. Chris Timothy was also very supportive because I had told him what I had to deal with.

I had had to tell someone because it was intolerable, otherwise; trying to appear normal after a phone call where I had been called a hundred foul names. And while it was lovely having Michael with me, it was just another thing to worry about so meant more stress.

I know that Robert Hardy used to get impatient with me some-times. He shouted at me one day because I had to leave early to get Michael from school, saying it was like trying to rehearse in a bloody crèche. I did understand his frustration, but what could I do? He is a lovely man actually, and very interesting to talk to. In the early days, when I first started, we used to go and have lunch in the executive dining room at the BBC, and he would tell me wonderful stories over a bottle or two of Burgundy.

In between filming for the BBC, I was still doing the Oxo commercials and I also did a six-month run in the West End in a play called *Look No Hans* starring my old friend David Jason. I was playing his wife who had very little to do except run on and off in a big brimmed hat and spotted dress. He was so funny in that play. It was a tour de force for him; the rest of us just came on and fed him lines really, so he could go into a comedy routine. There was a lovely actress called Anita Graham in the play with me. She was a six-foot blonde and very funny. We used to sit in my dress-ing room and knit and bitch about David taking too long to do a scene, because it was a Saturday night and we wanted to get home. The trouble was if the audience encouraged him, David would have gone on all night. Sometimes, if it got too much, I would actually go on to the stage in one particular scene, clap my hands and say loudly, 'That's enough, get on with it.' The audience would howl with laughter and think it was part of the script but David knew it was a message and we meant business. It was the first time I had my name in lights outside the theatre, and my dear sister Barbara took a photo that is framed and on my wall. I was so thrilled.

Alena used to bring Michael in on a matinee day and we would go and have tea somewhere. It was wonderful near Christmas because I would take him on an open-topped bus all round the West End, where all the lights were up, to look at the decorations.

It became a Christmas tradition. Into the West End and on to a bus to see the lights. Then down to Harrods to see Father Christmas. Then a McDonald's or sometimes tea in a posh hotel.

We did these things without Nunzio, not because we didn't want him to join us but because he was just not interested. He would go on and on to people about how he played with Michael, but he very rarely ever did anything; he would sit in front of the TV and watch sport most of the time. He did take Michael to Italy when I was doing *Look No Hans* and I missed his first steps. I was so upset. When they came back I came out of the stage door to greet them and round the corner came a little grown-up, tottering towards me!

In 1986, I also played The Inquisitor in a series of *Doctor Who*. Colin Baker was the Doctor, Michael Jayston was The Valeyard and Bonnie Langford was the Doctor's assistant. I had an extraordinary costume with a huge headdress that was attached to my shoulders with sticks in it to keep it upright. There is a photo of me looking rather like Joan Collins, with a great deal of eye make-up on and long false nails painted red. The nails were so long I couldn't get my tights on or off so a very sweet girl from the wardrobe department had to escort me to the ladies' loo and help me get them on and off each time. Poor girl! I opened the series by flouncing into a courtroom for the Doctor's trial. I then took my seat with great aplomb and stayed there for thirteen episodes, at the end of which I rose from my chair and left the courtroom with great aplomb! I have always been rather miffed that since they brought *Doctor Who* back, Russell T Davies has never asked me to come and be in an episode. I was a Time Lord, after all!

CHAPTER TWENTY

ANOTHER BUNDLE OF JOY BUT IT IS THE CALM BEFORE THE STORM

WHILE ON HOLIDAY in Italy in 1987, I found out I was pregnant again. Everyone was delighted. So was I, but there was a little niggle in the back of my mind. However, as an optimist, I just brushed it away. It was all going to be good. We had a successful business and Nunzio was so thrilled. For a while, things were calm.

Robert Ciro Peluso was born on Easter Sunday, 3rd April, 1988. He was luckier than his brother Michael in that we had more money so he was born privately at The Portland Hospital. Julie Walters was on the floor below. It was very posh compared to UCH five years earlier, but it could not make up for the fact that the cracks in my marriage were widening: even on the first night of our new son's life, Nunzio managed to reduce me to tears.

Robbie's birth had been quite eventful because he was early. Rosaria and her son Gennarro were staying with us for Easter, with the idea that she would be around again to help. The night before Easter Sunday, Nunzio had had a busy night in the restaurant, so when he came in late, he had fallen asleep in front of the TV. I woke in the early hours with terrible pains. I thought it was wind, so I went downstairs and made a cup of tea and sat talking to the dog. Star would always follow me round everywhere and he could feel something wasn't right. It slowly dawned on me that I was going into labour. This had not happened the first time because I had had an elective Caesarean. I suddenly panicked because it was Easter Sunday and I had promised Michael an Easter egg hunt in the garden. I couldn't let the little lad down so I got the eggs and wrote the clues, and in between contractions Star and I went round the garden hiding the eggs. I must have looked a very strange sight, practically bent double, stopping every few minutes to breathe and then crawling on all fours under a bush. My dad had always said that when we three girls went into labour it would be no problem as long as we had a bale of straw and some hot water!

I finally rang Mum at about 8 a.m. and she said I should ring the gynaecologist as soon as I could. I waited till nine and then got his answering machine. That's private medicine for you! I heard nothing for another hour so I rang the Portland and they said to come in. I then had to wake Nunzio, who was less than pleased as he had a hangover. He insisted we take everyone with us. Rosaria, Gennarro and Michael (but not the dog, who looked very forlorn as we drove away). We were like a band of travelling gypsies arriving at the hospital.

Peter Saunders, my wonderful gynaecologist, arrived and announced it would be ages to the birth yet, and did I mind if he went to lunch as he had friends coming round that day? I nodded weakly. Nunzio also decided to leave and go home as there was nothing he could do and the family wanted feeding. Fine. So I waited and contracted on my own. At about 3 p.m. the midwife decided it was time to sort me out and called Peter. I was now having full-blown contractions and it was very difficult giving me an epidural for the Caesarean as I couldn't keep still. We managed it in the end and away we went. Nunzio managed to get back in time to see the birth of son number two.

What a little sweetie he was with his mass of black hair. The Portland had a policy of giving new parents a celebratory meal in the room. So there we were, me, Nunzio, and Robbie in his cot, when suddenly Nunzio was having a go at me. I honestly can't remember what about, but each time the nurse came in, I would hide my head in my hands and Nunzio would sit and glower. At one point, the nurse dared to suggest that Nunzio give me a hug and stop making me miserable. The look he gave her sent her scuttling from the room.

When I brought Robbie home it was to a house full of people, and it stayed that way for weeks. It again meant I had no time to myself to think about my situation. Everything was stress. We had invited Nunzio's brother Michele to come and live in England with his family and work for Nunzio in the restaurant. I spent hours trying to find him a flat. I organised the deposit and the mortgage on a lovely flat in Barnet and then I cleaned it up and furnished it. Then, just as they were due to move in, Nunzio and his brother had a big fight and he decided to take his family back to Naples, leaving us with a flat to get rid of.

I don't know what the fight was about, but around this time we had an Italian girl who came to visit, and work in the restaurant. She was the daughter of a friend of Nunzio's family. Just what you need around the house when you have just had a baby: she was all long brown limbs and tossed golden hair. It is extraordinary how I put up with it, when you consider that Nunzio spent half his waking hours accusing me of being a slut and sleeping with all and sundry, yet here he was now working with a girl half his age who couldn't keep her eyes off him. He used to take her home after work, and I thought nothing about it until Michele, Nunzio's brother, said to me one day before he left, 'Don't worry about Teresa, she is not important. My brother is a fool.' I questioned him further but he wouldn't be drawn. When I asked Nunzio for an explanation he just smiled. I can see his face even now! He just smiled and shrugged his shoulders. Can you imagine if that had been me?

It was the last straw. I had done humiliation before. I got very beady and edgy. We now had a lovely girl helping me called Valentina. We had met her the year before on holiday in Sardinia. She was such a gentle soul and she understood the Italian mentality better than anyone. We were standing in the kitchen one day and I had Robbie in my arms, and Nunzio stormed in, screaming and shouting about something. I was not in the mood to listen and told him to go away. He swung round, narrowly missing little baby Robbie. It was too much. Even Valentina gasped and told me to give her the baby. She withdrew and Nunzio just ranted and raved at me. He finally went back to work but I knew he would be back later.

I was in pieces. Valentina was so kind and she knew how frightened I was. She suggested I went and stayed somewhere else for the night so Nunzio could calm down: 'Don't worry, I will keep Robbie safe. He would never hurt him.' She was right, so I went over the road to my friend and neighbour, Maggie Leonard. I knocked on her door at ten o'clock in the evening and she was great and took me in and calmed me down. I stayed in her front room all night, watching my house over the road.

The next morning, I watched Nunzio leave the house and go to work and then I went home. I had had enough. I gathered up the boys and bundled them into the car and drove down to my parents. They were shocked to see me. I had always tried not to tell them too much about what had been going on with Nunzio because I didn't want to worry them, but they knew really. Even so, I don't think they were aware of just how frightened I was of him. We talked and talked and I told them everything, and we all agreed I had to leave.

Then the phone calls started. Nunzio was screaming at me. Then my dad took the phone and he shouted at him. All day backwards and forwards went the calls. Finally, Nunzio said he was coming to get us. He arrived at my parents' house and took over. I still have a clear picture of it all these years later, of Nunzio standing in the kitchen with my mum and dad, shouting at us. He seemed to tower over us all, even my dad. His loud harsh voice bounced off the walls, making the children cry. My mum tried to reason with him, but she said all the words he didn't want to hear, like 'divorce' and 'better we parted for the sake of the children'. He turned on her and screamed at her: 'You know nothing, you are English! I will never give up my boys. I am Italian, my family is everything to me!'

'So why don't you treat them better?' was my father's measured reply. Nunzio was having none of it. After much arguing and then tears he agreed to leave me in peace to think about what to do for the best. I managed to stave off a decision for two weeks, but every day he was on the phone for hours. His rage had turned to pleading with me. He promised he would change. He would get help. He loved me. He wore me down and despite my parents begging me to be strong and leave him, I went back. We arranged to have therapy sessions, which we did for the next three years or more. It helped me to go and talk, sometimes, because at least someone knew the hell I was going through, day in day out. But I really don't know if it helped Nunzio, or our marriage. Going over old ground often just opened up old wounds and he would come home to me and have a go at me again.

I FEEL THIS IS the moment for me to take a break from telling my story and explain just how difficult this is for me. I think that if I go through the rest of my marriage to Nunzio, blow by blow, it just becomes a succession of depressing stories. It wasn't all depressing, anyway. We did have some wonderful moments but sadly, for every happy time, there was an even worse unhappy time. Domestic abuse is by its very nature a private and secret thing, usually carried out behind closed doors. That is why it is so difficult to discover. I have given many talks over the last few years to women who have been through far worse than me. But the same things always come up. The isolation from family and friends. The drip, drip of abuse. The control in terms of money and time. The unpredictability of the abusive partner. The desire to please and placate all the time and, most important of all: the fear. It is crippling. It permeates one's whole life. Everything is affected by it. Sleep becomes impossible and normal friendships suffer because of it.

There is no way for anyone who has not been in this situation to really understand because it takes so long to reach that point, but there always comes a day when you no longer have any control over your life. You have been made to feel so worthless that there is no option but to stay in that relationship because you think no one else is going to want you. I have watched films and plays that do not come anywhere close to explaining to the outside world what goes on. I just hope that anyone reading this who has had similar problem will know that you are not alone, and that the very best thing anyone in this situation can do is talk about it. Tell someone. Don't block out your family and friends. The more people who know, the better. Even in cultures where it is 'acceptable' to beat one's wife, it must be stopped. It is not acceptable. We all know that bullies are really cowards, but it's not easy to stand up to them when you are cowed, and beaten, after years of taking it on the chin. Literally. If society were really to take up the cause it could make a huge change.

Just like the drink-driving campaign has made it almost impossible for anyone to drink and drive in public and get away with it, so it should be with abusive behaviour of any kind. Whether it is in a marriage, or the work place. No one should live in fear.

WE MOVED HOUSE around this time as well, to a huge house round the corner in Muswell Avenue. It had five bedrooms and a huge playroom up at the top of the house in which there was a full-sized billiard table already. It even had a swimming pool. It was way out of our price range but we had to have it.

Nunzio was a perfectionist which is fine to a point, but we just didn't have the money to do up the house to the standard he required. I realise now that the other issue about making the house nice was that it was all about keeping Nunzio sweet. If he was happy he would be good to me, it was as simple as that. So furnishing it to his exacting standards was just another way of keeping the peace. Everything had to be the best. For example, we had no wardrobes in our bedroom and no chest of drawers for shirts and the like. It used to drive me mad to have to pick my way across the floor all the time to get dressed. But Nunzio insisted he only wanted the best for his house. He had found a Georgian chest of drawers which was going to cost about £3,000. We didn't have that kind of money to spend on drawers. Finally, I could take no more and went and found one for £1,500, which was a bargain. He was thrilled and carefully packed and folded away all his sweaters and under-wear into it, leaving no space for my clothing. My clothes stayed on the floor for another year!

We spent the next two years pouring money into the house and doing it up. It was magnificent when it was finished and a testa-ment to Nunzio's vision and good taste. For all his faults, Nunzio did have style. He knew exactly what he wanted that house to be – a palazzo in north London! The boy from the poor part of Torre del Greco was now living in a palace. It had blood-red walls and thick, enormous braided curtains. The fireplace in the lounge had been painted by the same artist who worked on Prince Charles's house at Highgrove. The kitchen, which took for ever to do up, was all wood floors and turquoise rugs and tiles, and led out to a pool area. We heated the pool so it was like a bath for the boys. It was like being in a hot country without the sun!

That bloody swimming pool was the bane of my life, and when he was about eighteen months old, it nearly took Robbie's life. We had always tried to keep the outside doors locked because of the dangers of the water but somehow that day he broke free. Nunzio was talking to me in the kitchen when suddenly he looked out of the window, shouted and ran outside and dived into the pool fully dressed. The image that is emblazoned on my memory is of Robbie's little body hanging in the water, his legs straight down and his mop of black hair. It still makes me feel sick to think about it. We laid him on the patio and, thank God, he coughed up a load of water and started breathing. We had caught him in time. He seemed none the worse for wear except he did not utter a sound for a full twenty-four hours. He must have been in shock.

After that incident, we were very wary of all children near the water and my dear dad paid for a fence to be put round it with a locked gate. Every summer I played swimming-pool attendant, handing out towels and guarding the gate. But the boys loved it so much and they learned to swim very quickly. At first they just swam under water all the time but then they learnt to swim, like the rest of us, on top of the water.

We had a big party when the house was all finished, and I remember going upstairs, looking out of the window into the garden and thinking, 'Wow, this is all mine!' It was heady stuff after so many years of graft. I guess we must have looked like we had everything.

CHAPTER TWENTY-ONE

LIFE MIRRORS ART

IN 1988, just after Robbie was born, I teamed up with Jan Etherington and Gavin Petrie, a husband-and-wife writer couple. They had just won a BBC Radio prize for comedy and part of the prize was to make a pilot radio episode of the script that won. They called me and we had lunch together and they said some lovely things to me about my talent as a comedy actress. Finally, after all those years of tits and arse, I was going to get the chance to prove my point that women can be funny, attractive *and* intelligent! They had written a series called *Second Thoughts* that was vaguely autobiographical, about a couple, Faith and Bill, reaching middle age who embark on a relationship, with all the problems of ex-wives and other people's children. When we started at the Maida Vale studios in 1988 on the radio, little would we imagine that it was to be the start of ten years together.

As I had new-born Robbie, I was a bit like a travelling circus, with Valentina and the buggy and all foodstuffs necessary for a long day recording. I also supplied the actors with croissants and coffee. James Bolam was cast to play my other half and it was a wonderful choice. We worked together well over the next few years, though sometimes I had to wonder: I'm sure James won't mind me saying this, but sometimes he could be a bit grumpy! So I had two grumpy men in my life! I left one at home and spent the day, at work, with another. I know which grump I preferred to be with, though. At least Jimmy's grumpiness produced wonderful comedy moments.

Belinda Lang – another wonderful comedy actress – played Jimmy's ex-wife, and Julia Sawalha played my daughter, long before she went on to find worldwide fame as Saff in *Absolutely Fabulous*. At one point, she was my lodger, and it sometimes felt like we were in another comedy series! I love her to bits. The radio series was a huge hit, and then we got the news that London Weekend Television wanted to make it. It was a real chance to get back up there again!

One of my heroines has always been Lucille Ball. She was a great American comedienne, whose style of comedy appeals to me because it involved a bit of slapstick. Physical comedy and women is, again, not the usual way female humour is perceived, but Jan and Gavin wrote some classic comedy slapstick moments for me. The series was a great success and we made seven more. It was a great team and when Jimmy decided he had done enough, the writers and I stayed together and created a spin-off called *Faith in the Future*. This was to be the life and times of Faith as a single woman, who suddenly finds herself living with her grown-up daughter, played once again by Julia. We had such fun and our director, Sylvie Boden, has become a life-long friend. The whole team was tremendous and we won the Best Comedy Award in 1998. It was, however, my usual bad luck that London Weekend Television underwent a hostile takeover around this time and was absorbed by Granada, and our show was one of the casualties.

During one season of *Second Thoughts*, in 1993, I was caught by Michael Aspel and the big red book. I had often said to Nunzio if ever they ask you whether I'd like to be on *This Is Your Life*, to please say yes. He always said he would refuse because: 'I don't want to sit on the television while they introduce all your fucks!' I tried to explain it was not quite like that, but to no avail. Thank God my mum got to hear about it and helped organise the guest list.

It was the last programme ever to be made at Thames Television Studios at Teddington. I had been to several sessions of *This Is Your Life* for other people over the years, some when it was still Eamonn Andrews, the original host, and a few with Michael Aspel. What the audience see in terms of surprise guests who appear on the screen is nothing to the party afterwards, where the studio is full of everyone who has ever been in your life. It was fantastic. What a night we had. It didn't finish until 6 a.m.

We didn't start filming it until after midnight because they surprised me while I was recording an episode of *Second Thoughts*. We had been told we had to do a retake and Jimmy was going to come in and start the scene again with the line, 'I just went to the pub to get a bottle of wine.'

I had my back to him on the sofa so I couldn't see him. The director shouted 'Action!' and in came Jimmy. I heard him say: 'I just went to the pub and you would never believe who I met.' I didn't really take in what he was saying because I thought he had gone wrong and was about to have a wobbly. I swung round nervously to see Jimmy standing there with Michael Aspel. The audience in the studio were all applauding and cheering. I thought it was Jimmy's *This Is Your Life* and I was thinking, 'Oh, dear, he won't like this,' because he's a very private man, but then suddenly Michael was talking to me and handing me the big red book. It was so wonderful.

I was driven from the studios at Waterloo to Teddington studios. All the way down in the car, I swigged champagne and mentally ran through everyone I could remember in my life. I didn't want to let the side down and not know who anyone was: it was always so awful on that programme when they introduced someone and it was obvious that the star didn't have a clue who it was! I had to be kept isolated because the producers do not want anyone to spoil the surprise or talk to you about anything. But in my case, they had to let me phone my mum because she was going to be unable to appear as she was very ill with pneumonia. Poor dear Mum, she was so upset – she would have loved so much to have held court! My dad spoke in his rather reserved way and also my sister, Jean, who was brilliant and gave a lovely account of the family.

They have a policy with *This Is Your Life* that you are allowed a couple of guests from overseas. Budget permitting, obviously. When I was waiting in the room to start the show I was thinking of two dear friends I hoped might fly over. Wally Michaels from Canada and Bryn Lloyd from California. No such luck. What Nunzio had done was use the flights available to bring over his mates from Italy for a freebie. As usual it was all about him.

When I came on and sat down next to him in the studio, I could feel the waves of tension emanating from him. This was going to be a nightmare. If anyone came on that I had slept with what was I going to do? I just crossed my fingers and prayed that Mum, Dad and Nik Grace all knew what he was like, and had arranged things accordingly. Michael Aspel told me years after the event that he had never seen a man so like a coiled spring. He said people were phoning in asking why Lynda Bellingham's husband never smiled. I was so nervous and so aware of everything I said. But we got through it OK and I had a fabulous time.

The next day we had a house full of Nunzio's family and friends. One of these was a man called Vittorio, a very flamboyant old queen. He was always good fun and he wanted me to take him out to lunch and show him the sights. Nunzio had to work so I agreed. We met up with Jack Tinker and we had a right old time of it. We got home late in the afternoon, a little the worse for wear. Nunzio was all smiles in front of Vittorio but after they had left, he laid into me, calling me selfish and insensitive. How could I go out like that while he had to work? But I was only doing it to please him. It was the last thing I needed to do after a late night and all the excitement. It made me so angry that he'd even managed to ruin that moment for me.

One job I managed to slip in around this busy time was *The Vision*, starring Dirk Bogarde and Lee Remick. I was playing a TV presenter who had to interview Mr Bogarde. While we were waiting for the crew to set up the shot I tried to make conversation with Dirk, and got short shrift. Then lots of children, who were in the scene, started coming up to me and asking me for my autograph. It was so weird because they were queuing for me and ignoring the real star. Dirk Bogarde watched this for a bit and then he said, 'Should I know you? You're obviously well known to all these people.'

'No, not really,' I stammered. 'It's because I do the Oxo commercials, that's all.'

There was a long pause and then he said, 'Really? I didn't know gravy was so popular.'

Another big star I worked with during these years was Sir Paul Scofield. What a charmer. I got the role of Mrs Lupin in *Martin Chuzzlewit*, a big glossy classic series. Once more I got all excited because I thought it might lead to greater things, and once more I was disappointed. Mind you, seeing what I looked like in one of those lovely period mob caps and no make-up, it's hardly surprising Hollywood wasn't knocking on my door. Julia Sawalha was in it as well, so it was lovely to be working with her again. We used to compete for Sir Paul's attention by taking him sweets. He said he loved different sweets so we kept taking him bagsful every day. He was so gorgeous and twinkled at you throughout a scene.

I also did a play during these five years. It was *The Sisters Rosensweig* by Wendy Wasserstein. We opened at Greenwich and then went into the Old Vic. It starred Janet Suzman, Maureen Lipman and me, and was directed by Michael Blakemore.

When we opened at the Old Vic, Maureen used to get cross because Janet would arrive after the half in the evenings. The half is the half an hour before curtain-up and an actor is supposed contractually to be in the theatre thirty-five minutes beforehand. Janet never was and it really irked Maureen. I was playing the youngest sister and my role crossed over into real life as I hovered between the two keeping the peace. It felt like Janet and Maureen were competing for who had the best guest in their dressing room. One night, Janet was entertaining Jonathan Kent, the artistic direc-tor of the Almeida theatre, while Maureen had Tony and Cherie Blair (before he was Prime Minister, though). Larry Lamb was our leading man and he very diplomatically kept everyone happy. Michael Codron was the producer, a very distinguished man, who must have had a constant headache keeping things sweet.

I enjoyed a special moment with Princess Diana during this time. There was a lunch given at St James's Palace for fifty famous mums and I was so proud to be included with the likes of Linda McCartney and Shirley Conran. I asked Nunzio to help me find a suitable outfit because I knew he had great taste, and I wanted to make him part of my special day. We trawled the shops and finally found a beautiful Yves St Laurent suit.

On the day, I did look good, though I say so myself. We were all introduced to Diana and then a bit later she came and asked me where my suit was from. I explained how Nunzio had helped me choose it and her response was that all Italians have such good taste. I felt like saying if only they were kinder to their wives!

CHAPTER TWENTY-TWO

'IF YOU CANNOT GET RID OF THE FAMILY SKELETON, YOU MAY AS WELL MAKE IT DANCE'

(GEORGE BERNARD SHAW)

WHEN BOTH MY children were born I went through the same feelings and insecurities. All those questions about inherited illnesses. Was there a history of heart disease in my birth family? High blood pressure? Since having Michael I had thought a good deal about my background, not just about the physical stuff either; more about my mental state, to be honest. All I heard from my husband now was that I was a slut and a drunk.

I couldn't understand how I had let myself get so low. I had no self-respect or self-worth. All through my childhood I had wanted to please people. First my parents, then my teachers and friends at school. My career was spent trying to be things I was not. When would it end? When would I be able to be myself? Whoever that was.

After having Robbie, I decided the one thing I could do was to find out the truth about my mother. If she had dumped me, better

I know for sure. If she could give up her baby, there must have been a good reason. I wanted to know why.

While I was filming *All Creatures Great and Small* and we were up in Birmingham, I was waiting in line at the hotel one morning to check out. In front of me was a stewardess from Air Canada, who was giving her address as Montreal, Canada. Before I could stop myself I was telling her that I was born in Canada. She was very polite and responded accordingly, but then I found myself asking if she knew any way I could trace my birth mother over there. She explained that it was very difficult in Canada because they had privacy laws, but she did know of a charity called the Missing Children's Network, that traced missing children, and they would probably be able to give me all sorts of information about how to trace people.

When I got back to London I decided to have a go. I opened a bottle of wine, got a pad and pencil and set to. I spoke to a lovely woman at the Missing Children's Network called Susan Armstrong. She explained that they did not trace parents as such; instead, they found children who turned up on the streets of Montreal. But she asked me to give her all the information I had because their organisation had several useful contacts. I had quite a lot, actually, because I had my birth certificate, including my mother's name, Marjorie Hughes, the name of the hospital where I was born, and the registration papers. Susan told me they had a contact in the files office at the hospital that might be able to get a sneaky look. We chatted a bit longer and she asked me what I did and I told her. Then she asked if she might have seen anything on TV that I had been in. I mentioned *All Creatures Great and Small* and she went bananas: 'Oh my God, you're Helen Herriot! That is so exciting, I can't wait to tell my associate! We love that programme.' I tried to explain that it was really important that we were discreet for several reasons, not least the reputation of my birth mother. She calmed down and said, of course, she would be very discreet and she would ring me back.

She rang me back almost immediately and said the girl in the records office had got caught trying to snoop, so that was the end of that! I suggested to Susan that maybe there would be records of my grandfather, as he was a doctor (this was my father's idea, the doctor in Montreal had mentioned it to him). Of course, Susan said, leave it with me. Within the week she had everything. There had been a report in the local newspaper in Calgary when he died, and an obituary. He had died in 1959. Susan said it was only a matter of putting all the pieces together and we would have everything we needed.

I decided I had better talk to my parents before I proceeded any further. Nunzio was all for me going ahead. I don't think his actions were entirely honourable, though: I think he wanted to drive a wedge between me and my family and keep them at bay. Ever since I had left him briefly that time, and Mum had suggested we should part, he had been very cold towards them. The idea I might have a mother conveniently far away in Canada appealed to him.

I drove down to my parents one Sunday. It was always so lovely to see them and very rare now. It wasn't that Nunzio stopped me seeing them but he just made it so difficult. If I wanted to take the boys he would make a big deal about how Sundays were the only day he could see them. This was rubbish as he was home every afternoon from the restaurant but usually he just fell asleep. Then if we did drive down he would be ringing my parents' phone all the time, asking what time we were coming back. It was just such a hassle all the time.

I sat with my parents on that Sunday and went through it all with them. I knew they would be upset and I really wanted them to understand that it was something I had to do because of the boys. I told them how much I loved them and that there was no way I wanted to start a dialogue or anything with my birth mother. I just wanted to set the record straight. They gave me their blessing. I drove straight home and phoned Canada. Susan said they were still working on it and to be patient.

The following week I was filming *All Creatures* and had chosen to stay in a B&B just outside Birmingham because I was taking the boys and the nanny and the dog. It was half-term so they were all off from school. It was about 7 p.m. and I was reading the boys a bedtime story, when the landlady came to tell me there was a phone call. It was Nunzio, in a great state of excitement, because Canada had rung to say they had the phone number for my birth mother. She was staying in a hotel in Victoria, British Columbia, with her sister, Shirley. I asked him if he would try and ring the number and at least warn the poor woman before I rang her. He rang back five minutes later in a grump saying he got the wrong number, and it was all too difficult, and he was missing the football on TV, and as it was my problem I should do it myself. So supportive. I sat for a good fifteen minutes trying to decide what to do. I had always seen these things on TV where there was either a counsellor present or the people had been primed beforehand. Could I really just pick up the phone and say, 'Hi Mom!'

I asked the landlady if I could use the phone to make a long-distance call. She said of course. So there I was at 9 o'clock on a Tuesday night, ringing a number in Victoria, BC. I had checked the time difference and it was about 1 p.m. their time, which was perfect. I heard the distinct dialling tone that you hear on American TV films. The phone was picked up on the third ring: 'Hello?' An old lady's voice with a slight Canadian accent.

'Hi. Is that Marjorie?'

'Who is this calling, please?' I froze. What should I say? Where to start? It must have been a long pause because suddenly Marjorie was saying, 'Is there anybody there? I'm sorry, I think you have the wrong number.'

'Please don't hang up!' I cried. 'Does the name Lynda Bellingham mean anything to you?' I thought maybe she would remember the name Bellingham from the adoption papers.

'No, I'm so sorry, caller. I think you have the wrong number.'

Before she hung up I quickly said, 'Does the name Meredith Lee Hughes mean anything?'

There was barely a pause before she said, 'Oh my Lord. May the 31st, 1948. Is it really you, dear?'

PART TWO
FOUND

CHAPTER TWENTY-THREE

MARJORIE

MARJORIE HUGHES WAS born in September 1918 in Calgary, Canada. Her father was a good man – the head of the Baptist church and a doctor. Marjorie was the youngest of three girls. Avis was the eldest, then Shirley, then Marjorie. She loved being the youngest because she was spoilt rotten, but as she got older she realised it had its disadvantages because she always seemed to have to rely on others. She was used to being looked after.

The social scene in Calgary was a little slow, as one can imagine, focussing especially round the church. Avis had found herself a husband who worked for petroleum oil. His name was Milton Moorhouse and his family were farmers from Edmonton. He was a good catch. He was hardworking and loved Avis. Shirley became a school teacher. She was rather a timid soul out of the classroom, and didn't mix easily in society. Marjorie was the dreamer. She wrote a little and over the years did various secretarial jobs. In 1945, just as the war was coming to an end, she met Bruce Bond. He was a pilot with the New Zealand Air Force and was out in Canada on training sessions. They fell in love and became engaged to be married.

On their wedding night Marjorie was excited and nervous. She was a curious girl and had asked her eldest sister, Avis, to give her a hint as to what to expect. She well understood the mechanics of it all as she was a doctor's daughter, but Bruce had seemed a little remote. On their wedding night his lovemaking was tentative and reserved. Marjorie was disappointed. She lay in the dark listening to his breathing and pondered. She decided not to pursue the matter for the moment. After all, the poor man was flying off in two days' time, back to Europe. That must be playing on his mind. She prayed to God to give her strength and understanding and fell asleep, glad to have made a decision.

Bruce left and life pretty much returned to the same routine. It was as though she had never been married. Marjorie felt restless. Her sister Avis was down in Montreal and that seemed to be so much more exciting, and when Avis fell pregnant, Marjorie and Shirley went to visit. Marjorie loved the bustling city. It was full of French-speaking Canadians, which gave it a European feel. The old town had some lovely buildings quite unlike the stark, plain buildings of Calgary. Avis gave birth to a little girl and she was called Sylvia.

Milton was not around much as he travelled the world with the oil company but Marjorie loved to hear his stories of other countries. She especially loved to hear about England and she vowed one day she was going to travel, and England was top of the list.

On returning from her visit to Montreal there was a letter waiting for her from Bruce. He was going to be on a troop ship that was docking in San Francisco sometime the following month (he was not allowed to say when for security reasons). Could Marjorie come down and see him for a couple of days? Her heart skipped a beat. She was so excited. She talked to her parents and they agreed she should go down by train. She was only allowed to take $50 but she would be very careful.

Marjorie loved the freedom of travelling by herself. People were so kind and helpful. She arrived the night before the ship was due in and booked into the YWCA. She prayed and prayed everything was going to be all right. On the train coming down she had decided to write her husband a note describing her feelings about their honeymoon night. It was a difficult subject and had to be handled with delicacy, but she was not someone to hide her head in the sand. If they had a problem, she thought it was better to face it now.

The morning arrived bright and clear. Marjorie made her way to the docks, marvelling at all the sights and sounds of the wharf. She was very early so she bought a coffee and sat in a diner and watched the world go by. She didn't feel quite so cavalier this morning, and as she had her prayer book in her bag, she brought it out and read until her heart slowed down.

On checking her watch for what seemed like the fiftieth time, finally the time had come to meet Bruce. She walked to the barrier and waited, hand shielding her eyes, straining for the first glimpse of her beloved. Finally, Bruce appeared at the end of the quay and she ran towards him, arms outstretched. He gave her a huge hug and swung her in the air, while she laughed delightedly and kissed him on the lips right there in public. Well, why not?

Then she noticed there was another man beside them, who had been standing back and letting the newlyweds enjoy their reunion. Bruce introduced him to Marjorie, explaining that they had flown together on their last tour and would be together for the next. Bruce suggested they all did some sightseeing together before they went back to the hotel. Marjorie wasn't thrilled at the idea. She had planned their day together down to the last detail and it didn't include some man trailing round with them. But she showed no signs of her disappointment and smiled brightly. So be it.

As it turned out they had a wonderful day. They all got on well and laughed and fooled around all afternoon as they explored the city. Eventually, they said their farewells and Bruce and Marjorie made their way back to their hotel. Marjorie lay on the bed while

Bruce took a shower, and thought about the night ahead. She took out the note she had written and laid it beside the bed. She undressed and caught sight of herself in the mirror. She had a neat little body. She was only five foot but she was in proportion. She traced her fingers down her throat and let them linger across her breasts. She had very soft, olive skin; it was one of her best features.

Tonight would be full of passion and romance, she had decided. If Bruce was a little shy, God would give her the courage to take control and show him the way. She brushed her hair and climbed into bed. Bruce came in drying his hair, with a towel wrapped round his waist. She watched him admiringly: he was a fine figure of a man, was her beloved husband. Marjorie indicated the note to him and suggested he read it. Bruce looked puzzled but sat down, opened it and read it. After he had finished reading, he sighed very deeply and turned and studied Marjorie.

'Darling Marjorie, you know I love you, don't you?'

'Of course I do, Bruce dear. I only wrote you that note because I wanted you to know that although I have no experience, I felt we were not as free together as we could be, and I wanted you to know I'm aware of that and want to help.' She looked at him sitting there on the end of the bed and realised how tired he looked. Almost grey with exhaustion. She felt guilty for bringing it all up now.

'Oh, Bruce, don't mind me. I am so sorry I brought it up. Let's go to bed. You look so tired.'

'No, you're right,' Bruce sighed. 'We need to get things straight. If I'm to expect you to travel halfway across the world to come and live with me after the war is over, the least I can do is give you an explanation. Marjorie, I am tired. You're right. But it is not just a physical tiredness. It's a mental thing. I've seen so much in the last three years. Seen my friends die. Seen terrible things. I've lost my faith in God and humanity. Being with you makes me realise how jaded I've become. It's so hard to let myself go. Please bear with me. Once the war is over and I get home, I'll be fine, I promise.'

Marjorie moved across to him and laid her head on his chest. She listened to his heart beating and tried to give him all her loving thoughts and hopes. They lay like that in the half light until Marjorie could feel his breathing had grown heavy. She slipped out from under his arm and looked at him lying fast asleep.

'Please, dear God, make him better. Keep him safe and bring him back to me.'

In the morning they made their farewells at the hotel and as she watched him walk away, Marjorie turned away to hide her tears.

Marjorie never saw Bruce again. Six months later she received a letter expressing great sadness in having to tell her that her husband Bruce was missing in action.

I T WAS A difficult time. Not only was she now a widow, but the family were all in shock at the news that her sister Avis was very ill. She had a tumour and was going to need treatment.

There was also a feeling of anticlimax hanging over the country. What was going to happen next? After the euphoria of the end of hostilities in Europe, there was an air of expectancy. People knew the world was going to change, but how? Marjorie decided to go and visit her husband's family in New Zealand. It was the least she could do to show her late husband some respect. She had a nagging feeling of guilt about her and Bruce's last night together, and maybe she could resolve things if she went and made her peace with his parents. So Marjorie joined the other wives and widows on the long voyage to New Zealand.

Bruce's family greeted her with open arms. They were so kind and friendly that Marjorie stayed for six months, but Avis needed her support back in Canada so she said her farewells and was back on the boat going home. She felt her loss more acutely now. Here she was on a boat going to nowhere. Home, yes, but home to what? Life in Calgary in her parents' home? Her sister, Shirley, was settling for the life of a spinster, but that was not for her. She couldn't bear the thought that this was it. She leaned against the railings on deck and watched the waves swelling around her. Suddenly, she felt someone at her elbow.

'Awesome, isn't it?' said a voice. She looked around and into the eyes of a tall, handsome man. His gaze rested discomfortingly on her. She could not put her finger on it but he made her feel uneasy, yet excited.

'Hi, I'm Carl Hutton, I'm part of the crew. If there's anything I can do for you don't hesitate to let me know,' he said and he turned and was gone.

Over the next few weeks, Carl Hutton would magically appear at her side every time they disembarked at some exotic location. She would allow him to escort her round because he made her laugh and he made her feel safe. He seemed to know everything about everything. He would offer her strange and wonderful cock-tails, which she always refused because, as she kept telling him, she had taken the pledge at a young age. Her father had warned her of the dangers of alcohol.

Carl would laugh and say, 'Christ, Marjorie, I have no hope, then, of seducing you!'

'Don't blaspheme Carl,' she would scold. But she couldn't be angry with him for long. He was so charming and boyish and full of life, he made her feel there was a life to lead. A life full of fun and colour and laughter.

When they docked in New York, Marjorie was going to stay with some friends of the family for a few days and do a bit of sight-seeing. Carl offered to take her round. What harm could there be in that? She accepted his offer and the next day she met him at his hotel and they set off. He was the perfect companion; again, he knew everything there was to know about New York. He flirted with her outrageously and kept trying to hold her hand or throw his arm around her and squeeze her waist. She would rebuff him playfully, but not before she felt the frisson of excitement between them. Was this what she had missed with Bruce?

Carl steered her through the crowds at the Statue of Liberty. He lifted her up to see over the railings at the zoo. He held her tight, up high on the Empire State Building and then he kissed her long and hard when they came to say goodbye at the door of his hotel room. She melted into his arms and all her fears and frustrations melted, too. It was as if she had spent her life waiting for this moment. She was frightened by the power of her emotions but it was so exciting. She could feel every hair on her head tingling. Her arms went round him and she pulled him to her. He carried her to the bed and made love to her. This was what she had known, deep down, that it was all about. All along, she had tried to catch this feeling with Bruce, but this was Carl and he was here and he loved her.

Each day was a blur to her. She was full of him. He took over her every waking hour. He was so intense. He devoured her greedily. He watched her every move, chiding her if she looked away. Pulling her back into him if she stayed to look in a shop window.

There were moments when he frightened her. His sarcasm when she wouldn't have a drink. What had been a joke between them on the ship now seemed like a wall. He loved to drink. He loved bars and the people in them. They would sit at night in a crowded bar and Carl would hold court to those around him. He was witty and charming and good-looking. People liked him. Women loved him. Sometimes Marjorie felt pushed out, especially when he made jokes at her expense. One night, he spiked her drink then told everyone about it and mocked her for being so pompous about being a tee-totaller. She saw another side of him, a cruel streak that she didn't like, but she put it aside. She wanted nothing to spoil these few days.

All too soon, it was time to leave. Carl woke her with roses and a proposal. She was to go home and tell her parents she was to be married. He would travel up later. They parted at the train station. She was amazed to see he was crying as he ran beside the train waving goodbye. He must love her very much.

Her family was delighted. Her sister Avis was recuperating at home with her parents so the sisters were together again, and excitedly began to make wedding plans.

CHAPTER TWENTY-FOUR

DOING THE RIGHT THING?

S HE STARED AT the doctor.

'Pregnant.' She whispered the word, though not as a question, because deep in her heart she had known the truth. Had known the exact moment in the hotel room in New York.

The doctor interrupted her thoughts: 'You must be so thrilled, Mrs Bond. Congratulations!'

Back outside, Marjorie walked along the streets. Winter was coming and the leaves were deserting the trees, their reds and golds turning to dirty brown on the sidewalk beneath her feet. She could feel the baby inside her. God's miracle. Why had He done this? Why had God decided to ruin her life? This was not supposed to happen. Would Carl be angry with her? Surely not? They were getting married anyway. The shame would be terrible for Mother and Dad, though. She would have to tell them because she never lied. That was one thing she never did. She never lied. And her father was a doctor; he had respect for life. She would be married as quickly as possible and maybe nobody would notice.

When she reached home she went straight to her room to gather herself before she told her parents. Avis appeared at the door and, looking at her, said, 'What's wrong, dear? You look so pale.'

'Can you get Shirley and bring her here?' Marjorie decided to start with her sisters and test the water.

The girls gathered round their sister and waited expectantly. There was no way to do this but come straight out with it: 'I'm pregnant.'

Shirley gasped and sat down on the edge of the bed. 'Oh dear, Marjorie, what have you done?' Avis shushed her quiet and kneeled down beside Marjorie.

'You poor girl. But don't worry, we'll get through this. But first of all, let me beg you not to tell Mother and Father. It would destroy them. I know you can't tell a lie, Marjorie, but we have to find a way that you don't tell them. First off, you need to tell Carl. I'll drive you to a phone booth so no one hears your conversation.'

She drove Marjorie to the phone booth on the corner by the coffee shop. Marjorie dialled the number and heard the connection. After a couple of rings a man answered.

'Carl, is that you?' she asked.

'No, Carl's not here right now. Shall I take a message?' Marjorie could hear music and laughter in the background and a woman's voice.

'No. Can you tell me when he will be back?'

'Oh, anytime now, I should think. Shall I tell him you called?'

'Yes, do that, thanks. Say his fiancée rang.' She heard him snort and clear his throat.

'Oh, right. Well, OK, ma'am.' As he hung up she thought she heard him laugh and start to say something.

She and Avis went and sat in the coffee shop and had a soda. Half an hour later, she tried again. Carl answered on the second ring.

'Hi, Baby! How are you? Sorry I missed your call before.'

'Carl, I'm so sorry to call like this, but I just had to tell you. I am having a baby.'

There was silence at the other end of the line. Marjorie could hear him breathing fast.

'OK. Well, that is news. Are you saying I'm the father?'

'Well, of course you're the father, Carl. What do you mean by that? Who else would it be?'

'Well now, come on, Marjorie. There were plenty of other men on that boat.'

Marjorie dropped the phone as her hands flew up to her mouth to stifle the anguished cry that found its way up from deep inside her. She all but staggered from the phone booth into Avis's arms. Her sister understood immediately.

'I'm so sorry, Marjorie. It's OK, we'll manage somehow.' They just stood there, the two of them, in the growing darkness. The sisters made a plan. It was just like when Marjorie was small and her sister would tell her what to do. Avis was going back to Montreal shortly and Marjorie would go with her, on the pretext of helping Avis look after Sylvia. She would stay for her confinement, have the baby, sort out the adoption and then come home. Their parents need never know.

Within the week Marjorie was packed and on a train to Montreal.

M ILTON SAT AT the kitchen table and listened to Marjorie's tale of woe. Milton was rather a stern man and he looked kind of scary to Marjorie now as she talked. He stared at her hard and said little. When she had finished he seemed to gather himself up and then launched into a speech that was both pompous and incredibly insensitive, in equal measures. He said he was sorry that Marjorie had found herself in this unfortunate position, but that she had only herself to blame. He'd like to help, but she must understand that in his position at the oil company, it would be very embarrassing for him to have to explain her pregnancy and lack of a husband, and he felt it was wrong to set any kind of example like this to his young daughter. He was also concerned for Avis's health, and did not want her to be put under any undue stress. So he felt it was better, in the circumstances, if Marjorie took a room somewhere. He would help her financially, of course, and Avis would always be around to support her.

Marjorie said she quite understood and thanked him, but she would not take a penny of his money as she would get a job. Avis was silent. What could she say? Milton was her husband and head of the household.

The next day Marjorie went and found a job. She was a skilled typist so it was not difficult. She found a room and settled down to the next six months. She still wore her wedding ring so everyone assumed she was married, with a husband at home. As soon as she could no longer hide the bump, she asked for some time off. She had enough money saved to get her through her confinement. She did manage to make contact with some old friends of the family whom she knew she could trust with her secret. Once the Cohens had heard her story, they insisted Marjorie go to live with them. She could help out with a bit of housework if she wanted to say thank you.

It was the perfect arrangement for all of them, and Marjorie was able to concentrate on her other plan: having her baby adopted. She had met a very nice doctor at the local Baptist church and was forming a plan to go and see him with her dilemma. The following Sunday, after the morning service, she approached the doctor and his wife. His name was Dr Gordon and he had noticed the young woman who sat in church and prayed so earnestly. This morning she was looking nervous and intense. Could she have some advice? She glanced at his wife. In private? His wife smiled kindly and left them alone. Dr Gordon led her to a bench and they sat down. Marjorie told her whole story with hardly a pause for breath.

Dr Gordon had heard similar stories many times before, but he happened to have heard of Dr Ralph Hughes, Marjorie's father, and he realised just how much this young woman was suffering. Her guilt and her love for her parents were at odds with her circumstances. She had made a mistake. She had surely suffered enough. Marjorie wanted Dr Gordon to help her have her baby adopted privately. Could he find her somebody to take the baby to England? She loved the idea of her child being brought up by a nice British couple in a country village somewhere.

'Do you know England then?' asked Dr Gordon.

'Oh no, but I've read so much about it and my brother-in-law has told me all about life there. Please can you help me?'

Dr Gordon said he would do his best. Then he told her not to worry and to concentrate on keeping healthy and safe until the baby was born. This she did, and on 31st May, 1948 at St Paul's Hospital in Montreal, Marjorie Hughes (Bond) was delivered of a baby girl. She called her Meredith Lee Hughes. She thought her heart would break with love as she held her in her arms.

Then the nurse took the bundle away and she was left alone, bereft.

The nurses in the ward knew that Marjorie did not have a husband, and the ward sister seemed to take delight in her unhappiness. She was informed it was policy, where a child was to be adopted, that the baby was removed from the mother as soon as possible. She had visiting rights once a week, until she had to take her baby to the doctor in charge of her case for private adoption. Her baby, her little Meredith, was in a big house just on the outskirts of town, being looked after by a very jolly lady from Yorkshire, England. That seemed like a good omen to Marjorie.

All she had to do was be patient and trust that Doctor Gordon would find her baby a good home.

Every Saturday, after a long week back at work as a typist, she took the bus out to the house to visit. She wasn't allowed to be left alone with the child. Marjorie found herself longing to look in a mirror at herself and her baby, to see and remember the sight of the two of them together, but it was never possible.

After six weeks, she got a call from Dr Gordon. He had found a suitable couple to adopt Meredith. One of his other duties was as the Medical Advisor for BOAC and its staff, when they were stationed in Montreal. He had recently seen a young pilot and his wife who were newly married and wanted to make sure they could have children as they had been trying for a year. He had been happy to tell them that all was well and that they just had to be patient. The young woman was desperate, and he suggested adoption, because he did happen to know of a baby that was in need of a home. He knew the family history and felt that the baby would have all the same physical attributes as their own children. He suggested they went to see the child. They were entranced, and the adoption would go ahead. Mr and Mrs Donald Bellingham were to become the proud parents of a baby girl.

Marjorie collected Meredith Lee on that fateful morning and climbed into the taxi with her bundle. She kept whispering to the child, 'I love you. Remember, I will always love you. You must know I love you.'

She took the baby to Dr Gordon's surgery and handed the little girl over to him. She did not shed a tear and she held her head high. She gave him a letter addressed to 'The Mother' and asked him to pass it on. Then she turned and left. She made her way across the road and waited. She watched the couple come out with her baby and get into the car and drive off. She ran into the street after it, as her tears flowed, howling like a wounded animal. A passer-by stopped and took hold of her as she crumpled to the ground. Once she recovered, she took a taxi back to work but they had to send her home because she was in such a state.

'Whatever is the matter, Marjorie?' they kept asking her. 'Has someone died?'

Someone might just as well have done, as far as Marjorie was concerned. She had lost her baby as surely as though it had died. She knew she would never see Meredith Lee again. Until she picked up the phone forty years later.

CHAPTER TWENTY-FIVE

'WHEN I DISCOVER WHO I AM, I WILL BE FREE'

(RALPH ELLISON)

'IS IT REALLY you, dear?'

I cannot put into words what my feelings were at that moment. Maybe relief. She did exist. I would get some answers.

We talked for half an hour. Her first question to me was, 'Are you a Christian?' Yes.

My first question to her was, 'Do you have any other children?' No.

Marjorie's sister, Shirley, was in the room with her and all through our conversation Marjorie kept shouting to her, as she was obviously deaf. I explained how I had found her and she was aghast because she thought she had covered her trail pretty well. But she had not taken into account that her father had been quite a celebrity in his own way and worthy of press coverage, so quite easily traceable.

Susan Armstrong at the Missing Children's Network, and her work associate, Marcele La Marche, had read the newspaper piece that said that Dr Ralph Hughes had died leaving two daughters,

Shirley Hughes and Marjorie Moorhouse. Further investigation showed a family burial plot in Calgary. Avis had died, leaving her widowed husband, Milton Moorhouse. The girls put two and two together and surmised that Marjorie had married Milton. They had found Milton Moorhouse in the phone book and rung him.

Susan had made up a story that she had been at school with Marjorie and lost touch and would it be possible for him to tell her where she could find her? Milton explained that she was his wife now, and that she was with her sister, Shirley, on holiday in Victoria. He gave her the number and wished them well. Milton told Marjorie afterwards that he somehow had a feeling that the story did not ring true.

I asked Marjorie if she would mind if I came to visit her. She was very excited by the idea but said she would have to discuss it with Milton first. I could not believe she had married the man who had virtually thrown her out of his house when she was pregnant, but I thought it best to leave all that for another time. We agreed I would ring her in three days' time when she would be home in Edmonton.

I put the phone down and burst into tears. I went into the bedroom, looked at my two little cherubs fast asleep, and wondered what the hell I had done.

I RANG THE GIRLS at the Missing Children's Network and arranged to come and see them on my way to Edmonton. I also agreed to attend a big charity event they were having; it was a way of saying thank you. Then I rang Marjorie to make a plan. We were both much calmer now and more guarded. She started to back off the idea of me visiting, saying she wasn't sure they had the sort of place in which they could entertain an actress. I explained that I wasn't Sophia Loren or anything, just a working actress. Then Marjorie said that *All Creatures Great and Small* was one of Milton's favourite TV shows, and I actually think that that was the key that opened the door into their lives!

I told her about the girls and their charity. That made her very nervous because she didn't want anybody to know who I was. She had never told a soul about the adoption except a minister from England she had met, and even Milton didn't know she had told anyone. I got the distinct impression that it was Milton who wanted to keep everything under wraps, suggesting that his attitude hadn't changed much since the day she got pregnant. I didn't think I was going to like Milton.

Marjorie finally agreed and we set a date. Then I had to go and break the news to my parents. They were shocked at how quickly events had happened, but they were supportive, as always. I told them the story so far and said that Marjorie had mentioned she wanted to thank them for looking after me so well. My dad just said brusquely, 'She doesn't have to thank me. You're my daughter and always will be.'

One thing we talked about was how Dad had driven away that day they picked me up at Dr Gordon's surgery.

'The trouble was, Lynda,' my father explained, 'I saw her in my driving mirror, running after the car, crying, and I had to make a split-second decision. Whether to step on the brake or the accelerator; I chose the accelerator. Please say to Marjorie I hope I made the right decision.' I also asked Mum about the letter that Marjorie had given the doctor. She told me she destroyed it because she really felt at the time it was better for all of us to make a clean break. She did write a letter to Marjorie, a few months later, and I was to see that letter when I went over to Canada. They also agreed with me that it was very strange she ended up marrying a man who had had so little respect for her.

And so the stage was set. The boys were to stay under the watchful eye of our lovely nanny, Natalie, and our flight awaited me and Nunzio. I was very nervous and Nunzio seemed very jumpy, because he hates flying. We had a great flight over, though, and we were upgraded to Club Class because the head steward recognised me. We drank lots of champagne and talked about what was going to happen when we met Marjorie. But the first stop was Montreal.

The girls from the network charity met us at the airport. They were lovely and so excited. Marcele had brought her husband, and Susan was a single mum with a daughter. We had Sunday brunch, and they told us more about the charity and filled us in on what would happen at the do the following night.

We spent the next day touring the city. It was a strange mix of old and new. All the shopping malls were underground and were so characterless and dull, with piped muzak and strip lighting. But up above, outside, there was a vibrant quarter of the town with little restaurants and markets. It was autumn, just like when Marjorie had given me away and, as I walked the streets, I imagined what she must have been feeling. I went back to the hotel feeling a bit weary and emotional as the jet lag set in.

I decided the best thing to do was just to keep going so I had a bath and started to get ready. Nunzio, of course, went to sleep and I couldn't get him to wake up. He complained he had a headache and he was not interested in going out. I spent the entire time trying to chivvy him along while preparing myself for the charity ball that night. It was work as far as I was concerned.

We had a terrible evening. We had too much to drink just to get through the night. At eleven we made our excuses because we had to be up at 5 a.m. to get an internal flight to Edmonton, which was going to take five or six hours. Nunzio was already panicking about the flight. As we left I gave Susan a cheque for £500 for the charity. It was the least I could do: they had done such marvellous work.

As we rode the lift to our room, however, Nunzio started on at me. How dare I give away our money without consulting him? I explained coolly that actually it was my money. Well, that was it. He was off, ranting and raving at me. I think it was a combination of alcohol and nerves about the upcoming flight.

Then suddenly, in the middle of this tirade, there was an earth tremor. Unheard of in Montreal! We were on the seventeenth floor (an unlucky number in Naples I later learned), feeling the earth move. Back in our room, Nunzio was a wreck. He completely went to pieces and hid under the sheets. He said he was not coming on the plane and that he was going to stay in Montreal. I pleaded with him but to no avail. So I got up and dressed in the morning, and set off for the airport. The next thing I knew, Nunzio was running after me, screaming for me to wait. To think that I had hoped for some support from him!

We arrived in Edmonton completely wrecked, having had no sleep during the flight. It was a very weird feeling as I scanned the Arrivals lounge for someone who looked like my mother. I suddenly felt a hand on my arm, and looked down into the brownest eyes I have ever seen. The face was long, and framed by white fluffy hair. It had never occurred to me that she would have white hair. I was looking at a little old lady and trying to see myself.

Behind her, tall and stiffly straight, was Milton. He stuck out his hand to shake mine as I rushed into his arms for an embrace that felt like I was holding a tree trunk. We stood there, the four of us, looking at each other, while people swirled around us. Nobody said anything, then Marjorie broke the spell: 'Oh, Lynda dear, you look so darling. You're much too pretty to belong to me.' We all laughed and Milton turned and strode out of the airport towards his car.

Marjorie Moorhouse, 1947

Marjorie and me in Edmonton, 1993

Second Thoughts, another of my families, 1993

Being caught by Michael Aspel for *This Is Your Life* (on the *Second Thoughts* set), 1993

Czarina Alexandra in *The Romanovs*,
1998 – a far cry from making gravy

I do love a corset – *My Uncle Silas*
with Albert Finney, 2002

With my best friend,
Nickolas Grace

Meeting HM Queen
Elizabeth, with Harry Hill
and Nicholas Parsons, 2005

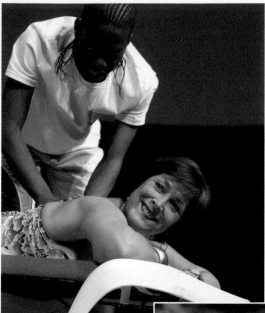

Sugar Mummies, 2006
– it's tough at the top

This is scary!
Playing Irene Radford
in *The Bill*, 2004

Third time lucky! Michael and me on our wedding day, 31st May, 2008

My new family: Michael and Michael, Robbie, stepson Bradley, stepdaughter Stacey and stepgrandson Cooper, who looks less than sure about us all

The lovely Loose Ladies – don't they brush up well!

Michael and me in Paris
for our first wedding
anniversary, 31st May, 2009
(he is such a smoothie)

Loose Women at
work. We look
very genteel here –
very deceptive

Strictly Come Dancing
with Darren Bennett –
you can't see the terror
behind my eyes!

Calendar Girl – hardly Playboy centrefold!

Marjorie took my arm and urged me forward with Nunzio following on behind. For once he was speechless.

I T WAS A difficult few days, made even more difficult by Nunzio and Milton. Both men seemed to feel threatened in some way. I worked very hard to thaw Milton: I talked about farming and my dad being a pilot and tried to show him that actresses were human. Nunzio spent the whole time complaining of jet lag, just enough each day to stop me relaxing.

And Marjorie and I? Well, we talked and talked. She lived in a bungalow in acres of bungalows. Edmonton is completely flat and from a tall building you could see for miles, if there was anything to see. The house was spotless with lots of knick-knacks from travels abroad. In a way, it was too tidy, like so many people's houses who do not have children or grandchildren. We talked about my boys and I showed her photos. She told me about Avis's daughter, Sylvia's children. She was married but was now divorced, and had two adopted boys. So my sons were the only blood relations in this extended family, which was interesting.

Perhaps understandably, Marjorie only talked about my father, Carl, out of earshot of Milton. She seemed very embarrassed at first but then, as the memories flooded back, she became much more animated. She had a wicked sense of humour and could tell a good story. She showed me the letter from Ruth Bellingham and it made me cry. My dear mum was always so caring of other people and had obviously wanted to make Marjorie feel better about giving up her baby. It was kind and caring and very sensitive.

We all went out for dinner each night, and that had its comic moments. Marjorie suffered from deafness like her sister, Shirley, but whereas Shirley was profoundly deaf owing to a burst eardrum in childhood, Marjorie simply had a hearing aid due to old age.

However, it did make conversation difficult, especially if we were talking about me and the adoption. We all had to shout to be heard above the hubbub of conversation, and I was still meant to be a secret!

Then, one evening, we were approached at the table by a Scottish lady who recognised me, and wanted my autograph. The look on Milton's face! You'd have thought we had been discovered snorting cocaine. He was still insistent that nobody knew of Marjorie's 'shame'. It was so sad. As for Marjorie's guilt, it seemed to have increased her religious fervour. She was a born-again Christian and tended to preach at every opportunity. Milton was an atheist so her words of wisdom fell on deaf ears, and she was delighted to have new converts.

When we were alone it was very hard because she liked to hold my hand and just gaze at me. She wanted me to call her Mum but I just couldn't bring myself to do so. It would be a betrayal to Mum and Dad. But as Marjorie pointed out to me, it didn't feel odd to her: 'Lynda, dear, when I held you in my arms the first time, I felt the floodgates open, and I had to dam all those feelings in order to part with you. Seeing you now, all those feelings have returned. All my maternal emotions that were locked away have resurfaced. But to you, dear, I'm a stranger whom you need to get to know.' She was right, of course, and I was grateful for her understanding.

I tried to talk to her about why she gave me up but never really got a satisfactory reply. She talked about the shame on the family, which I understood, but which I also knew other people had risen above; including my granny in England, as I told her. But she seemed to think it was different. I didn't push it, because I thought we would be able to have many conversations over the coming years and we needed to relax with each other.

I asked Marjorie how it came about that she married Milton. She explained that after Avis died, Milton would often visit the family because of Sylvia – as he was often away, working, Sylvia spent a good deal of time with the Hughes family and Shirley even taught her for a while. And apparently it was not unusual in those days for brothers and sisters to marry their in-laws if someone had died. Nothing wrong with that, I agreed, but he had been so horrible to her. She laughed and said he was right, though. She had only got herself to blame.

I began to see a very strong similarity between me and my birth mother, the link of very low self-esteem. She must have seen it too, as one day she said to me, in one of our heart-to-hearts, when I had given a little too much away about my current problems with Nunzio: 'Lynda, when I held you in my arms in that taxi going to Dr Gordon's, I kept telling you I loved you because I did not want you to feel unloved or bad about yourself in later life. I had no idea you could inherit no self-worth.'

I knew that was true. I had spent my whole life trying to please everyone, to make everyone love me, and here I was again, trying to create a good impression.

The time came to say goodbye and we parted with promises to try and get together again soon. As I turned to Milton he came forward and gave me a big hug, which was lovely. Marjorie bade me goodbye with tears in her eyes and I had such mixed emotions.

All the way home on the flight I tried to sort out what I was feeling. A mixture of relief to have finally found out about my roots, and terrible guilt about betraying my parents. Confusion in how I felt about Marjorie. I couldn't love her because I didn't know her, but I felt a sense of responsibility towards her. Would I be able to like her enough? I had to take it one step at a time.

THE NEXT TIME we saw each other, Milton and Marjorie came to London and met my parents. I discussed the meeting with Mum and Dad and we decided they would have lunch with Marjorie and Milton. Just the four of them. We chose the restaurant in Liberty's because it was quite discreet. In a wonderful gesture, Mum made up an album of photos of me from when they had me to the present day. The meeting was a success and went smoothly, although my father did not take to Milton. He thought his attitude to Marjorie was controlling and rather unkind.

That evening, we all had dinner together. We went to the River Café, which is a lovely place but very noisy. It was a stupid choice for the occasion, and I don't know why I chose it. It made conversation difficult for Marjorie because she couldn't hear and, at one point, I realised that everyone was talking to each other except Marjorie. She was just sitting there looking rather forlorn, with a tear in her eye. Milton kept making rather bad jokes at Marjorie's expense, until my father finally asked him to stop. They were not amused. Well done, Dad.

Marjorie loved the boys and they loved her. She told them all sorts of stories about bears and Indians and moose! We agreed that we would go and visit the following year and go skiing. And that is what we did for several years. It worked well because we spent a week skiing at Jasper or Lake Louise, which are both beautiful resorts, and sometimes Marjorie joined us. But we had a bad trip one time with Nunzio. We were in the Banff Springs Hotel, which is a fabulous old hotel that was built for the railways; it nestles in the mountains like a shrine to Victorian architecture. Nunzio got cross with a waiter and Marjorie, half jokingly, told him to shut up. When we got upstairs we all said goodnight outside the rooms. We were with the boys in one room and Marjorie was next door. As soon as we were in our room, Nunzio started shouting at me and the boys were getting very distressed. Suddenly, there was a knock on the door and there was Marjorie in her nightie and curlers.

'Nunzio, you stop your bullying,' this five-foot-nothing granny said. 'I know what you do to Lynda, and if you lay a finger on her you will have me to answer to!'

Unbelievably, Nunzio then just laid into her, and told her she was a slut, just like her daughter. We were both sluts and had no respect. I know Marjorie was really shocked. Most people were when they were confronted by my husband in full flow. It was also incredibly hurtful and insensitive, after all she had been through. After that incident Nunzio didn't come again, which was a huge relief.

The first time I went on my own to see Marjorie, it was a very emotional experience. The day before my flight was Easter Day 1994, and I had done an Easter egg hunt as usual and made a lovely lunch with roast chicken and all the trimmings. As we sat down to eat, Nunzio decided to throw a wobbly. I cannot remember the reason; there probably wasn't one. All the food went everywhere, a chair got thrown which caught me on the head. The boys were crying and it was mayhem. I went to bed and was woken, later in the evening, by little Michael standing at the edge of my bed, with a cup of tea for me, and Nunzio with Robbie in his arms. Nunzio apologised, as usual, and said he was nervous because we were all flying tomorrow, me to Canada and he and the boys to Italy.

I was in such a state by the time I got on the plane. I had left the boys at home, crying, and I was crying now as I buckled up for the flight. I had a huge egg-shaped bump on my forehead as a reminder of another happy Easter.

When I arrived in Edmonton, Marjorie launched into a cross-examination of what had happened to me. I told her it was an accident. She was not convinced. She tucked me up in a single bed in the guest room and fussed over me for the next twenty-four hours. It was so claustrophobic, I thought I would go mad. The houses are very over-heated in Canada because of the tremendous cold, and it can be suffocating. The cold also means the air is very dry, and every time I touched the nylon sheets I got an electric shock. I was so low and just couldn't hide it from Marjorie. We talked about Nunzio and his jealousy and his controlling nature.

Marjorie started talking about my real father, and said he had been the same. He had had a cruel side and would accuse her of all sorts of horrible things: 'Probably because he was doing them himself, dear.' He was controlling and very jealous and was always accusing her of wanting other men. We talked about the similarity between them. Marjorie seemed to think she could have changed him. I knew better. She admitted she had had very low self-esteem and that she was so sorry I inherited that rather negative quality. She insisted that she was quite different now and that no man was a match for her. But I have to say that is not how it looked to me. I saw a woman who was very much under the thumb of her husband. Partly because of their age and the society they came from but also because I perceived Milton as being quite controlling. She tried so hard to understand and give me love and comfort, but I just wanted my parents and my sons. I was so homesick it was ridiculous.

I also got a bit irritated by her insular view of the world. Marjorie was so cosseted, and really had no idea what was going on in the real world. She and Milton had their careful mapped-out life, and it was a selfish life. They had their routine and nobody could interrupt it. Dinner at 6.30 p.m. Church on Sunday. Then there was their immaculate house: you could never imagine small children ever being allowed to play amongst the myriad china ornaments. Don't get me wrong, of course they were entitled to it.

Milton had earned it. But Marjorie had taken on Milton's slightly preachy, smug attitude towards others and that got to me. I tried to love her as my mother but I couldn't.

I also spent the time thinking how different my life would have been if I had been brought up in Edmonton. The small-town mentality was frightening. I don't want to be disrespectful of this place but I realised just what a wonderful upbringing I had had with my mother and father. I had a real overview of life and even though I was failing miserably in many respects, I did know right from wrong and, fundamentally, had respect for other people and their way of life. My parents had also given me the chance to express myself. I couldn't imagine Marjorie ever agreeing to me being an actress.

I returned from that trip with the realisation that I really did not have a great deal in common with my birth mother. I also knew that I had a hell of a lot more to worry about on the home front. Things were seriously falling apart.

CHAPTER TWENTY-SIX

TIME TO MAKE IT STOP

THE LAST FOUR years of my marriage are a blur. How I managed to run the house, look after two small children and star in *Faith in the Future* on TV will for ever be a mystery. Faith I did not have in the future. Everything was chaos: the house, which we were doing up; and the restaurant, with which I was still very involved.

The restaurant was doing OK but Nunzio knew he should really move on: capitalise on its success, and buy closer to the West End. I encouraged him but he was a great procrastinator. He loved the fame and the money, but I think he was actually too frightened.

He was always going to Italy to show off and, at the end of these trips, we would have guys from Naples coming to work for him. Either friends or sons of friends. Nunzio was obviously pulling the boss card and telling his mates he could help them, including giving them a base at our home for a bit until they found their feet in London. I still had my duties as run-around for the restaurant. Sometimes at 10 o'clock at night Nunzio would call up and ask me to drive to Green Lanes and buy more vegetables. If there was no help around I would have to put Robbie in his car seat, strap Michael in the back of the car, half asleep, and drive round looking for bloody mushrooms!

I tried to be there for Nunzio, even though our work schedules clashed so badly. I would sit up and wait for him to finish at the restaurant and make him a meal and listen to all the problems. I would get up early to deal with the boys before I went to rehearsals, then be back in the afternoon to pick them up from school, do homework and cook dinner! I had help from a succession of lovely girls, but I still wanted to be hands-on.

For most of Robbie's early years, he had Natalie, God bless her. We had met her at the local riding school and, just as I had done with Alena, I recognised someone with the right nature to look after my sons. She was so kind and gentle. The only problem was she suffered from epilepsy. The poor girl had been too frightened to tell me in case I would not have her for the job, but, ironically, I knew all about epilepsy because of my eldest son, Michael.

When Michael was about thirteen, we drove to Birmingham at five in the morning, one Christmas morning, so I could do the breakfast TV show with Anne Diamond and Nick Owen at the BBC. The boys wanted me to do it because they wanted to meet Frank Bruno, who was also going to be on. The producer had promised me we would be back in time to have our Christmas lunch.

Halfway up the M1, I suddenly noticed Michael was shaking – it looked as though his seat belt was choking him. We stopped on the hard shoulder and got him out of the car. He woke up but had no recall of anything. He was very pale and shaky. So were we. I rang the studio who told me they had a doctor on call and, as we were halfway there, it seemed sensible to carry on, and have Michael checked out up in Birmingham. It was a terrible morning. We did the show, and the boys were so thrilled to meet Frank, but all I could think about was what was wrong with Michael. The doctor thought it had been a fit and said that we should take Michael to a specialist straight away. All through Christmas Day, and when we put him to bed that night, we watched him like hawks, while trying not to show him we were concerned.

I got an appointment as soon as I could. Michael had an MRI scan and it confirmed he had had a fit. The specialist recommended we leave things be for the time being, and see if he had another one.

Nothing happened for a year, but then Michael suddenly had two fits in a row, and the specialist recommended we put Michael on medication for epilepsy. He told us that once the brain got into a habit of fitting it would continue to do so, but by stopping the fits, with drugs, there was a chance that would be the end of the problem. Fits in puberty, especially in young boys, are quite common and they mostly grow out of them.

I was so worried. It's always the way, isn't it, when your children are ill? It's unbearable. We were also told that while he was on these drugs, and it was a three-year course, that Michael must get plenty of rest, and avoid stress and alcohol. He was now fourteen and about to start his GCSEs. Not a good time! My stress levels were pushed to the limit anyway and then to top it all, Nunzio blamed me for Michael's condition, saying it was down to me giving him too much apple juice. What?!

I'd also had another very frightening experience of epilepsy because my dear friend Jack Tinker's youngest daughter had the condition. She was very good about taking her medication, but the problem can be that because the person feels so well while on the drugs there is a strong inclination to want to stop taking them. Jack's daughter did this, with absolutely tragic consequences, as she had a fit one evening and drowned in her bath. I had the difficult task, with my son, of trying to make him understand the importance of taking the pills, without making him incredibly scared.

Then Natalie had a fit while I was at work and Nunzio was at the restaurant. The boys were on their own with her in the house. It must have been awful for Michael, who could understand what was going on, but was helpless to stop it.

A few weeks later, dear Natalie came back from holiday feeling great, didn't take her medication for a few days and, she too, tragically, had a fit and drowned in the bath. I still feel so bad for her family.

If it means anything, she did my son a huge favour, because he never forgot to take his drugs after that. After three years without a fit, he was able to come off them and has been fine ever since. Thank God.

OVER THOSE YEARS I could not have survived without the support and companionship of some of the mothers I met through my sons. These are friendships that are born in the playground: women who initially come together because of the shared interest in their children but discover a good friendship on top of that.

Sandra Horley, the head of Refuge, the charity for women and children suffering domestic violence, was a mother at my son's school. I would see her at the gate and wish I could talk to her. But I still had to keep my personal problems under wraps, because of my Oxo contract. If I lost that now, there would be no money for all these extras in the house that, sometimes, kept Nunzio quiet. As the face of the nation's favourite mum, I had to keep the perfect-family charade going.

I KEPT MY HEAD down and kept going. I made sure my sons did all the stuff the other children did. We had the birthday parties and the special cakes, thanks to my sister Jean. She made amazing themed cakes, and once did one for Robbie based on Michael Jackson. There was the little Jackson, as a werewolf, standing on top of the cake, in front of a huge moon that she had made out of a melted glacier mint. She put a candle behind it and it made the moon glow. The boys loved it. Another year we had a Ghostbusters van, and another year a huge dinosaur cake. That was a disaster, because we went to the park and left the cake on the table and when we returned later, we discovered the dog had eaten it. Star had green poo for days!

My career seemed to have a life of its own at this time. *Second Thoughts* continued to be a big success and, thanks to the support of Jan Etherington and Gavin Petrie, I not only had great scripts to perform, but also a shoulder to cry on. They knew what I was going through and did everything they could to make life easy for me at work.

There was also an interesting moment when dear Lynda La Plante rang and told me she had written a series about a police-woman, and that she had suggested me for the role. I realised I would not be free and had to pass. The series was called *Prime Suspect*. Let's not even go there! I remember standing in the new kitchen, trying to talk to Nunzio about my disappointment over not being able to have a crack at the role. His attitude was very much why was I making such a fuss? I had got Oxo and *Second Thoughts*. But he just couldn't see that much as I loved doing comedy, I longed for a dramatic role, and that it was so important to me that the industry took me seriously. The discussion then moved on to why was it so important to me that I still had a career? Didn't I care about my family? Weren't my children important to me? Nunzio then suggested I just wanted to be a success so I could go out and fuck lots of men. But this was how it always was these days. It was like a broken record over and over again.

Slowly but surely, I was becoming aware that Nunzio's cata-logue of recriminations, paranoia and behaviour towards me was getting worse. Much worse. Around this time, he locked me in the living room and spent the next several hours pacing the floor and screaming at me. If I tried to respond, it made him worse. So I sat rigid on the edge of the sofa for most of the night while he prowled round me like a caged animal, hurling abuse at me and yelling into my face that I should be dead.

I wished I was dead. God I wished that. The hatred that was emanating from him was tangible. I have never been so frightened. I honestly hoped that I might pass out with fright. Or that he might collapse, have a heart attack. Anything to make him stop. After several hours, as it was getting light, he suddenly stopped and sat down opposite me and without moving his gaze from my face he just sort of fell asleep. I waited until I was sure he was really asleep and then crept to the door, unlocked it, and fled the room. I was still shaking as I woke the boys up for school. My head was ringing with his taunts and screams. I wished there was a way I could help him. Make him stop.

There was another similar incident one morning in front of the builders where he chased me round the kitchen shouting that women like me deserved to die. The men just stood there, open-mouthed.

I tried to joke about it. Nunzio would then joke about it with me, sometimes, and I could see the confusion in people's faces. If I didn't have enough self-respect to stand up for myself, why should they worry? If I didn't seem to take it too seriously it must be fine.

The trouble was, I was just too frightened and too cowed. I kept hoping that Nunzio would see how much I loved him, and how much I wanted to please him, and everything would be OK. He must have despised me. I despised myself. At one point, I decided to take a knife to bed with me as protection. What a stupid thing to do. Thank God, I never lost control – it could have ended up with me in prison.

Even now, I sometimes ask myself if I created this whole scenario? If I had been stronger, and stood up for myself, and been more Italian, maybe we would never have got to the state we did? Just another symptom of the slow grinding down of my self-esteem.

Dear Catharine would come as often as she could. She tried so hard to keep me sane. We started to write an idea for a TV series together about a woman who runs a refuge for abused women. Nunzio asked us what it was about one day, and we were rather thrown, because we felt he wouldn't exactly appreciate the subject matter. We hedged a bit and quickly made up a story. That was a big mistake because, in Nunzio's paranoiac mind, we were plotting against him and Catharine was trying to turn me against him.

My new series, *Faith in the Future* – the spin-off series from *Second Thoughts* – seemed to be a success. I knew I needed to keep pushing on, but my agent, Sara Randall, was just not getting me the work I wanted. I know this is always a tricky situation with actors and their agents, and perhaps all my upsets had made me a difficult client to place. I loved Sara; she was, and is, a fantastic woman, loyal friend and good agent. However, I had the feeling it was time to move on.

Leaving Sara was going to be hard for a number of different reasons. I talked to Sylvie Boden, who was the director of *Faith in the Future*. She recommended I talk to Sue Latimer, who was then an agent with William Morris. I did, and liked Sue very much. She was savvy and tough, and had children of her own, so knew all the problems of juggling a career and a family. She had no idea just how much juggling I was doing at the time! We agreed to give it a go and all I had to do now was tell Sara. I was not looking forward to that.

I SAT IN MY car outside Sara's office for a good hour. I had consumed half a bottle of vodka and could not stop crying. I wasn't just upset about leaving her; I was upset about Nunzio and everything that was going on. My life was a mess and I felt I was letting it all pass me by.

I finally plucked up the courage to go in and tell her. I sat there and blubbed and said it was all my fault, and I was sorry, but I needed to move on. She was lovely, and gracious, and let me go. I drove home, still blubbing. Nunzio came in and asked me what the matter was and I told him. He gave a laugh of derision; something inside me snapped and I turned on him: 'I'd be careful if I were you, Nunzio. I have got rid of my agent, I can get rid of you.' He just laughed.

The next day was Saturday 6th April, a date that will be for ever emblazoned on my mind. I woke up feeling wrecked, thanks to the vodka, and an evening spent dealing with Nunzio's put-downs. After lunch, I found myself standing at the bottom of the stairs. Michael had gone to football practice and Robbie was playing in his room with his friend, Felix. Nunzio came down the stairs on his way to work. He passed some comment – I really do not remember what it was – but I flipped. I turned on him and told him to fuck off. His face turned black as thunder and he picked up the broken newel post on the end of the stairs and raised it to hit me.

I just didn't care any more.

'Go on, hit me,' I said, dully. 'Go on, Nunzio, I don't care any more. I'm sick to death of being frightened of you. Put me out of my misery.' He put down the post and his eyes held mine. I was so tired of feeling scared. My heart always in my mouth, and being on my guard. It had to stop. Someone had to make him stop. I had to make it stop. A light turned on in my head.

I ran into the kitchen and called the police. Nunzio followed me and pulled the phone jack out of its socket, but it was too late. The call was logged. Five minutes later, the police arrived. They put Nunzio in one room and me in another, and interviewed us separately. I sat there, sobbing, and kept saying, 'I'm so sorry. Please don't tell anyone. Please don't tell the press or I'll lose my job. If they find out Mrs Oxo is being abused they'll crucify me. I'm so sorry.'

They calmed me down and, as they left, they told Nunzio to watch it. That was it. I stood there looking at Nunzio, who seemed to be in shock. He picked Robbie up, went into the kitchen, sat down on the sofa and turned on the TV. Michael arrived home and ran in to sit with his dad. Whoever had brought him home very kindly agreed to take Felix back to his house.

I shut the front door and stood in the hall. That was it then. It was all over. Finally, I had let in the outside world. Just that fact was enough. To face those policemen and admit defeat was enough to show me it was finished. I went into the kitchen and looked at Nunzio sitting there on the sofa, with an arm tightly round each child. They looked at me with bewilderment. What was going on, Mum? Nunzio then said, 'You see, boys, what your mummy has done? She is very bad; she wants to send your daddy to prison. Daddy will go to prison; he will have to leave you.' The boys started to cry.

How I hated Nunzio at that moment. The emotional blackmail and manipulation. It was suddenly all so clear. Everything boiled down to him; it was all, and only ever had been, about him. He didn't love his children if he could put them through this. He certainly didn't love me. It was time to go. As I had said the day before, I could leave my agent, so I could leave him.

While he was sitting with the boys, I ran upstairs and got our passports and shoved them in a bag. Keeping an ear out, I packed up some of the boys' clothes, and put the case under the bed. I was able to go out of the front door, round the side of the house to the back garden where the car was parked without being seen. I made two or three journeys and filled the car and threw a rug over everything in the back. Then I went into the kitchen. They were all sitting just as I had left them, staring at the TV.

'You'll be late. You need to open the restaurant,' I said. No answer. 'Come on, Nunzio. I'm going to take the boys out.'

'You're not taking my boys anywhere. I will stop you, you bitch.'

'I'm going to take them to the park.' I hoped my shaky voice wouldn't betray me. 'You'd like that, wouldn't you, guys? We can get a McDonald's, too.' The boys jumped up and seemed relieved that the tension had been broken.

'OK, you can go, but you do not take the dog. The dog comes with me.'

Nunzio stared at me and I felt my heart sink. Did he know what I was planning? Was he going to come back and catch us? I held his eye and he got up and went out into the hall. I followed him, keeping my distance. I didn't want to look too eager to get him out of the house. He went upstairs to the bathroom and I held my breath. He came down and went back to the kitchen. It was as though he was teasing me. Finally, he kissed the boys and started for the door, throwing a: 'You walking to the park?' over his shoulder.

I swallowed and held my breath, then replied, 'No, because we're going to stop at McDonald's.' Nunzio stood there, looking at me. Then he seemed satisfied with my answer, because he called the dog to him and left. I stood just inside the front door, until I heard his car start up and leave. I waited a good ten minutes and then I called to the children: 'Come on, guys. Quick, quick, we need to go.' They were faffing around trying to find their football boots and their hats, and I was getting more and more nervous.

'Please, hurry up!' Finally, we got in the car. I put the key in the ignition and tried to keep my hands from trembling. I crashed the gears and stalled the engine. Come on, Lynda, get a grip. We set off up the road. I didn't look back. I was doing it. I was going to be free. It was April 1996, I was nearly fifty years old and had no husband, no agent and at that point in time, no job. But I was going to be free!

CHAPTER TWENTY-SEVEN

FROM RUSSIA WITH LOVE

I MANAGED TO MOVE us all to a beautiful new home in Highgate. Mum and Dad, Jean and Barbara, and Barbara's husband David, were all brilliant and helped me so much. Dad had driven me back up to London the day after my flight from home with the boys and we had parked the car round the corner from the house, waiting until Nunzio went to work. Then I slipped in and got some clothes and paperwork and, most important of all, our dear Star!

It took some adjusting, downsizing from a seven-bedroomed house to a three-bedroomed flat. The boys moaned all the time about giving up their swimming pool and their billiard table, but I ploughed on with all the adrenalin-fuelled energy that comes with major emotional upheaval. Our new flat was on two floors: the ground and basement. We had a lovely garden that backed on to a tennis club, which the boys would join eventually, and they each had their own rooms with a bathroom, so they were hardly slumming it! They didn't have to change schools or give up their friends, so all in all things were pretty good.

Then, out of the blue, came an opportunity of a lifetime: to star in a movie to be made in Russia. It was a love story, called *The Romanovs*. It was based on the diaries of Czar Nicholas about the last year of his and his family's life, in 1918, when they were under house arrest.

I first heard about the film in October 1996, when I was down in Dorset spending a couple of weeks on a film called *The Scarlet Tunic* starring Jean-Marc Barr (swoon) and Emma Fielding. It was adapted from a short story by Thomas Hardy and directed by the lovely Stuart St Paul. I was to play a housekeeper who was having an affair with the boss, played by Jack Shepherd. I would love to say our story was the nub of the piece but the reality was we were the subplot. Other notable actors in the cast were Simon Callow, and Gareth Hale taking a break from his partner Norman Pace (working partner, I hasten to add; that is how rumours start). We were all working for peanuts and staying in a brilliant B&B in West Bay.

One day, the first assistant came and told me there were two gentlemen to see me – a Mr Big and a Mr Pants-Off, apparently – who had come down to Dorset to discuss a big film role with me. I thought it was probably Noel Edmonds trying to do a 'Gotcha' on me for his programme, *Noel's House Party*.

I got back to the B&B to find three men waiting. A producer called Mr Baig, a director called Gleb Panfilov, and another huge bear of a man, who was introduced as Mikail the lighting cameraman, who had a video camera clutched permanently in his hand.

They wanted to video me for the leading role in a film about Nicholas and Alexandra. They spent two hours filming me and then returned to London. The cast all took the mickey out of me and said it was probably a porn film. The next day I talked to my agent about it and she was quite excited because this was a big Russian film, and the director had originally approached Meryl Streep for the leading role, but she was not keen on the possibility of filming in Moscow. More fool her! It was a big leap of faith from Meryl to me I know, but that's showbiz!

As it turned out, however, there was no point in me getting excited because the director did not think I was right for the role. Well, that was a red rag to a bull. This was the first chance I had ever had of coming near a decent role in a film and I was not about to let it go without a fight. I told my agent to get me an interview with them on Sunday, and I would come up from Dorset.

Everyone knows what the Sunday rail services are like. Limited, to say the least. I got on a train at 9 a.m. and seemed to stay on it for most of the day. I finally made it to the hotel in Bayswater and was shown into a suite. There was the director, Gleb Panfilov, and the producer and the cameraman and various others. They were all sitting behind a big table. I sat down opposite them and waited. Then a lady in a dark suit and enormous horn-rimmed glasses came in and introduced herself as the translator for Gleb Panfilov.

I had decided to show them a scene from the film I was doing, as it had a wonderful moment in it where I stood at a window talking and a tear rolled down my face. It was very moving and just right for the kind of emotion that would be required in a Russian film. When it had finished, there was a long silence and, suddenly, the director was out of his chair and applauding me and coming round the table and giving me a big hug, chatting nineteen-to-the-dozen. The translator was also applauding and translating: 'Gleb says you are wonderful. He never thought that English actresses had any soul but you have it. He loves you and wants you to be his empress.'

Everyone was laughing and crying, and I had got myself the job! When things had calmed down the translator said to me, 'Mr Panfilov wishes to know if you have any questions about the script or any problems with the role?'

Now, I did have one concern, because in the scene I had read for, it said that the Empress sits up in bed and 'offers up her beautiful naked breasts'. Naked! I tried to make light of it by saying,

'Does the director really think the audience needs to see these tired old tits?' The translator looked aghast and asked me if I really wanted her to translate those exact words.

'Yes, please,' I replied, watching the director. She repeated my words and the director just turned to the cameraman and said something in Russian. Mikail nodded. Gleb then said something to the translator and she turned to me and said, 'The director says you please him and the lighting cameraman says there will not be a problem.'

This was not quite the answer I had hoped for and I didn't really understand what they were saying. But I decided to leave well alone for the time being. I had got the job; that was the main thing. We all kissed and hugged farewell and I was back on the slow train to Dorset.

The next day I couldn't believe it had all really happened, but later that day I got a call from the producer, explaining I would be required to travel to Prague the week before Christmas for make-up and costume tests.

I rang my mother and father with the news. My mum, God rest her soul, put her foot straight in it by saying, 'The czarina? Alexandra? Are you sure, dear? Alexandra was very tall and very beaut...!' She stopped herself.

'Beautiful?' I broke in. 'Yes, that's the word, Mother. But I'd like to point out that I'm playing her in the last years of her life when she's under house arrest, and prematurely grey!'

Gleb had wanted a British actress because Alexandra was half-English and half-German. He had been told that the film would appeal to Europe if they had someone British in the role. Everyone else in the cast was Russian, apart from my maid who was going to be played by Rebecca Lacey, a super actress who was the daughter of the late Ronald Lacey. We would be filming in Prague and St Petersburg.

I finished the film in Dorset and came back to London to get busy. The first thing I had to do was get a visa and sort out who would look after the boys. It was also coming up for Christmas and I was determined that this was going to be a special one. It would be our first Christmas in our new house, and although Nunzio was, as usual, doing his best to spoil things for us, I was not going to let that happen. I organised the whole Christmas before I left, including the dinner table and stockings for the boys. I rushed round buying stuff for the Christmas meal, and even set up and decorated the tree, laid the table and bought the crackers. Then I locked the dining room door so that the boys would not see anything until I returned on Christmas Eve.

Alena was back working with me, which was fantastic. She had had her fair share of ups and downs and was now the mother of two children herself. A boy and a girl. Billy was a year older than Robbie and Katy was four. Alena was probably the only person who really understood what I had been through and was going through, and she had dealt with Nunzio before so I knew the boys would be safe with her.

The day of the departure to Prague dawned and I was ready. I gave the boys a big hug and told them I would be back before Father Christmas arrived, to hang up their stockings and to sort out the mince pies in time. They were more impressed by the big Limo that had come to pick me up.

We drove over to pick up Pat and set off for the airport. I had asked if Pat could come as my make-up person and they had agreed. It was so great to think we would finally work together on a big project. It was like having a security blanket for me and just made the whole job so perfect. Sadly for Pat, the budget did not stretch to a first-class ticket for her so at the airport, she turned right for economy class and I turned left. Which I felt bad about, but what a lovely feeling it was to be going first class!

I was flying with the other British actress, Rebecca Lacey, and we got on like a house on fire. When we touched down in Prague we were both intoxicated with excitement and champagne. Well, it had seemed churlish to refuse the free bubbly...

We were met in Prague by an even bigger Limo and whisked to a five-star hotel in the city centre. It had that wonderful look of the sixties about it – all a bit orange in décor, with lots of chunky lights and stainless steel. It was all very retro, although the bedrooms were like a standard Holiday Inn. I unpacked what little I had brought with me and rang Pat's room, and we arranged to meet in the bar.

The producer and director were already there and were very solicitous. The producer handed me an envelope with my expense money; how good was that? Not only was I being paid a salary but on top of that they paid for my hotel and all my meals. It was a pity this facility did not extend to my mobile phone bill. One week it was £750. I just kept ringing home because I was so homesick and worried about the boys. We all went out for dinner and drank lots of vodka; I found that when I drank vodka my knowledge of the Russian language improved remarkably! I fell into bed in a wonderful state of euphoria and fell deeply asleep, dreaming of those little wooden Russian dolls, one inside the other.

THE FOLLOWING MORNING Rebecca and I were driven out to Barrandov Studios. As we left the old town of Prague, with its beautiful churches and bridges, the landscape became much bleaker. Sixties concrete apartment blocks were stark against the steely sky.

The studios looked like a prison. There was concrete everywhere, and long dark corridors that led seemingly nowhere. My dressing room, in contrast, was all decorated in Versace and had a bathroom with a sunken bath – bright glaring Versace tiles, with bling gold taps on the bath! The seating area, by contrast, was quite small with a dressing table and easy chair. I later discovered that my dressing room was in the bathroom section of a suite of rooms that had been Tom Cruise's dressing room while he was filming *Mission Impossible*.

The director had summoned Pat and a Russian make-up designer to discuss the idea of contact lenses. Alexandra had had very distinctive grey eyes and mine were hazel, so Gleb wanted me to wear coloured lenses. He was obsessed with the idea that all the actors looked exactly like the real people or as near as damn it. All round the walls of the make-up room were photos of the real Romanov family and, over the next few weeks during filming, we all seemed to morph into their likeness. It was scary.

Pat had brought a selection of contact lenses and proceeded to try them in my eyes. It was hopeless; I just couldn't deal with them and my eyes became redder and redder. To make matters worse, when they were actually in my eyes, they gave my face a dead look. You could see no emotion. The lenses hid my soul! Thank God, the director agreed and they were discarded.

The hair proved more of a problem. Pat had brought lots of hair pieces and bits to put in my hair, but the director wanted a full wig that would fit to the front of my head, with my own hair combed through the wig hair to disguise the hairline. The lovely Russian make-up lady, Olga, could speak no English, and Pat could speak no Russian but somehow they managed to communicate, and the upshot was I was whisked away to a hairdresser and spent the next five hours having my hair dyed blonde at the front. Again! Thank goodness Pat was on hand, because at the first attempt, we watched aghast as my hair turned orange.

The final result made me look like an old hooker (which didn't really go amiss in Prague because there were a lot of them about). Olga arranged to meet us the next day and have a wig ready to show the director. The next morning, she produced an incredible wig that she had made virtually overnight. She then sprayed my new blonde hair and combed it through the wig. You couldn't see the join at all – it was fantastic!

The costumes were equally amazing. They fitted me for three hours, bringing out endless swathes of silk and swatches of velvet. There was hundreds of pounds' worth of material and everything was being made by hand. I was fitted with shoes with incredibly high heels to make me taller. My mother was right as usual.

By the time I arrived back in the UK on Christmas Eve, my head was buzzing. It was so good to see the boys and because I felt so much better about myself, I was good company that Christmas. I felt hopeful for the first time in months.

I was back on the plane after Christmas without Pat. My dear friend had been offered an amazing job, as make-up designer on a film, *Richard III*, starring Sir Ian McKellen. She was so worried about letting the side down, but it was an opportunity not to be missed, and when we discussed it, we decided that Olga was a genius and would look after me a treat. I had been to John Lewis and Marks and Spencer at Christmas, and stocked up on sweaters and jackets for Olga, and Pat had doubled up on all her make-up, so she could leave Olga a set of everything. Money was tight for the likes of her.

Back out in Prague, filming began straight away. I had no idea what to expect. Rebecca and I had got on the coach in the dark and freezing cold at 5 a.m. All around us were the unfamiliar voices of the Russians. But it is amazing how the language of film is international. It took no time at all to pick up what was going on and learn some words. Cameras and microphones and lights are all the same. They had given me a man to translate for me but he got in the way in the end: it was irritating to have this shadow permanently at my shoulder and I preferred to find my own way. I had spent a long time over Christmas, and now in my room, reading all the books I could get my hands on about the Romanov family, steeping myself in all the stories, both real and hearsay.

The girls playing the daughters arrived. They were stunning: they all had long, beautiful hair, but it was going to be cut off! This had happened to the daughters in real life, because when Alexei, their little brother, got chickenpox, he had to have his head shaved, so they all did the same to give him support. Rebecca and I had to stand in that first scene and watch these gorgeous girls have their heads shaved. It was not difficult to cry real tears for them. The girls then had to wear wigs for the rest of the film. It was bizarre. But as all the actors sat in their chairs in the make-up room it became obvious just how clever the director had been. His vision, and Olga's talent, had combined to make those people come alive again.

Filming was magic. We worked strange hours but it didn't matter. Sometimes I would be acting at midnight. Then, the next day, at eight in the morning. There were no union rules here. Sometimes the director would talk about a scene and I would worry that I would not be able to grasp what he wanted, but we seemed to be perfectly in tune and each time he called 'Cut!', he would beam at me and give me the thumbs up. I spoke the dialogue phonetically and learned the other actors' lines so I could recognise my cues more easily; I hardly ever slept as there was so much to absorb before a day's shoot. But I didn't care. I loved every moment. I lived the character.

All the crew were very kind to me and, bizarrely, they seemed to think I was royalty. They were always so careful round me. Nodding and bowing. Of course, if this had been a British film, I would have spent the whole time telling dirty jokes in the pub, but

I couldn't do that here. The best thing I could do was act like a queen. I felt like one.

Every Sunday I took all the actors out to lunch. They were earning so little money, the girls especially, they could hardly afford to eat properly. We would all assemble at a wonderful restaurant below the Charles Bridge. It had a buffet and you could eat as much as you could pile on your plate; the girls would stuff food in their bags for later. They would drink and laugh and end the afternoon with a singsong. The snow outside would sparkle from the lights in the trees, and I used to walk back to the hotel feeling magical and happy.

I missed the boys terribly, but they were able to come out every other weekend, so it wasn't so bad. Robbie was still quite young, only nine, so Alena came with them and I paid for her to bring her son who was ten. When they did come it was often very hard, because I had to forget the film when I got back to the hotel, and be Mum again. But it was worth the exhaustion. Prague has a tradition of puppetry; there were puppet shops on every corner, selling beautiful, hand-made figures. The boys adored them and over the six months they acquired quite a collection. It was wonderful to have them with me: emotionally, I was still very vulnerable and I was also very alone. While I was away, Nunzio had taken the boys to live with him in his flat, and would not let me ring them there.

One evening, we were finishing a scene in the house where the family were imprisoned. When they had been there, there were guards with them all the time and even as they ate their evening meal, they had had to endure snide remarks and taunts from their captors. As a family they were incredibly close and that helped them to be strong.

It was a very moving scene and, as often happens with a cast, there was a great sense of togetherness by now. I looked up at the camera at one point, and my eye was caught by a movement just to the other side of the camera. Suddenly, the director shouted 'Cut!' and turned and gave the young man standing there a hug. There was much kissing and hugging and we were all introduced to Ivan Panfilov, Gleb's son. He was very handsome, but too young for me! He came across and shook my hand and gave me a radiant smile. What a charmer.

We all had dinner that night and, to my delight, Ivan spoke perfect English. It made things so much easier when talking to Gleb. Over the next few days, Ivan would come to my dressing room to chat about England. He loved London, and wanted to study there, eventually. He also used my room to smoke in, something he was not allowed to do in the presence of his father. He told me he was planning a birthday party in two weeks' time, as he was going to be eighteen. I told him about the restaurant where we all went on a Sunday and invited him to join us. 'The girls will love having you there,' I told him. He laughed shyly.

The following weekend all the young actors and some of the crew were going clubbing. I bumped into them all in the bar. Ivan seemed to be in charge. He was like the Pied Piper, being followed by a happy band of girls. I envied them their youth and energy. There was no way I could do that and get up and film the next day.

My boys had come to visit, and brought me some videos to watch. Ivan was very interested in them and, the following week, he turned up at my door with a bottle of champagne and asked if he might join me to watch a film. I was rather taken aback, but agreed. We watched a video and had some dinner and it was fun. He was good company. Very bright and with a wicked sense of humour. I told Rebecca about the evening and she gave me a knowing look.

'It doesn't mean anything. You've got a dirty mind,' I laughed.

But later in my room, I wondered. He did flirt with me some-times and he was always very attentive. I decided I was being ridiculous; I was old enough to be his mother. And, in fact, we stayed in touch and he is good friends with my son Michael today.

GLEB CAME TO me one morning, with Ivan to translate. He was preparing to film the scene where the whole family are herded into a small room and shot. He smiled sadly as Ivan explained to me that his father had put off this moment for as long as he could, because he did not want to kill off his beautiful family.

I was very touched by Gleb's very real involvement in the film. To him, this film was a personal mission. He wanted to show the world, but especially the Russian people, that the Csar Nicholas may have been a fool, and naive about the state of his country, but he was not a bad man. He loved his country and, most importantly for this film, he loved his family.

The room in the house in Yekaterinburg where the executions took place had been recreated in the studio in Prague. The morning of the shoot, Gleb had handpicked the soldiers who would shoot the family. He was emphatic that none of these soldiers, all played by Czech actors, must talk to any of the family before the moment they saw them in that room. He wanted them to feel the moment they looked into the eyes of these people, and shot them in cold blood.

There was an air of anticipation over the studio that morning, a sense of imminent disaster that was palpable to all. I felt anxious and jumpy. The girls were unusually quiet, waiting to start. In the make-up room, everyone was talking in whispers and giving each other hugs. I sat in a corner with the boy playing my son, Alexei, and waited for the call.

Before the scene we all had to be wired with small explosives. As we were shot, tiny capsules would explode on our bodies like gunshots. No one spoke as the firearms technician worked on the devices. Across the other side of the studio, the soldiers were being given a lesson in how to shoot their rifles. I could hear the guns being locked and loaded.

Then we were led across the vast wide floor of the studio to the place of execution. We walked through a long, low corridor to get there, and the walls seemed to press in against us. As we passed the crew no one spoke. Everyone seemed to look away, frightened to break this amazing atmosphere.

We had rehearsed the scene the day before so we all knew what we were doing. In all the books I had read about the Romanovs and their history, this story was the most emotive. The family doctor had been told by the rebels, the night before, that the family would be called together early in the morning for a group photo before they were taken on the next part of their journey. However, this was simply a way of getting them all together without arousing suspicion. The plan was actually to shoot them. The rebels had given the doctor the choice to stay or leave. His loyalty to the family was absolute. He stayed.

The young princesses had prepared for the journey, and all the women had sewn their jewels into small cushions that they always carried with them. So, as they gathered for the photo, each girl had a small satin cushion on her lap. The family group prepared for the photo. Very quietly, the photographer arranged them. Moving an arm here or a hand to a shoulder there. The Empress was seated with her son on her right and her husband behind her with his hand on her shoulder. To their left was one of her daughters. The photographer retired behind the black cloth over the camera. Someone counted to three and as the camera flashed the doorway was filled with faces. Eyes wild and staring.

It was a real shock, and made me jump, even though I knew it was going to happen. I looked up and happened to catch the eye of one of the soldiers. Time stood still. He was so young and looked so scared. He almost tried to speak and in his eyes I could see his apology hovering, but it was gone in a moment and, suddenly, the room was filled with tremendous noise and smoke. I felt my device pop and, as rehearsed, I fell forwards to the floor. I could hear screams and shouting all around me as I lay there. It seemed to go on for ever. Then, suddenly, complete silence and, through the heavy, smoke-filled air, came the sounds of whimpering and moans. It was heartbreaking. One of the girls was jerking violently, her body in spasm. A single gunshot and then nothing, just a pile of human carnage. Blood was everywhere. Splashes all down the walls, and pools forming on the floor. When the scene had happened for real, shots had hit the jewels in the cushions, and the bullets had ricocheted off, causing devastating mess and making the deaths of several of the family more painful, because the bullets did not enter their bodies cleanly.

After Gleb had cut the scene, I got up slowly and looked around. It was, indeed, a blood bath. The director came into the room and just held out his arms. We all went to him as one. Some of the girls were crying quietly. I just felt drained. I saw the handsome young Czech actor, who played the soldier whose eye I had caught at that last moment, and went over and kissed him. He seemed to be grateful that I hadn't taken it personally. It was only a film, but it was a very special moment and we all felt it.

THAT NIGHT THE whole crew went clubbing. I decided to hell with it, and joined them. I had not danced for ten years, never mind been to a club. I drank vodka and danced and danced. It was fantastic. Filming that scene had made us all aware of death, and death makes the living want to feel alive. Here I was, surrounded by gorgeous young men and women. Perhaps the vodka had made me crazy but I grabbed the handsome Czech guy who had played the soldier and we danced and danced. He was an actor who worked mainly in the theatre and spoke quite good English. It felt as though we had a kind of bond between us after the day's filming and got on really well. It just felt so great to be free. The music was pounding in my head and the bass was throbbing through my body, down to my toes. Suddenly, the lights dipped very low and I found myself slowly going round the floor with my head pressed to the guy's chest. I sneaked a look up at him and there was his beautiful face. I had an overwhelming desire to kiss him. I lifted my face towards his and found myself in a tight embrace. It made me feel giddy.

I ran to the toilets and went to the basin and ran the cold water. I doused my face and looked up at the mirror. All around me girls were laughing and giggling and jostling each other for space to redo their make-up. I looked shell-shocked, but there was something else in my eyes. Hope. I was alive, so very alive, and I was going to bloody well stay alive! I clenched my fists and mouthed, 'Yes!' to myself before going back to the dance floor. My lovely young man was waiting for me and we walked back to the hotel as dawn was breaking. He kissed me once more, very gently, and said goodnight.

I sat on my bed and tried to make sense of it. There was nothing to make sense of, Lynda. He had been a charming date. I was bloody lucky to get a kiss from the lad. What more did I want?

Quite unexpectedly, my young man became quite a regular thing while I was on the film. We were very discreet and spent a good deal of time in my hotel room. He made me laugh and he made me feel special. I had no expectations of anything long term, but for those few weeks my faith in myself was restored. It was perhaps the simplest and purest relationship I have ever had. When I finally returned to the UK we said our goodbyes without any drama or tears. It was a perfect, natural end to an amazing experience, and the beginning of a new life for me alone. From now on it was just me and my boys.

CHAPTER TWENTY-EIGHT

HANGING ON BY THE SKIN OF MY TEETH

I T IS 20TH JANUARY, 2000 and Nunzio leaves court with a £4,000 fine and an injunction against him not to come anywhere near me, or my home, for seven years.

There was no sense of relief for me. I knew it would not end here. The last three years had become one long nightmare of fear. In the press release it says that in court, the prosecutor said: 'It was a violent marriage. Miss Bellingham was forced to call the police several times after he [Nunzio] threatened to kill her. She believed his threats would be carried out.'

It was a relief to see these words written down. It made it real for me. When you have been ground down by hate for so long, you begin to think you have imagined it all, that things are so bad they cannot possibly be real.

It may sound dramatic, but it is only now, all these years later, that I can dare to let myself go and admit to the horror of it all. At the time, I just had to ignore the threats and the tirades of abuse on the phone, otherwise I could not have kept going.

From April 1996, when I left Nunzio for good, until the hearing that was almost four years later, I had lived like some kind of fugitive. Every time I left the house I was looking over my shoulder.

My kitchen window at the back looked out over tennis courts, and Nunzio would sit on a wall by these courts looking up at my window. I nicknamed him the black crow because that is exactly what he looked like. A black crow sitting on the wall. Waiting. Once I came home and was unpacking the car outside the flat. I was leaning into the boot of the car and suddenly felt something on the back of my legs. He had driven right up behind me so I was trapped between the cars.

The divorce had gone through very quickly in September 1996. Unreasonable behaviour was cited. An understatement, indeed. My dear friend, Richard Lane, who is also my accountant, helped me through the finances. But really it was simple. I gave Nunzio half of everything I had. But even then he wouldn't believe me, and was convinced that Richard had helped me salt away some kind of fortune. If only I had! Even after we had actually divorced and he heard I was doing the film in Russia, he went after me for more money. I paid a barrister £1,000 to be told that as I was the bread-winner, maybe I should just settle a sum and be done with him. But why should I? We had done the deal when we divorced. No one could give me a straight answer and I was so harassed by Nunzio, I spent the whole time in a panic.

Much against Richard's judgement I decided to hand over the only money I had left: the boys' school fee trust. The tax was paid on it, so it was a lump sum just sitting there, except I now had no money at all to pay for the school fees. Nunzio took it.

Over the next years he didn't pay a penny towards the boys. I remember one time he was taking them for a pizza. He picked them up and then, five minutes later, Michael came back and rang the door bell.

'Can we have some cash for the pizza, please? Papa hasn't got any money.'

Thank God, I made some money from the Russian film, and thanks to sound advice from Richard, I bought the flat at the top of the house. Now, at least, I had a source of income for my old age, and this was when Julia Sawalha moved in, which was wonderful. She was going through a very bad relationship at the time, as well, so we helped each other.

Nunzio had bought a flat about a quarter of a mile away so that he could be near his children. More like spy on me. I was effectively a prisoner in my own flat. He would patrol the road outside and every time I looked out he was there. If the lights were on after a certain time, he would ring and ask who was there? Or he would want to know what the boys were doing. Why weren't they asleep? Then other times, he would come to the house at ten or eleven at night, and insist I get the boys out of bed so he could see them. There was no thought for their welfare at all. He talks about love, all the time, to them, but it is only on his terms. I would leave the phone on loudspeaker, and do my housework, while Nunzio was on the other end screaming for an hour at a time: 'You're a cunt! Women like you die in my country. You deserve to die. I'll kill you. You are a bitch, do you hear me? A bitch and a slut.' It went on and on. Even when I told him I was recording the phone calls, for evidence, it didn't stop him: 'Fine. I don't give a fuck what you do. You can record me and tell all your friends, but will you tell them you are a cunt and a slut?'

The police came one day and, while they were there, he rang. I let them listen as Nunzio threatened to kill me. But the police told me they were powerless to do anything until he actually attacked me. So when he drove over the pavement in front of me and Pat as we walked along the road, that was OK? When he jumped out of the bushes as I came up my garden path and screamed at me, that was OK? If I went to the shops in Crouch End and he opened my car door as I was sitting there waiting for Michael to buy a bun and said: 'Remember I am watching you. Everything you do. I am watching. I will destroy you,' that too was fine, apparently.

Unless they've experienced it themselves, no one has any idea what it feels like to live with this kind of fear. My dear sisters and parents accused me of being theatrical. 'Stand up to him,' they said. 'Don't be such a wimp.' In fact, I did feel pretty pathetic, until a situation arose that confirmed I was not being completely useless.

London Weekend Television had hired a bodyguard for me, to live in, and help me deal with the daily onslaughts from Nunzio. I had asked for a woman because I knew that if it was a man it would just exacerbate the situation. My sister, Barbara, and her husband, David, had come for lunch and we were all discussing the situation with Nunzio and how I should deal with it. Barbara and David were criticising me a bit and suggesting I should just stop being so dramatic and stand up to him. Suddenly, my bodyguard came to my defence: 'You middle-class people make me sick. You have no idea what a man like Nunzio could do to Lynda. She has every right to feel fucking scared, and I hope you never have to go through what she is going through.'

I love my sisters deeply and I have lost Barbara now, so nothing is worse than that. But I really do think they never understood how bad it was.

Certainly my sons do not realise. It was so hard for them because Nunzio is their dad after all, and they love him. I tried to keep a good deal of the personal abuse of me a secret from them. This resulted in them not understanding the situation at all, and if I called the police they had a go at me: 'Don't do this, Mum. Why do you want Papa to go to jail? You make him angry.'

Oh my God, that hurt me so much. It is the classic answer of an abusive man to his wife, or girlfriend: 'You're the only woman who has ever made me do this. I am not a violent man really. It's all *your* fault.' And here were my own sons accusing me of causing this pain. There were many times I wanted to set them straight. But the poor boys heard nothing all day from their Dad except rantings and ravings; they didn't need to hear it from me as well.

During these years, I was also trying to keep the situation out of the press as I still had my Oxo contract till 1999. The police were fantastic. They are often accused of being indiscreet and leaking stuff to the press, but they were brilliant with me and incredibly supportive; even the usual Panda car guys, who must get so frustrated when they are called to domestic scenes, time after time, and nothing changes, were always very helpful and positive.

After I got back from the film in Russia I thought I was on the mend. My wonderful experience out there had given me a second wind. But not for long. I just couldn't fight the barrage of abuse I was taking on a daily basis. I could go away for a couple of months, on a job, and find some respite, but that often meant the boys were left alone to deal with it. Not that Nunzio would harm them in any way, but he just battered their senses with his constant stream of hatred against me. It was wrong. I knew it was wrong, but how could I stop it?

The years from 1998 to 2003 were a weird mixture of ups and downs. I did a lovely little film called *Don't Go Breaking My Heart* starring Anthony Edwards of *ER* fame, and Jenny Seagrove. It had a stellar cast including Charles Dance as a smooth dentist. George Layton and I played a lovely north London Jewish couple and Michael, my son, played our son! Never one to miss an opportunity I suggested him for the role. I made some lifelong friends on this shoot. I had returned from Russia with my terrible blonde hair and, thanks to the very talented Carol Hemming, a film hairdresser, she made me look perfect for the film and then restyled my hair completely afterwards. She also introduced me to the fabulous Andrea Schaverien who gave me back a hair colour that was human and who now continues to make me look acceptable for a woman of a certain age!

I then went off to the Isle of Wight and did a six-part series for ITV called *Reach for the Moon*. It was a fabulous location and we were in a beautiful hotel called the Priory Bay which had its own private beach. Even the weather was good that year. I gave a birthday party at the hotel; a hog roast for all the crew. It was great fun, only marred by a phone call from my son, Michael, saying he had been suspended from school.

This was just before he was to take his GCSEs. I rang the school and spoke to the headmistress. She knew quite a lot about what we had all been through, and were going through, and I begged her to have some compassion. It wasn't even as though he and his mate had done anything really serious – they had skipped a class and gone out in the lunch hour and were late back. We were not talking drugs here! She would not budge. Poor Michael was terrified that Nunzio would find out. I could do nothing, stuck on the Isle of Wight, except wrestle, yet again, with my guilt. Fortunately, Michael was allowed back to school in time for his exams and managed to scrape through them, bless his heart!

So, every time I came home I was faced with the torrent of hatred coming from up the road as Nunzio's constant harassment continued to rule our lives. I had managed to leave him yet here I was, two years on, still living in fear.

I found myself shut in the kitchen day after day drinking and smoking and bemoaning the fact that men were all bastards. A neighbour from across the road was going through a bad time with her husband, and another friend, Brenda, had discovered her husband was having an affair with her cleaner. Alena was suffering abuse from her partner. Can you see a pattern here? It was the classic situation of like finding like.

I had also started smoking again in Russia, and was trying to hide it from the boys. Talk about role reversal. They were now at an age when they were trying things out and smoking was the big thing. I was desperately trying to stop them from doing it while lighting up myself. Every time they came in the kitchen I had to drop my cigarette into my mug of tea. How pathetic was that?

I did try to keep things on an even keel. I met a fantastic aerobics instructor called Beverly Kaufmann who took me on and sorted me out. Well, physically at least. She came twice a week and we would exercise in my front room. Nunzio would drive by all the time and peer in. Or he would be outside watching. He once shouted across the street that he knew why I was trying to exercise and lose weight. It was because I wanted to fuck men! That was the last thing on my agenda. Beverly put me on a diet and over the next two years I lost three stone. However, my new health kick didn't stop my alcohol intake; it just kept a complete breakdown at bay.

I am proud of the fact that no matter how much I was battling with myself and my demons, I continued to provide a home for the boys. They may not have appreciated it at the time, but now Michael often says to me that he realises how well I managed to look after them. My sons were at a difficult age. Michael was sixteen in 1999 and was going through all sorts of difficult stuff. Robbie was only twelve and having to listen to a constant barrage from his father about me. He was at Aldenham School in Hertfordshire as a day boy. It cost me a fortune but I was trying to keep Robbie away from all the shit and give him some discipline. At one point he expressed a desire to board on a weekly basis because lots of his friends were boarders. This would have been ideal for me because I could work, knowing he was safely tucked away, and then we could all have our weekends together. Nunzio put the kibosh on it, of course, the inference being that I wanted to get rid of Robbie to have a good time. It was so disheartening that every time I tried to organise our lives we were dragged back into the fog of Nunzio's hatred and paranoia. They were very dark times and I must confess there were nights when I sat in my kitchen in the dark thinking about ending it all. But every time the thoughts began, I would try and imagine what would happen to my boys if I died. I could not do that to them. So I would take another sip of wine to help me sleep and edge closer and closer to the brink of despair.

THERE IS A Jean Rhys quote, from *Wide Sargasso Sea*: 'The only time she felt excited or happy was when she had had a drink, because then anything might happen. The feeling of insecurity became exciting.' This perfectly describes my life as a drinker. Everything, for me, arose from insecurity. I drank to be funny, or sexy. I drank because I was afraid or happy or sad, and I drank for anything that required emotional commitment. I know that now. I had chosen a profession that thrives on insecurity, and is never far from some form of social intercourse that involves alcohol or drugs – the profession involves intercourse, period! I have some wonderful friends who still enjoy a drink and manage to stay in control, and I admire them, but I have also lost many dear friends to it.

Most of my early love life was conducted under the influence of booze. I just felt better when I had a drink inside me and, over the years, I think I associated drink with sex. I never drank, though, when I worked. I was completely professional about that and, of course, ironically, I never needed to drink when I was acting, because I was happy doing what I was doing. I was in control.

The trouble for me was that I had a strong tolerance for alcohol. If only it had made me sick like it did some of my friends! But

I could throw it back. It wasn't like I was on my own with a bottle in a brown paper bag; all my friends drank. We had fun. The social scene was about eating and drinking. In fact, we were very well behaved compared to a lot of what goes on now. You would never see me fall out of a nightclub or catch me snorting cocaine in a toilet. But one did follow the herd and you had to be in it to win it. Acting is really the hardest career for anyone who is in the least bit sensitive or insecure, and yet I would say ninety per cent of actors are sensitive and insecure. It is rarely about being talented. It is about surviving the knocks, pushing through the rejections, and ignoring the crap that is everywhere you turn. Nowadays, it is even worse because celebrity today means a brand name. Everything celebrities do or say is fed to us by the media. Alcohol just helps one wade through the miasma of bullshit. I don't mean to sound bitter and twisted and indeed I'm not, now. But I was getting that way, very slowly.

SOME OF MY drinking was brilliant. There is nothing like the camaraderie one has with fellow drinkers. It is a club you never leave once you join. Well, certainly not willingly or easily. After my marriage ended, there were some wonderful times when I was out with the girls. The gang was often headed by the glorious Sally Bulloch, whom I had rediscovered when I came back from Russia. This was a woman who could hold her drink! She ran the Athenaeum Hotel with an iron rod (well, cocktail stick), and I have never known someone consume champagne in the quantities that she did, and still carry on all evening, chatting and networking, as if she were as sober as a judge. I have never laughed so much or found myself in more bizarre situations than with her. Once, in Mexico together, we sat in a mud hut underground being reborn, and in Prague, I followed her round as we stopped at every bar for a local tincture, known as *becherovka*, so that our friend, Lynda Berry, who could not cross bridges (is there a medical name for that?) got pissed enough to forget her phobia so we could all get back to the hotel. The sight of Sally wobbling over the cobblestones, in her impossibly high heels and long mink coat, is for ever emblazoned on my mind.

They were good days, and Sally Bulloch was never far away. She died very tragically two years ago. Anyone who knew her and loved her knows it was so wrong for her to go like she did, but we all make choices and, whether we like it or not, sometimes our loved ones have to pursue their own destiny. Alcohol was her killer; she couldn't give it up.

I did some good work around this time, in 2000, in a series called *At Home with the Braithwaites* and made some fantastic friends. Amanda Redman, who starred in the series, is a great actress and a good mate. Sylvia Syms, who I also met on that series, has become a good friend. We had such fun and we did get to go out and get drunk from time to time, but only after hours and I was in control because I was working. I also had some wonderful Sunday lunches when I wasn't working, and the boys joined in as well. It was a great way of finding out what they were up to because normally they were very tight-lipped with me – I was their mother, after all. But get a few friends round and after a glass or two, we would all relax and be telling stories, and they'd open up and relate their adventures to everyone.

Also around this time, I had done an episode of *My Uncle Silas* which starred Albert Finney, and we had had a wonderful two weeks. Sue Johnston, who was an old friend, was also in it and I was playing a fabulous role. I played a wicked widow whom Albert had to chase round an orchard in her petticoats. It was great fun until I slipped and fell over and pulled a muscle in my back. The next day we had a sexy love scene to do, where Albert untied my bootlaces and threw me on the bed. I discovered that it's very difficult to be sexy when one is in agony with back pain: the director kept saying to me, 'Lynda, dear, do try not to show the pain in your face. It's wrong for the scene.'

Albert was so kind to me that I wanted to thank him, so I organised a lunch at my flat. I asked Mitchell Everard, the then manager of the Ivy, what Mr Finney's favourite red wine was. Barolo. I took myself off to Majestic and spent a happy half-morning ordering wine and champagne. There were six of us to lunch, including Sally and Lynda La Plante, and Albert's now wife, Pene Delmage, and the wine bill came to £500! I did Wensleydale cheese soup (from my B&B days for *All Creatures*), followed by rack of lamb, with bread and butter pudding to follow. Then loads of smelly cheeses and After Eight mints. The lunch started at noon and went on until twelve that night. Albert is an example to us all. He works to live. Too many of us live to work.

I was so lucky to have the friends I have to help me get through those Nunzio years. Catharine had got married and moved to Shropshire with her husband, Rupert, and the boys and I would often go and spend a weekend with them. She had started a wine business so there was many a glass raised by a roaring fire. And my friend Gabrielle Lloyd would have to listen to me for hours on end when I was in my cups, poor girl. Anna and Albert Ferrante invited us to France for wonderful summer weeks spent in their garden next to a field of sunflowers. We were surrounded by vineyards and tiny villages with markets full of cheese and wine and *foie gras*. These were happy days amidst the gloom.

But I couldn't ignore the fact that, slowly and steadily, I was beginning to lose control of my life, and that drink was taking over. I look back over the years just before and after my divorce, and a good deal of the time I was not sober. I wasn't drunk but I wasn't sober. I am sure that anyone who supports Alcoholics Anonymous would say I was in denial, but I don't think so. I knew I was going wrong.

I can remember, absolutely crystal clearly, moments when I knew I was out of control, but couldn't, or didn't want to, stop myself. It was as if I was going to push it as far as I could and see what happened: the moment I left my parents' house to return to London when I was married to Greg and I was in my car, driving with a bottle of cheap sherry; a morning with Norman Eshley, when we got up and drank vodka and orange juice instead of a cup of tea; the time I tried to kill myself after Greg; but perhaps one of the most humiliating moments in my life was after a night out with Sally and the gang, and I took a bloke home with me that I had met that evening; he was some City type, complete with red braces. He started to make love to me and suddenly said, 'I can't believe I'm going to fuck the Oxo mum.' I was mortified. I got up immediately and told him to leave.

Writing this now, it makes me want to weep. Some people are going to question why I have confessed this to all and sundry, but I think it is important that you know just how far down the line I was going. Where was my guardian angel now?

CHAPTER TWENTY-NINE

THESE THINGS ARE SENT TO TRY US, BUT WHY ME?

WHEN JULIA SAWALHA moved out of the flat above me in 1998, I had various tenants moving in and out from then on. I hated having to deal with it all but it was necessary. I had a master plan that the man who lived in the middle would one day sell to me and then I would be the owner of a huge house in Highgate and be set for the rest of my life (but that would have been far too simple for my life; surely I knew that!)

In 2000, I interviewed the girl who cleaned for Dill, the man in the middle flat, to take over my top-floor flat with her new boyfriend. Julie explained that she and George had only been together a few weeks but this was the real thing, and they wanted to live together. Fine with me. They both came to see me to discuss rent and the terms, and during the meeting I found George to be a bit reserved and very cautious. He felt they could not really afford the council tax on top of the rent so, being the big-hearted, stupid woman I am, I said I would pay the council tax for the first year and they could see how they got on.

They moved in and alarm bells first rang when I went up with the gas man to sort out the boiler and I realised they had made the flat into two separate bed-sitters. I found this rather strange for a young couple in this day and age, but when I was talking to Dill about it he told me that Julie was very religious.

All was quiet until a month later, when they both came down to talk to me. George did the talking and told me that my eldest son, Michael, had been harassing Julie and shouting at her from the window. They said he and his friends were making life very uncomfortable for them. It sounded very unlike my son. Don't get me wrong, he could be a pain in the arse about some things, like all teenage boys, but he wasn't a hooligan. I talked to him about it and he had no idea what the problem was. We decided to let it go.

Then a few days later, a police poster appeared by the front door in the communal hall. 'Rat on a Rat' was the message, referring to drug abuse. This really annoyed me; I took it down and rang Julie.

'Did you put that poster up?' I asked her.

'Well, George thinks there's drug dealing going on in the road and your son may be involved,' was her reply.

I was livid. 'That is absolutely not true! And please tell George that if he has any more concerns to come directly to me next time.'

A few days later Michael and I were having a row, as you do, and there was a knock on my door. It was George, saying that some boys had been shouting at Julie again. I turned to Michael and asked him if he had any idea who it was. He categorically denied any knowledge and stomped off. After he had gone there was an awkward silence and George suddenly moved towards me. He was so close I honestly thought he was going to kiss me. I stepped back, a bit flustered. He tried to offer me a word of comfort saying, 'Don't worry about your son. Teenage boys are all difficult. I was awful to my mum but I loved her really.' And then he left.

I heard no more for a couple of months. Then, one Sunday, I was giving a Sunday lunch and we were all sitting round enjoying ourselves when the phone rang. It was George complaining that Michael was shouting obscenities out of the window again. This was a downright lie because the poor boy was sitting with us! I told George that and hung up. But he rang again and started complaining. That was enough for me. I told him I thought he and Julie should leave and gave them two months' notice. They left. I found it strange, though, that Julie didn't come to say goodbye, and I never saw her again.

I forgot all about them until we had a phone call in the summer from Tottenham police station, saying there had been a complaint made against Michael, from a George Millar. Apparently Michael had been shooting at him with a pellet gun. Fortunately, we were able to prove that Michael was in Italy with his dad when this incident was supposed to have taken place, so no further action was taken. It was all very odd. Then, one morning, I noticed the tyres on my car had been slashed. A few weeks later, a window was broken. I thought it might be Nunzio but decided to put it down to 'normal' life in London. These things happen.

In November, however, I received a solicitor's letter saying that if I and my son did not stop stalking and harassing Mr George Millar, he would be forced to take out an injunction against us. What?! I decided to ring the Tottenham police station for advice. I was lucky enough to speak to the policeman who had dealt with George's complaint about the pellet gun. I told him about the solicitor's letter, and I told him about all the complaints George had made when he was living above us. The policeman agreed that he had seemed a bit flaky and suggested we take no notice, but I decided to write a response. I informed the solicitor that there was no foundation for any of these accusations and that I had spoken to the police about the matter. I went on to say that if their client continued with these ridiculous claims I would counter-sue for harassment. That was the end of it. We heard no more.

Then one night in the following February, I was woken by Michael and his friend, Martin, shouting to tell me that there was a smell of petrol in the front room. The window had been smashed in and there was a rock in the middle of the living-room carpet: a rock with a white T-shirt tied round it, soaked in petrol. Attached to this was a firecracker.

I called the police and they arrived very quickly (they knew exactly where we lived, thanks to Nunzio's escapades). Three detectives sat in the kitchen, all having a cup of tea, and regarded me with interest. They, of course, thought this is the work of the ex. Michael and I tried to explain that while Nunzio may have hated me, he would never harm his kids. They took some details and, as we were talking, I suddenly thought of George Millar. I told the detectives about how he had accused Michael of all sorts of things and that I had thrown them out of the flat, and I knew he lived somewhere in the area. Thank God one of the detectives listened to me. The other two just thought I was a sad, victimised ex-wife who was in denial.

The police rang the next day and said they had arrested George Millar. I then had to wait for details. Finally, the detective who had believed me came round to take my statement and filled me in. When they had gone round to George's flat they had found ripped T-shirts all over the floor and a petrol canister and printouts, from the internet, on how to make a bomb. On his screen saver was the message: REVENGE LIKE OXO IS A DISH BEST SERVED COLD.

I couldn't believe it. I didn't understand it. What had I or Michael ever done to this guy? I had done nothing but try to help him and Julie. The detective explained to me that George was a paranoid schizophrenic with a history of not taking his medication. Julie had gone back to her parents even before they left my flat, which explains why I never saw her again. I just wish she'd told me of the problem.

When you're in the public eye, it makes you very nervous about people knowing where you live. In fact, I sometimes get letters addressed to Lynda Bellingham, Actress, North London. Who said the Royal Mail is inefficient? It was very scary, though, because after what happened to Jill Dando, you just never knew. We were so lucky the firework went out when it hit my curtains, because all the bedrooms in the flat were downstairs. We might not have woken up in time.

The case took a year to come to court and when it finally came to trial, the judge ruled that George was obviously mad, so there was no point in bringing the case before a jury. George was accused of attempted arson, with intent to harm, or something like that. The judge suggested we drop the case and he would section the man for a long time. So that was that. Until two days later, when I was visited at home by a policeman who had come to inform me that because George had been in the hospital all the time before the trial, it had now been decided by the doctors that he was fit to leave! The policeman apologised and said he would send a patrol round from time to time to check we were OK. Great.

The boys and I stayed up all night expecting a visit from him. Then I got a call to tell me that George had been taken into hospital again because he was not taking his medication. This time, Julie, who had stood by him through all this, had reported him to the authorities.

But, a few days after *that*, the police were at my door again, saying they were so sorry but George Millar had broken out of the secure unit. He had bashed someone over the head with a chair.

They told me again they would drive by from time to time to check on us.

You couldn't make it up!

It took a week for them to find him sleeping rough in the woods nearby. He was then safely locked up, but a few days later he hung himself. I would be a liar if I did not admit I was relieved. But my condolences go out to Julie and his family. It is a terrible illness and affects so many families.

I WAS STARTING TO struggle to make ends meet. Television work was scarce, and when I did do an episode of something, it was so badly paid, it hardly touched the debts. I always knew it was going to be tough once I got to a certain age, but I reckoned after a career spanning thirty years I would survive. After all, it wasn't as though I had had to rely on my looks. Quite the opposite, in fact – I had been waiting to grow into my face! I was a character actress. What I had not taken into account was just how many actresses, like me, were still hanging around at fifty-something, waiting for the odd role. And as the roles are so few and far between, it means the likes of Dames Judi Dench and Helen Mirren get all the jobs going! The only way a job was ever going to come my way was if everyone else had either turned it down or were not available. And it would be offered to so many other ladies before it even got to me.

I recently did a test voice-over for Vodafone. I was very excited because it was for the TV and would be well paid. After I did the test everybody seemed really pleased and I went away thinking the job was mine. About two weeks later I was in the kitchen, and I heard the music from the advert. I called to Michael to come and listen to 'my' ad. To my horror, the voice-over was in the dulcet tones of Judi Dench. I am her number one fan, but she doesn't need the money like I do! If a Dame is happy to do a voice-over, what chance do the rest of us, mere mortals, have of earning a crust?

Ageism has always been around in show business. It is the nature of the beast. Gone are the days where longevity counts for anything. The television and film industries are run by Youth, who only want to see youth and beauty. Their idea of someone's mother is Demi Moore or Sharon Stone. The only acceptable face of a grandmother is Jane Fonda. These women look fantastic but they are not representative of the average woman; they represent an unrealistic ideal that can only be achieved with help. British television is not quite as bad as US television, but the problem is that writers do not write parts for anyone over fifty because the youthful Powers That Be are rarely interested in anyone not of their demographic.

I DECIDED TO SELL the flat upstairs. I hated it after all the business with the stalker and as it was highly unlikely that my neighbour in the middle was ever going to move, I reckoned my dream of being a property tycoon was well and truly scuppered. Around this time, I did an episode of *Dalziel and Pascoe* and met an actress called Katy Cavanagh, who was trying to buy a flat. My guardian angel was back as she loved it, and bought it. Thankfully, it meant I had a bit of money now to keep us going.

CHAPTER THIRTY

MORTGAGE OR MARRIAGE, MY LOVER?

MORAIRA IS A lovely fishing village between Alicante and Valencia on the Costa Blanca. I had gone there for a long weekend with Pat. She was going to look at a little villa that was for sale near her sister in Moraira. Her sister, Alma, and her husband, Robert, had been going there for eighteen years. I knew absolutely nothing about Spain and had no expectations of it.

This proved to be just as well because the drive from Alicante to Moraira along the motorway was pretty grim. Coming out of Alicante airport, which was just a seething mass of humanity, even in November, we were met by a flat brown landscape. Pat was sitting in the car chatting away to Alma, and I was staring out of the window, thinking there was no way I'd want to live here. I was looking at the area as a potential resting place for my twilight years and, so far, it was not encouraging.

We arrived at Alma's flat and unpacked our few bits and pieces. It was a nice flat but a bit dark in the way so many places are where the sun shines hot. We went round the corner for a meal and, again, I can't honestly say I was very impressed. As we walked home I turned to Pat and remarked that it was all a bit wrinkly.

'Bellie, *we'll* be wrinkly by the time we live here,' was her frank reply. I was horrified by the thought. I was fine about getting old but I wanted to do it disgracefully and with style. I wanted a balcony, or a café in the sunshine, where I would sit wearing an elegant hat, with a large glass of *vino tinto*, and watch the world go by. Beautiful young men would come and flirt with me, and beautiful young girls would ask for my advice about their lovers...

The next day was more encouraging. We went into the town and I discovered that although there were quite a lot of older people, Moraira was really rather nice. The sea was great and there were some nice shops and restaurants. We had a coffee and then set off to see Pat's possible pad. It was in a *communidad* of about twelve small villas that were two up, two down, but Spanish style. Actually, Pat's had three bedrooms, a bathroom, a living/kitchen area and out of her back door there was a patio that you could sit on, by a communal pool. It was perfect. Three houses up from there, was another one with a 'For Sale' sign.

'I should go and look at that,' I said. 'Can you imagine how perfect it would be if we were next door to each other?' The more we thought about it, the more it seemed like a good idea. So I made a viewing appointment and we went to see it in the early evening.

The apartment was the top half of one of the villas, so it was tiny but perfect for me. Living room/kitchen, bedroom and tiny bathroom. The owners were offering it fully furnished, with a car! Yes, a Renault Megane thrown in. I put in an offer straight away, which galvanised Pat into action (she would have taken years to decide otherwise), and we went to dinner to celebrate. I ordered a drink and experienced the shock of a Spanish vodka tonic. Half a pint of vodka and a tablespoon of tonic. No wonder everyone was pissed all the time! After three of those I was plastered. But very happy!

The next morning, however, I was very ill. Feeling like death, I ordered a fry-up at the local café (very Spanish, I know), and we sat and discussed a plan of action. We had been told by a guy in the local bar that if we needed a mortgage, the man to call was Mickey Pattemore. While I was slowly working my way through the large greasy sausages, Pat rang his number. The conversation was short and sweet and she announced he was on his way. Five minutes later, a red sports car roared to a halt and out stepped Mickey Pattemore.

'Oh my God, look at him. He's been round the block a few times. He looks like a right Jack the Lad!' I said, *sotto voce* to Pat.

'Yes, Bellie, and you'll probably have had him by Christmas!' was her tart reply. Not what you'd call an auspicious start, perhaps.

Mickey Pattemore was like a whirlwind. His handshake would have cracked a walnut. He had a broad Somerset accent and a nose that suggested he had had one too many beers. But I have to say that when I looked into his brown eyes and broad charming smile, despite my hangover haze, I was a little bit smitten.

He asked all sorts of questions about Pat's finances and then, before you could ask, 'fixed rate or interest only?', he whisked her off in his car to the bank. Alma and Robert sat there, stunned for a few moments before Robert remarked in his broad Scottish accent: 'I do hope Pat will be OK. For all we know he's taken her for the white slave trade.'

'In her wildest dreams,' I said.

She was back within twenty minutes.

'All sorted,' said Mr Mortgage Man. 'Now what can I do for you, Miss Bellingham?' So he recognised me. I was rather chuffed! I didn't think I was going to need a mortgage, but we agreed it might be better to have one.

'OK, fine with me. But I need to ring Richard, my accountant.'

'Not a problem. Ring me later,' and he was gone in a roar of petrol fumes.

We were all sat looking at each other for a good few moments: 'Well, he doesn't waste any time, does he?' said Alma.

That afternoon we made all sorts of plans, and I spoke to Richard, who gave me all the information I needed to complete my purchase.

We were off back to London the next day, Saturday, as we had already booked our flights, but now we had to return on the following Monday to deal with all the necessary paperwork. I felt good. I had a plan, and I like a plan. Pat and I could spend our old age in a beautiful place.

For the past couple of years, my mother had been ill, fading away more and more into that awful abyss that is Alzheimer's disease. She would sit in her prison, locked inside her own mind, but sometimes seeming to know Dad, which made it worse for him. I had watched, when he arrived at the home, how she would turn her head to him and a smile would light up her eyes. Seeing her decline, I had been forced to face the future. I had so many girl-friends who were in the same position as me: no man in their lives, not to mention no pension and not many prospects of earning over the next twenty years. I could let these facts depress and overwhelm me, or I could make a plan and be positive, and this is what I intended to do. Better to be poor in the warmth of Spain, than cold in a flat in London, I reckoned. The boys would be leaving home eventually and that was another thing that had started to niggle in the back of my mind. I did not want my sons to feel I was a burden to them as I grew older; I wanted them to enjoy my company. I was determined to view this purchase of a pad in Spain as the prelude to the next chapter in my life.

So Pat and I turned around on the Saturday, and flew back on the Sunday evening, ready to meet Michael Pattemore bright and early on Monday morning.

He was outside waiting for us at 8.30 a.m. on the dot. First Brownie point to him: punctuality is very important in my book. Then we were off to the police station to get our NIE numbers. This is similar to a National Insurance number, and you need one for practically everything in Spain. We had rather a long wait in the police station and Michael entertained us with lots of stories. He was very charming and funny and we got on like a house on fire.

Driving back to Moraira I was sitting in the back and he kept looking at me in the driving mirror. Was he flirting with me? He asked me how old I was and, when I told him, he pretended to be shocked. He said he thought I was younger. Yeah, yeah! In fact, he confessed later that he had looked at my passport in the police station so he knew exactly how old I was. I told him I was divorced and he told us that he was divorced, and had come to Spain to get away from his ex-wife, who had been having an affair that had split their marriage of twenty-five years. He said he was with someone now but that it wasn't serious. Well, they all say that, don't they?!

While we were in the car Michael was planning our return, after Christmas, for the completion date on our properties. In Spain, you all go to the notary and sign the papers on a nominated day. Michael was suggesting the first week in January.

'But I can't. I'll be doing a play,' I said.

'Can't you get the day off?' asked Michael, blissfully unaware of how theatre works (nobody has a day off unless they are dying). I explained this to him and he said to Pat and me that this was a problem because the papers all had to be signed on the same day: 'Could you give Pat your power of attorney? Then she can sign for you.' We agreed that was the best way to do it.

Pat and I began to appreciate more and more the powers of the Pattemore and what an ally he was to have. Had I been trying to do this on my own it would have been a nightmare. There was so much red tape to get through. But Michael took us through everything with ease and we finished up in a tapas bar with a large glass of *vino tinto*.

Pat now had power of attorney to return and sign on the dotted line for me.

'Brilliant. You sorted my flat,' I said to her, 'now all you have to do is find me a man!'

We had a very long lunch and then said our goodbyes. That night I fell into bed and dreamt of a notary who looked like Michael Pattemore, and had an office like a tapas bar. *Hasta la vista!*

B ACK IN LONDON, life went on. I was getting a fair amount of publicity as I was appearing on *The Bill* twice a week. I had landed a great part thanks to Paul Marquess, who was the producer at the time. He saw beyond the obvious and cast me as a real villain. Irene Radford was a widow whose husband had been killed by a cop and had taken over his criminal activities of sex, slavery and drugs! It was a fantastic opportunity for me to play a completely different kind of character and I attacked it with relish.

It started out as a couple of episodes and ended up with me doing a six-month stint. I had a terrific time with the cast, especially Roberta Taylor and Beth Cordingly.

I also had a very exciting outing around this time. ITV was celebrating its fiftieth birthday. There was a big do at the Natural History Museum, attended by the Queen, and I discovered when I got there that I was to be in the line to be introduced to Her Majesty. I was sandwiched between Nicholas Parsons and Harry Hill.

Harry was wearing one of his trademark shirts with a huge collar, but no black tie. An ITV executive pulled me aside and asked me to persuade him to put his tie on as it was protocol. I duly went up to Harry and berated him as though I was his mother. He agreed to put the tie on with the retort, 'God, I never thought I'd be told off by the Oxo mum!'

We all stood in line for hours waiting for the Queen to reach us and, as is typical of theatrical people, we were all chatting nineteen-to-the-dozen and had to be told to pay attention as our monarch drew nearer. Harry was hysterical and gave Her Majesty a card that his daughter had made for her. This is not done, apparently, and the Queen looked rather bemused, looking round for someone to take it from her. I stepped in, quick as a flash, 'Allow me, your Majesty,' and took it. She gave me a radiant smile, thanked me and wished me luck.

TOWARDS THE END of November 2004 I found myself, one evening, sitting in my trailer in a car park in Bushy (the way you do with these glamorous TV locations). I was filming an episode of *Murder in Suburbia*, a crime series, when my phone bleeped at me. A text.

'How's it going, Miss B?'

It was Michael Pattemore! My heart gave a flutter.

'Sitting in a car park near Watford,' I texted back.

We exchanged a few more words but then I was called on to the set and that was that. Then, one evening, Pat was round for supper and, fuelled with a few glasses of wine, I rang Michael to see how things were going. He flirted outrageously with me while Pat just nodded sagely. I invited Michael to call in at any time if he was going to be in London. Maybe around Christmas?

He told me he would be in Manchester with his girlfriend. Which rather put the dampener on things, so I left it at that.

I had started rehearsals for *Losing Louis* at the Hampstead Theatre Club and was grateful for the diversion. The play was written by Simon Mendes de Costa and directed by Robin Lefèvre. He was a terrific director and I had worked with him a hundred years ago on *Richard II*, starring my dear old friend, Nik Grace.

I love rehearsing almost more than performing. Trying things out with the character, and getting to know the other actors and how they work. Alison Steadman and David Horovitch were brilliant together. I had worked with my other half, Brian Protheroe, in the play we did with Janet Suzman and Maureen Lipman, *The Sisters Rosensweig*, and we had the same producer now, Michael Codron. It was good to be working with Brian as someone I trusted, especially as I had to flash my fanny at him! We worked very hard before Christmas and were looking forward to a few days off.

The day before Christmas Eve, I was running round getting everything sorted. This year, though, was not quite so busy because Robbie had gone to America with his friend, Aaron, and his family, and Michael was going to Italy with his dad, on Boxing Day. I had decided Michael and I would go and see my father on Christmas Day because he had been taken ill in the last week, and Barbara and Jean decided it would be better if we all came down to see him, just in case things did not improve.

I was pottering in the afternoon and decided to give Michael Pattemore a ring and wish him Happy Christmas.

'Where are you?' I asked.

'In England,' came the reply.

'Oh, great! Are you going to call in and say hello?'

'Well, that could be difficult just now as I'm on the M6.'

'Oh, right.' I tried to hide my disappointment.

'But I'm going to pick my daughter up from Windsor,' Michael continued.

'Well, that's just down the road!' I said. 'Come and have a drink.'

'I'll see how I go for time,' Michael hedged. 'We have to get back to Manchester.'

Of course, the girlfriend. But he and I could have a drink just as friends, couldn't we? I put the phone down and wondered what to do next. What if he came? I had better make myself presentable.

It was now mid-afternoon, and at six o'clock I got a call to say the traffic had been terrible and that Michael had only just picked up his daughter.

'Well, why don't you both come for dinner and stay the night?' What am I like?

I rushed around making up the beds in Robbie's room. I knew I had some steaks in the fridge as I always have food in my house, because you never know how many boys will turn up at any given moment. The phone rang again an hour later.

'We're lost on the North Circular.' I talked them through the last bit of their journey and, five minutes later, they were standing in my kitchen.

Stacey, Michael's daughter, was lovely. She was a similar age to my Michael. She was very attractive and had a lovely smile like her dad. We had dinner and drank lots of wine and then watched me in my penultimate episode of *The Bill*, which was showing that night. How tacky is that? Making them watch me on the telly. Poor Stacey could hardly keep her eyes open, so I showed her the bedroom, and left her to it.

Michael had had an overnight bag which I had put in the room, but after he had been to say goodnight to Stacey I noticed the bag had moved to outside the bedroom door. Hmm!

Michael and I drank lots more wine and had a lovely evening. It was so relaxed as he was so easy to get on with. I, however, was in a dilemma. The wine had made me amorous, but my brain was telling me to leave it because he had a girlfriend, even though it 'wasn't serious'. Then I was trying to convince myself that even if we did go to bed together it probably wouldn't be that great, and that this would be a good thing, because then I wouldn't be interested any more and we could all go our separate ways, no harm done.

But there was a nagging voice in my head that was telling me that this wouldn't be true; that everything about Michael attracted me. He was the first man I had met in years who was a proper human being; I really liked him and wanted him to like me. But he had been through so much in the last five years, since his wife left him, and he was obviously wary of relationships. I just wanted to hold him and feel his energy around me. That is still one of the things I love about him, his lust for life and positive energy. So many people in my life had taken my energy along the way. You are either a giver, or a taker, but here was a fellow giver.

It was no good, I was going to have to succumb to my baser instincts, and test the water. I leaned over and kissed him. That was all it took. As we went to the bedroom, I remarked that his overnight bag seemed to be making its own way to my room.

'It hoped it might get lucky,' said Mr Pattemore, with a wink.

Suffice to say, it was neither a shock nor a revelation to me to find that I had met my match in every way. It was as though I rewound my entire life that night, and started at zero again. It was fantastic, and for the first time in my life I wished I had not had so much red wine. I wanted to be sober!

In the morning I sat in the bath, while Michael stood at the mirror, shaving. I felt so comfortable. I am extremely insecure about my body, but with Michael I felt no shame, no fear, and no guilt. Just complete contentment. He seemed rather subdued and I suddenly felt very vulnerable. Was he regretting his actions?

I waved him and Stacey off from the gate and went off to walk the dog. I was feeling very confused. I had spent an amazing night with a great guy, who seemed to like me, but where was it going? I did not want the answer to be nowhere. But what could I do?

As I was walking back I suddenly saw Michael standing by his car in the distance. They had forgotten something. Stacey ran into the house to get it and Michael and I stood on the pavement in silence.

'I don't want to leave you,' he said. 'I don't want to you to go,' I replied.

He gave me a hug and, as Stacey came back, he got in the car and gave me a wink.

'I'll ring you very soon, I promise.'

I waved them goodbye and actually believed him.

I went inside and tried to put Michael aside, for the time being at least. It was Christmas Eve, usually my favourite day of the year, but this year there was a cloud hanging over it. My dear dad was fading.

My son Michael and I set off on Christmas morning with the car full of goodies. My father was living with Ba and David by now. I was going to cook, as Barbara had been doing all the work looking after Dad, and visiting Mum in the home she had had to move into.

When we arrived, I could tell from Barbara's face that things were not good. I took Michael upstairs to see his grandad. He knew who we were but he seemed very weak. Michael was shocked: when you don't see someone very often, the different changes are much more marked.

I have a huge regret that as a result of all the bad feeling from Nunzio, our sons never knew their grandad or granny as well as they should have done. I remember looking at all the artwork on the door in my parents' kitchen. Jean's children, Laura and Martha, had done loads of pictures for Granny and Grandad and they were pinned up every visit. There was nothing from my boys. We had so few visits over the years because Nunzio made it so difficult and, once we were separated, he had told the boys that Granny had made Mummy leave him. He also told them that Granny and Grandad didn't love them as much as their other grandchildren because they were not blood relations as I was adopted, so that made things difficult. How wicked can anyone be? If only they had spent more time with my father they might have had a different take on what being a man is all about.

I sat with Dad, after Michael had gone downstairs, and held his hand. It was the moment I always dreaded. Seeing my father as a weak old man. He had always been so strong and true, my knight in shining armour. Suddenly, I realised he *was* my knight and had always been my knight. I couldn't live without him. I just held his hand and couldn't even talk to him. He wanted me to straighten his pyjamas, which I did, but I felt it was such an intrusion. It had been fine to wash Mum and dress her but somehow pulling the clothes round this proud man just felt wrong. He held my hand tightly and I could hardly hear him when he spoke. He was always very softly spoken, even when he was telling me off, which had made it all the more effective. Now he was trying to wish me a happy Christmas, and I was trying not to cry. I fixed on his moustache. It was white now but still the same as it had been all my life and it tickled me when I kissed him, like it had always done. Please don't die, Dad! That was all I could think. I felt like I was screaming it at the top of my voice. Please don't die.

We are so selfish about death. We grieve for ourselves. My father had spent the last few years without the woman he loved so much. He had had to watch her mentally slowly leaving him, without being able to break free from her. Sitting with my father now I realised he must be so tired of hoping. The spirit keeps going against all the odds but I think Dad just decided he couldn't wait, any more, to go.

We all had a rather solemn meal together and then Michael and I drove back to London. I was going to see Amanda Redman on Boxing Day, for lunch, and Michael was off to Italy with his dad. Mr Pattemore rang me to wish me a happy Christmas, which just made me feel even sadder. I would have loved to have sat with him and listened to his stories. If I was honest I would love to have taken him to meet my father. That is one thing I regret very much, that neither of my parents ever met him.

I went back to rehearsals for *Losing Louis*, determined to keep my life on track. There was a good deal to think about, not least my opening night. Michael Pattemore rang me every now and then for an update. I was hoping he would be able to find a way to come down for New Year's Eve, as he had said he would try.

I had missed using my dining room this Christmas and wanted to share the tree and all the bits and pieces I had made, so I invited all the cast to supper at my house towards the very end of the year. Everyone had a lovely time; we had all bonded by now and were ready to show our play to the world.

I was clearing up after they had all gone; I always put the music on full blast and open a bottle of champagne as I wash up. I had some very steep stairs in my flat that went down to the bedrooms and time and time again I had said to the boys not to run up and down the stairs in their socks, as they might slip. So what did I find myself doing? I ran down the stairs in my tights.

I fell really badly, landing in the small space where the stairs turned the corner, and lay there winded. Had I not been drinking I may well have hurt myself even more, who knows? On the other hand if I had been sober I would not have slipped in the first place. I went to get up and let out a yell – the pain in my back was excruciating. Then the panic set in. What the hell was I going to do? I just couldn't move.

I have no idea how long I stayed there but, eventually, I managed to turn myself round and I got down the rest of the stairs on all fours. I got on to the bed and lay there until I fell asleep.

As soon as it was a reasonable hour in the morning I crawled to the phone and rang my sister, Jean. She came and took me to A&E. They couldn't tell me much except I had probably bruised my back very badly and should just rest. Great. Jean got me home and into bed. She rang the theatre and they were wonderful and wished me well. I had to get better quickly as I had a play to do.

I was feeling very wobbly. Then Michael phoned to say he was so sorry but he couldn't come down to see me. It was impossible. That was the last straw.

New Year's Eve of 2004 was spent lying on my back in agony. I got several calls from Mr Pattemore making sure I was OK and, as the evening progressed, he kept telling me what was going on at his end, including how some woman was trying to chat him up. I didn't want to know! I finally turned my phone off, had a good cry and went to sleep.

I did feel a bit better the next day, and the day after I went back to work. I spoke to Michael who was on his way back to Spain but I was beginning to think that the chances for my hoped-for reunion with him were fading fast.

Oh, me of little faith. He was soon back on the phone telling me he was coming over next weekend.

We had a fantastic couple of weekends after that. I was suddenly nervous about anyone finding out about us because I didn't want the boys to know, unless I was sure of the relationship, and I certainly didn't want Nunzio to find out, because he would put the mockers on it straight away. I wouldn't let Michael come to my opening night because of all the press. He did come to the show one Friday night, when he arrived from Gatwick. I asked him to buy a bottle of wine to drink in the bar with the girls and a bottle of wine for us to have in the hotel. I was so nervous I rushed into the bar and went straight past him!

After some confused episodes when I was talking about Michael Pattemore to the few people who knew of him in the early days – because of my son being Michael as well – I coined the name 'Mr Spain' for him. It somehow seemed to go well with our clandestine meetings in the Marriott Hotel, Swiss Cottage.

Michael had left his girlfriend by now, and we seemed to be getting very close, very fast. Early on, I completely freaked because he had booked some weekends in advance, without consulting me, and I suddenly felt I was being taken over. We had a row and I told him to cancel the flights. He went back to Spain and didn't call me for a week. I panicked even more and realised that was not at all what I wanted. So I rang him and asked him to come the following weekend. I booked into the Marriott to make it special, and this set a pattern.

Mr Spain used to arrive quite late on a Friday night with his wheelie hand-luggage bag crammed with bottles of red wine. This time I was very nervous, because I hadn't seen him for a couple of weeks, and I had tried hard to make myself be less intense about the relationship as I felt we needed to calm down. But I opened the door, saw him standing there, realised how much I fancied him and forgot all about my good intentions!

We were going through a great deal in these first few weeks, especially with it all being played out in hotel rooms. And we also had another problem, which I discovered on one of our 'Friday Nights'.

I was waiting impatiently for Mr Spain to arrive. I had booked the Athenaeum because if I could get away from North London sometimes I felt more secure. It was also such a lovely place to be and I reckoned we deserved a little luxury. I answered the knock on the door and there was my beloved with his hand luggage as usual. I gave him a big hug and proceeded to open a bottle of wine. I was so busy running about that I didn't notice he hadn't taken his jacket off. I turned to give him a glass of wine and he told me to sit down and listen to what he had to say: 'You may not want to ever see me again after you hear what I have to say, Lynda.' Oh my God, what now?

Michael began to tell me his story from the beginning. His early days as a roofer in Crewkerne. Meeting his wife, Jan, and going to live in Cornwall. Getting married and having his two children, Stacey and Bradley. He opened the biggest nightclub in Blackpool in the eighties called the Palace, and was at the top of his game. Then disaster struck, recession hit and he found himself penniless. He tried, unsuccessfully, to run a nightclub in Florida. He then met a man who introduced him to a man … It was an incredible story and ended with him being wanted by the FBI in 1997. And the next time he had returned to the UK he had been detained at Gatwick airport, picked up by the police and then taken to the nearest police station. He had been forced to go to court charged with 'Recklessness' because the British police couldn't think of what to charge him with. His wife was also being charged with him so he was given the option of pleading guilty, even though he was innocent and prepared to fight the case, so that he could go free. With two small children they could not face a long-drawn-out court case with the possibility that they might both go to prison.

The lawyers, and even the police dealing with the case, were convinced that Michael would only get a suspended sentence. He had no criminal record and had never had a whiff of trouble in his professional life. So he took their advice and pleaded guilty. However, the judge had other ideas and had decided to make an example of Michael. He sentenced him to twenty months.

By the time Michael finished telling me his story, dawn was breaking. He stood up to go. I grabbed him and gave him a big kiss.

'Don't be ridiculous! I don't care what you did. It's in the past. Let's forget about it and get on with the present.'

(I actually had dinner with the policeman who was in charge of the case at the time. He and his wife came to see *Losing Louis* and then we went out for a meal. He was a lovely man and couldn't stop telling me how shocked the police had been that Michael was sent to prison.)

We embarked on our affair with gusto. Sadly, we couldn't enjoy the start of it for long because my father died in January 2005. Once again, Michael and I were at the Athenaeum. It was a Saturday night and I had done two shows and was feeling very tired. I knew Dad was failing and I was intending to go down the next day, Sunday, to see him. Michael and I were having supper in our room and I was really edgy and giving him a hard time. I felt guilty being there when I should have been with Barbara and Jean and Dad. I told Michael I wanted to leave early the next morning. Poor Michael. He was being so understanding, and I was being such a bitch. In the middle of the night I woke up with a terrible feeling of dread and I just could not go back to sleep. I got dressed and left with hardly a word to Michael, simply that I would ring him later.

'I hope your father hasn't died, Lynda, because you'll always blame me for keeping you here when you should have been there.'

He was right. But it was in no way his fault. I knew that. I drove home to change and get some things, but the next thing I knew, my mobile phone rang, and it was Barbara telling me that Dad had died in his sleep.

My world went dark. I rang Michael and told him. I told him it was not his fault and I would love to see him next week. I needed him.

CHAPTER THIRTY-ONE

MY BELOVED PARENTS TAKE THEIR LEAVE

That Christmas of 2004 was a turning point in so many ways. As if meeting Michael Pattemore was not emotional enough, I was aware all the time that my father was dying. For the last six weeks of the year he could not leave his bed. He stopped eating and it was as if he had decided he had had enough. The last twelve years had been so painful for him in so many ways...

The last time I remember seeing my parents together was for my fiftieth birthday party. Mum and Dad had always come to all my parties: Mum loved to chat to all the actors and I think Dad enjoyed standing back and just watching. I held the party in my garden at Avenue Road in 1998. It was a lovely sunny day and I had a hundred people who all had a special place in my heart. Dill, my neighbour, had a jazz combo and agreed to play. I, of course, insisted on singing. Jean had made me a lovely cake and I did all the catering. I also wrote a poem mentioning almost everyone there by name.

We had a lovely day and it was so good to have Mum and Dad there as usual. I think the Alzheimer's was beginning to kick in then as she was starting to forget things, but she was in her seventies and we thought it was just the aging process. Her mother, my granny, had suffered from dementia and my mum had had to look after her. I remember her saying it was such hard work because my Gran was very independent, and insisted she could look after herself. But she couldn't. She would go to the village shop, for example, and buy stuff, then get home and realise she had forgotten most of the things on her list. So then Mum would have to go again. Everything had to be done twice.

As far as we can ascertain, Mum started showing signs of Alzheimer's in 1993 but dear Dad kept it from us. It only became really apparent after my father had a fall in 1999. When he had given up the farm, he had kept a couple of fields on because he just loved to be out doing things. I think that it also helped him deal with Mum's dementia because he had somewhere he could escape to for a few hours.

The day he fell, Dad, typically, was cutting down a tree, standing on a log in the back of a minivan, in the middle of a field. At the age of 80! As he landed, he said he heard his neck go, and there he was, just him and his Jack Russell dog, who sat faithfully at his side and would not budge. He had been lying there for four hours, when a couple of walkers passed and found him. He was taken to Stoke Mandeville Hospital where he was X-rayed and pronounced fit to leave, but for the next six weeks he was in agony.

My sisters and my mother nursed him, and that was when Barbara and Jean realised that not only was Dad very poorly, but that he had been hiding the fact that Mum was struggling to maintain her normal life. What clarified it for them was when Mum asked Barbara how to use the washing machine.

Jean had been a nurse at one point in her life and whenever the family needed medical attention, it usually came down to her to sort things out. So she arranged to take Mum to see the GP. Jean said it was awful because Mum seemed to know something was wrong and was trying to hide it. Whenever the doctor asked her a question she turned to Jean and asked her, until eventually the doctor had to ask Jean to wait outside the room.

Alzheimer's was diagnosed. My father was devastated. He'd managed to look after her really well until he had his accident.

Dad was normally a terrible patient and a bit of a hypochondriac (what man isn't?), so when he complained that his neck was not getting any better, Barbara and Jean didn't take much notice. But after six weeks it did cause concern. Finally, Barbara had a discussion with a physiotherapist who thought it was a good idea to get him checked out, and Barbara decided to get a private X-ray done for him. Lo and behold, he had broken his neck and had been walking around in grave danger – if he had fallen again he could have either died or been paralysed for life. He was taken back to Stoke Mandeville and had to be put in traction because his neck had set incorrectly in the weeks he did not get treatment. It was incredibly painful and he was so distressed. By the time they got him on the operating table he was very weak and he crashed. This resulted in making him very frail, and he never fully got back up to speed again. The doctor told us he probably had a stroke as well and this in turn made him forgetful. Not badly at first but enough to trouble him.

He definitely started to deteriorate after this. He had always been such a strong man, physically and mentally, and it was awful to have to see him struggle to keep things together. When I was young, I remember stories about his flying days. Not that he talked a lot about the war, but he did mention the odd incident, and this one has always made me feel proud. My father was flying bombers and on one mission was being harried by a German fighter plane that was trying to shoot him down. Dad was able to put in some good defensive manoeuvres, limited as he was in a bomber, but he was lucky because eventually the German pilot had flown alongside my Dad's plane, tipped his wings at him, given him the thumbs up and flown away. Maybe the pilot's heart just wasn't in it. But now, my hero dad was starting to slowly lose his grip on things, and became very emotional, especially about Mum.

And so the dreaded moment arrived when we had to decide what to do for the best. Mum had recently had a fall and broken her hip so she was now very disabled, and Dad just did not have the strength to lift her.

It was decided that we had to put Mum in a nursing home. Like most families who have to go through the pain of putting elderly relatives in care, my sisters and I saw over a dozen before we chose what we thought was the right place for Mum. But it turned out to be more of a respite home and they could not deal with the dementia. This is the trouble with so much of the care available – it is not specific enough for Alzheimer's. It takes a very special kind of carer to deal with these patients. I do a lot of work now with the Alzheimer's Society and it is vital we, as a society, recognise the importance of care for the elderly, particularly those with dementia. It is going to affect so many of us in the next twenty years because we live so much longer now.

Mum then went to a horrible place where they drugged her and mistreated her. It was awful. Then, finally, we found Chiltern View Nursing Home and it was brilliant. The staff were just fantastic and the whole atmosphere in the place was caring and loving.

I recall a wonderful moment once when I went to visit Mum. There was a lovely man who used to come and sit next to her. We were sitting together and he came and joined us, and took Mum's hand and gave it a kiss. She looked at him for quite a long moment and then she turned to me, smiled and said, 'I know it's the wrong man but it doesn't really matter now!'

It was so sweet and touching and funny. One grasped those moments because they just helped one get through all the pain.

Mum was a very easy patient in some respects. One of the most difficult aspects of Alzheimer's is the aggression that many patients exhibit towards their carers. Fortunately, Mum was not like that, except the day she was taken to the first home we had found for her. I cannot begin to know how terrible it must have been for our father, but my sisters told me that Mum just kept screaming at him, 'Why are you doing this to me? You said you loved me. Don't leave me. I want to stay in my home. I looked after my mother when she was ill; why can't you look after me? If you really loved me you wouldn't do this!'

Poor Dad had just wept. But it was impossible for him to manage because of his neck. He could hardly push her wheelchair, never mind lift her into bed. He was also starting to make mistakes with his driving. This was the hardest thing to tell him.

He used to go off to Tesco and have his breakfast in the café and chat to the ladies who worked there. They got to know him. One day one of the ladies took my sister aside and said she was concerned because he had been in and had breakfast, then come back an hour later and ordered another one. This was followed by an incident in the car park when Dad hit another car. Finally we had to break it to him that it wasn't safe for him to drive. He hated not being able to go off when he felt like it, and it was very hard on my sister Barbara as she had most of the care to deal with.

Those last few months that Mum was at home, my sisters bore the burden of most of the care but I did get down, sometimes, spending a few days with my parents and helping. I was grateful, in a way, to have those intimate times with them both. It is a cliché, I know, but we do revert to childhood as we get older, especially if we have to be cared for, and it is very touching as a child of an adult to have the roles reversed.

The hardest thing when dealing every day with dementia is the repetition. The same conversations over and over again. It drives one mad and it is very difficult not to get cross with the person. It was easy for me in a way because I was not there all the time, but I did make a special effort to never get grumpy. I loved making Mum laugh and would tell her stories and jokes and cook her all her favourite foods. I cherished those moments with her and they are the memories I have in my mind's eye, now. One memory that will always stay with me is that Mother had incredibly soft white skin. She never sunbathed and she was remarkably free of wrinkles. She had one of those walk-in baths and she would sit there quite happily chatting away. She loved all things purple so there was lots of mauve around. Her towels and soap, and always a lingering fragrance in the air of lavender.

I was not much use at this time as I was trying to keep things going in London. I had to work to keep all the bills paid and, even after the injunction on Nunzio, he was still giving me grief one way or another. Jean helped as much as she could and would drive down most weekends. However, we both decided that Barbara needed a rest and persuaded her, and her family, to take a break. Barbara was a bit of a control freak and left copious notes and instructions for feeding the dogs and cats and generally running the household.

I spent a very happy week with Dad. We would go for walks and then visit Mum. Dad would get very sad then and we would have a cry together over a glass of red wine. We would light a fire and sit in front of the flames with our toes toasting nicely and talk about everything from childhood days to the war, and my troubles with Nunzio, and how the boys were doing at school.

DAD DIED IN mid January 2005, and Mum died the following month. Apparently, the staff at her nursing home had been discussing the death of Mr Bellingham and, that night, Mum had a stroke and never regained consciousness. It was as if she knew. Yet for the past year she had been completely unresponsive. There was no recognition in her eyes at all and her health had deteriorated so much we had all been expecting her to go.

I let myself down very badly over Mum's final hours. I was invited to the christening of Lynda La Plante's adopted son, Lorcan, in February 2005. It was on a Sunday afternoon and I was not sure that I should have been going as I really should have been visiting Mum. I only had the Sunday off as I was in the West End appearing in *Losing Louis* at the Trafalgar Theatre. I talked to my sisters and they agreed I should go to the christening because Mum loved Lynda La Plante and would have wanted me to go and support her. During the afternoon I spoke to my sisters, who told me Mum was fading fast.

I'm afraid to say I got very drunk, and decided to get a mini cab down that night to Aylesbury to be with her. I sat in the back of the car with a bottle of wine and cried all the way to the nursing home. I must have arrived in the early hours of the morning, but the staff were fantastic and made me loads of cups of coffee. I sat with Mum and tried to tell her everything was OK and that Dad would see her very soon. Talking about it later to Jean, she told me that Mum had not been distressed until I arrived drunk and sat and poured my heart out to her. Typical me, I guess. Selfish to the end. I pray I did not really cause my mother distress in her last few hours. She died the next day in her sleep.

For us girls it was a numbing few weeks. Two funerals in the space of a month. The services were wonderful, though, and all credit to Barbara who organised them, with Jean. I was not much help as I was doing the play and as anyone who knows anything about the theatre will tell you, the play stops for nothing. Not even a death in the family. I had to go to both funerals while I was performing in the evening.

They were incredibly moving occasions, the village church full both times as a testament to my parents' popularity. For my father's funeral we filled the church with wild flowers, and the RAF sent a flag to go over the coffin. This is normally only reserved for people still in the service. My sister organised a bugler, also from the RAF, to play the Last Post and it rang out through the little country church, pure and strong. The church was packed to the rafters. My dad would have been so touched and probably embarrassed by the scenes of emotion he prompted in the congregation. My friend Jenny Puddefoot (married to Rod, the folk singer) sang 'Daisy, Daisy, give me your answer, do', as it was Mum and Dad's song when they were courting. Mum had chosen the 'Airmen's Hymn' to be sung for him too, in her better days, and it was very moving to hear. It was a fantastic service and did Dad proud.

But no sooner had we recovered ourselves, than we were back in the same pews waiting for Mum's coffin to arrive. Once again the church was decked with flowers, this time all purple. My son Michael sang 'Jerusalem', unaccompanied. I was so proud. Again, the church was packed. Lovely.

Both my parents had given so much to the village through the years and it was wonderful that so many people turned out to pay their respects.

When we had first arrived in Aston Abbotts people were suspicious, as they always are, of the newcomers. Then it was announced that the village was in the flight path of the proposed Wing Airport, and my dad came into his own. He headed the campaign against the Government's plan to build the third airport near our village and nearly achieved hero status because he knew all the ins and outs of the business, and could answer all the relevant queries and objections. The airport was eventually built at Stansted, thanks mainly to local objections.

Mum had been a member of the local ladies' club and ran a weekly craft group at home. She was always first in there with the ideas for the fete or church jumble sale, and loved organising everybody. When all her friends got older, and became widows, Mum also would insist on lending Dad out! He was kept very busy driving ladies around.

They were also of another generation that is now sadly nearly all gone. A generation from another kind of life, lived simply in the country in a way that was incredibly genuine and without guile. I mourn the creeping loss of that society of country folk and that way of life. But every day I mourn for my parents. I owed them so much. I could never have repaid any of their kindness or support but I just wish they could have been around to see me grow up. It took me so long, but anything I have achieved or learned is thanks to them, and any kindness or goodness in me is thanks to them.

Donald John Bellingham died 17th January, 2005.

Ruth Bellingham died 22nd February, 2005.

May they rest in peace.

CHAPTER THIRTY-TWO

I FACE MY DEMONS
AND EMBRACE
MY FATE

AFTER MY PARENTS had both passed away, I felt completely alone. Everything I had been through so far in my life I had coped with because they were there in the background, supporting me, but now it was just me against the world. Or so I thought.

Michael Pattemore was there for me every step of the way. I have been so unbelievably lucky to have met him. Our relationship moved very fast and became, for me, very intense. I clung to Michael and our sex life was incredible. It was as though I was trying to reaffirm my whole existence.

But we also had to keep our relationship under wraps. I was so worried that the press would get hold of the story and Nunzio would go mad and then the boys would have a hard time. My ex-husband still had that kind of control over me. I had lived with the fear of upsetting him for so long I knew no different.

Michael and I were spending so much money now on hotel rooms we decided we had to find a flat somewhere. Dear Pat Hay offered us her place for the summer, as she was going off to film *Doc Martin* in Cornwall. We had a wonderful time during those summer months. I was going to the theatre every night to do

Losing Louis, while weekends were spent meeting Michael in our secret flat.

I would get up on Sunday mornings and drive back home, which was only round the corner, and sort out the boys (they never got up before lunchtime so I was always able to be there when they got up) and cook them lunch. I would make enough for Michael as well, and afterwards I would drive back to Pat's with the rest of the Sunday lunch and we would have it in the evening. Talk about meals on wheels! The boys had no idea about my secret life!

More importantly neither did Nunzio. Then, in September 2005, we met Richard Lane, my friend and accountant, for a dinner at Langan's Brasserie. After a few glasses I was a bit too demonstrative towards Michael in the restaurant, and we were papped. Suddenly the *Daily Mail* – who had obviously done their research – was running headlines about my criminal lover: 'WANTED BY THE FBI' ran the headline. We were 'outed', and I had a decision to make.

The last six months had made me realise that I was deeply in love with Michael. We had spent a great deal of time together and he had been so strong. Although I was nervous about committing completely to our relationship, I knew I didn't want to lose him. I wanted to make a gesture of commitment to him during this bad time but now was not the time for him to move in with me. Nunzio would have made the boys' lives hell.

So we decided I should buy a little flat as an investment for my old age. I talked to Richard about it and he agreed it was a sound financial plan. Michael would contribute to the costs and we would have a place to be together. So we bought the 'Love Nest' in East Finchley. It was a one-bedroom flat in a sixties block. We had such fun decorating it and buying furniture for it and it was just so wonderful for me to share something with a man who didn't moan constantly and who could do things like plumbing and decorating. Heaven! Every weekend I would troll up there on a Friday with my shopping for the next two days, and while Michael was winging his way from Spain, I would be cooking and preparing for our weekend. It was like playing at being a family without the hassle of the children. My boys never asked me where I was going as long as their dinner was on the table. What did they care? I was only a phone call away.

It was the perfect arrangement. Christmas 2005 was hysterical. Two Christmas trees, two sets of decorations, two Christmas dinners. The boys love Christmas Eve as I do, so I stayed with them for that. Although now they were older, twenty-two and seventeen no less, it was more a question of getting up early on Christmas morning and taking their stockings in to them while they were asleep, and then waiting until they woke up bleary-eyed and hungover to open the presents.

This Christmas I went to Midnight Mass with Michael and then went home to my flat and organised the day to come. I delivered the stockings to the boys and spent the morning cooking the lunch. Michael had driven down to Somerset to see his parents and we were going to meet back at the Love Nest in the evening.

The boys and I had a lovely lunch and opened our presents and then they went off to see their dad. I cleared up and set off for East Finchley. It looked so pretty. We had a lovely Christmas tree and lights. Everything was very neat and tidy after my house. I put the presents under the tree and champagne in the fridge, and the dinner was in the oven. Michael drove like the clappers and was back in London by the early evening and we sat down and spent a wonderful Christmas evening together.

It was all working wonderfully well and we would probably have gone on like this indefinitely, when some friends of ours came round for dinner at our little flat and pointed out how ridiculous it was that we were in a one-bedroomed flat while my sons were in the lap of luxury in a three-bedroomed flat in Highgate, with all their meals cooked and their washing done and a cleaner who came in once a week. They had a point!

We decided to make a change, and when my son Michael saw the flat in East Finchley he wanted to move in straight away. That would have been fine if we could then move back to my flat but this was going to cause a problem with Nunzio, who would not let Robbie sleep under the same roof as my lover. So we bought a sofa bed for Robbie and the two boys moved into East Finchley. I thought this was the perfect way for them to learn to look after themselves, while I kept an eye on them from a distance.

The arrangement lasted about three weeks until Robbie got fed up and moved back with us. But big son stayed there for the next three years. It cost me a fortune because he was a student and couldn't afford rent, but he learnt to fend for himself in many other ways.

LATER IN THE year, I did a play called *Sugar Mummies* at the Royal Court, on Sloane Square. Written by Tanika Gupta and directed by Indhu Rubasingham, it was all about women going to the Caribbean for sex. I was playing Maggie, a less than sympathetic character from Manchester who finds a young black guy and tries to have sex with him on the beach, and when he can't manage it she ties him to a tree! (Obviously there was a good deal more to the play than that.) It was a fantastic take on this kind of abuse of young black men. Everyone knows about Thai brides but when it is young men involved, and women doing the buying, it doesn't create so much outrage for some reason, which shows appalling double standards in society today.

The cast was outstanding. A young actor called Jason Frederick played opposite me. The big scene where we are rolling around on the beach was a bit of a headache, and the poor guy was so nervous I suggested, one lunchtime, that we go and have some wine, and then rehearse the scene. He was worried he would get into trouble for drinking at work but I accepted full responsibility. On the back of that rehearsal, we decided it worked best to do the scene doggy style!

The set was fantastic – it was of a beach, using six tons of real sand. This had a drawback as, of course, the sand got everywhere, as sand tends to do, and after every performance rolling around in the first half, I had to spend the interval showering.

One day I asked Jason if he had told his mother he was doing this scene with me.

'Oh no,' was his reply. 'She really likes you and I don't want to upset her by telling her I am having sex with Mrs Oxo!'

The audiences were great during the run, and used to get really involved. One young actress, Heather Craney, had a scene where she called her black lover a nigger. There was always a stunned silence from the audience. One night, after this line, a single voice rang out in the theatre: 'Beat her!' It was extraordinary.

We got a huge round of applause every night. Great stuff. Again, though, the enjoyment was marred, because one of the directors at the Royal Court, a theatre which takes its image very seriously, remarked to me that it was unusual to see 'an actress like you' on its stage. Why? Just because I am well known commercially doesn't make me less of an actress. Just because the play got huge laughs and was sold out is not a matter of shame. It makes me so cross!

Again, I was disappointed when nothing came of the play for me personally, and no further roles arose because of it. Every job seemed to end and take me nowhere.

But I was always busy. I did an episode of *New Tricks* which was such fun as I was with all my old mates. Amanda Redman was on great form, as were Dennis Waterman and James Bolam. And Alun Armstrong was very naughty. I had last worked with him in 1970 on *General Hospital*. He had a wicked sense of humour then and he hadn't lost it.

In one scene for *New Tricks*, I had to do a long speech that was pretty intricate in terms of the plot, and making sure the audience would know what was going on. It's always hard when you come into a long-running series as a guest, because the guest gets all the boring bits of story-telling while the regulars get all the gags. We were all in the scene, which we'd had to do about five times so that each actor got his close-ups done. Of course, by the third time every-one was very bored with my speech, including me! Alun's character had got a broken leg so he was using a crutch and, when it came to my turn for a close-up, he decided to stick the crutch up my skirt while I was talking. I refused to stop, or laugh, so I spent the whole speech wrestling – out of view of the camera lens – with his crutch!

OVER THESE FEW months, Michael had taken a major decision and given up alcohol. He had been for a check-up and been told by the doctor that if he didn't stop drinking he would have a heart attack in ten years' time.

We had gone to the surgery together, and when he had come out and sat in the car and I had asked him how it all had gone, he could-n't tell me at first. Just said, 'Right, that's it, I've stopped drinking.' I must have looked amazed because he told me that even the doctor had thought it would be impossible for him to stop, just like that.

'He offered to find me a counsellor!' Michael said indignantly. 'I told him no way. I'll stop now from this minute, you watch me.' I didn't say anything but I secretly didn't believe him.

Michael's whole life in Spain revolved around drinking. All the socialising he had to do with clients, not to mention the fact that everyone drank in Spain, whatever they were doing. Since we had got together we were as bad as each other. We would sit out on the patio with a bottle of Amaretto and drink it dry.

So I wasn't holding my breath as far as his ability to stay off the juice went. How wrong could I be! He went back to the doctor three months later and all his tests were great. The doctor couldn't believe it. I was so proud of him and he looks a million dollars now.

I should have given up with him, of course, but I decided to 'soldier on'. My decision created a good deal of tension between us, however, and threatened to destroy our relationship.

The problem, of course, is that when someone doesn't drink they become very aware of everyone else getting drunk and talking rubbish around them and there is nothing so boring as going to a party or out for a meal with a group of friends because if they all get plastered, they get stupid, repeating themselves and getting aggressive and shouting over the top of each other.

I, of course, was doing all these things in spades. Poor Michael would come over from Spain to spend a weekend with me and we would go out to a friend's lunch, or a charity do, or a first night or something, and I would happily get a bit sozzled, or worse, and end up ignoring him.

One of the things I always used to do when I was drunk was come home and start ringing friends. Normally I hate talking on the phone for hours. I think it comes from when I was young and Dad would go mad because I was always on the phone, and he trained me to just deliver my message, and hang up. But when I had had a few, I was always happy to chat. It was a way of catching up with people, especially when I was going through all the problems with Nunzio and never got to see anyone.

But now, unfortunately, I was doing it at Michael's expense. He would go to bed and I would be in the kitchen on the phone. He tried telling me nicely that if I didn't calm down he would have to make a few decisions about our time together, but I took no notice until one day we had a big row and Michael told me he was not going to bother to come over for the weekends if I did not stop drinking. I was shocked. I wasn't that bad, surely? But he told me that I was starting to be a real pain. Sometimes, now, when we had been out I would come back and be sick, or just go to bed and pass out.

He was kind but firm. If I wanted to drink that was fine, but he would not be with me.

I had a lot of thinking to do. It seemed so unfair to make such a big deal of it because it didn't actually happen that often. Most of the time now, because Michael didn't drink, neither did I, and it was fine. But if I was honest with myself, there were the odd lunches where I seemed to get drunk very easily. Certainly my tolerance for alcohol had lowered considerably. But the thought of not having a glass or two of champagne or a glass of red wine was horrific. That lovely thing of getting tipsy with the one you love and making love all afternoon; I just couldn't imagine life without it. But obviously the time had come to call time on my drinking and, if I needed any more persuasion than losing the best thing that ever happened to me, my guardian angel also stepped in to give me a much-needed kick up the backside.

We had been to lunch with Amanda Redman at her house. Pat Hay was there, and some other friends, and it was a great day. It went on all afternoon and I was well away, telling stories and throwing back the red wine. Michael finally managed to drag me away and take me home. As we got into the house, the phone rang. Jean had been mugged, right outside her house, and was lying in the road. I was so drunk I couldn't actually stand up by this time, but

I registered the horror of it and through the fog I was struggling to get myself together to go and help her.

Michael just told me to shut up, sit down and stay there. He would deal with it. He left me sitting there, and I was still in the same place God knows how many hours later. I spent the whole time trying to sober up. I was sick to my stomach and my soul. As always in my life, things have to go to an extreme for me to actually do something about it.

When Michael returned he could hardly bring himself to talk to me. He told me Jean had broken her arm and been taken to The Whittington Hospital.

My poor dear sister had been having a hell of a time recently. She had discovered that her husband was having an affair and her twenty-eight-year marriage was in tatters, and now this. And where was her supporting family? Round the corner in a drunken stupor. Michael was so disgusted with me he left for Spain very early the next morning without even saying goodbye. When I rang him later he basically told me again that if I wanted to drink that was fine but he would not be coming back to visit me. I begged him to forgive me and pleaded for another chance. Thank goodness he relented, and I too stopped drinking there and then.

And so I began my new life. It sounds very dramatic, doesn't it? But it was a new life. In writing this book I have been shocked at just how much alcohol played a part in my life, and none of its influence was good, or constructive, in the end. Yes, it's great to have a few glasses of wine now and then. If you can do that, no problem. But some of us can't have just one glass. It's the same as smoking – if I could have had the odd cigarette after a meal, fine. But I could never stop at one, so it was easier not to do it at all.

And stopping drinking doesn't mean my life is a misery, or that my sex life is ruined, or that I have no social life. But it does mean

I can see life clearly now. I love my life and I intend to keep living it for a long time with Mr Spain.

WHILE I WAS doing *Sugar Mummies* I went on *Loose Women* on ITV to talk about the play. I had always loved the programme. It had started ten years before as a lunchtime chat show with a panel of four women, from an idea taken from an American show called *The View*. It had been moved to different time slots over the years but, for the last couple of years, it had found the perfect spot, at lunchtime, Monday to Friday.

I loved the format of women being able to chat about almost anything. The regular panellists were very open and honest and it was good fun to be on as a guest, as well.

I knew Denise Welch a little, and when I found myself riding a tandem bike with her for a charity event, I asked her to put a word in for me at *Loose Women* in case they needed any new permanent contributors. As I've said before, this industry is all about timing and sometimes the timing was right for me: I got a call asking me to go for a trial.

I was thrilled and nervous. These ladies were not to be messed with. I went on the show with Coleen Nolan, Carol McGiffin and Jane McDonald and the host, Jackie Brambles. I loved it. I think I probably tried too hard to be witty and amusing for the first few programmes, but everyone does that. Jane and I hit it off immediately but I felt that Carol and Coleen were sizing me up. In those early programmes I felt excluded or shouted down when I tried to join in. Carol is very much the rebel on the panel. She has the reputation for hard living and going out and getting pissed. Actually I discovered she doesn't hold her drink very well so it doesn't take much for her to have a good time. Coleen is brilliant at undercutting any discussion with a quip. I knew Sherrie a bit from our acting days and Andrea and I have a mutual friend in Penny Smith. I realised that the way forward in the show was to find my own niche and not try and compete with the other girls. I think that is what works for all of us. The combination of personalities at any one time.

As the weeks went on I discovered I had a good deal in common with all the girls in different ways. When we go into the meetings every day, to discuss the content for the show, we sometimes get really heated and really honest. It's like going to group therapy. At first I tried to hold back, and not be too open because you don't want everyone to know your business, but it doesn't work like that. You have to be up front. I had been a drinker, so I could relate to Carol, but also she and I agree on quite a few things, like the role of women in society, and family values. I was happy to let Coleen do the jokes and I would slip one in sometimes, but mainly I found my own anecdotes to tell, and became a kind of elder stateswoman of the piece. We are all so different and what works for the show ultimately, in my opinion, is when we work as a team, and everyone gets a say.

The production team is also fantastic and a complete mix of the young and not so young. Karl Newton, who is the executive producer, has been with the show from day one and is a very canny operator. The producer, Sue Walton, is a wonderful woman and very good at her job. And we have an editor called Emily who has the toughest job, in a sense, because she has to make sure the content of the show has a balance. That means she not only has to keep an eye on what we talk about, but also, sometimes, keep our egos in check!

It is very difficult when we have a heated discussion not to end up all talking at once, as it does not make good television. We have earpieces so that Emily can talk to us at all times and this can take some getting used to. Sometimes when I am off about something,

Emily tells me to shut up (not in so many words, but she does some-times tell me to get a move on because time is running out). You will know when this happens because if you look closely enough, you will see my eyes glaze over and I sort of slow down and run out of steam!

As the show is broadcast live, we also have to be very careful about bad language. I have been caught a couple of times: I said 'bollocks' once but I have no idea where it came from (I was talk-ing about cuckoos of all things, and suddenly out it popped!)

The worst moment I have witnessed was the live show starring Joan Rivers. She is amazing and once she starts talking there is no stopping her. She was going to be on for two parts of the show with a commercial break between the two parts. As we approached the end of the first half Miss Rivers was in full flow telling a story about Russell Crowe. Before anyone could stop her she was saying, 'He was a fucking little shit.' The studio audience gasped and I honestly thought I was hearing things. There was a moment when everything seemed to stop and then pandemonium reigned. The editor was screaming in our ears, 'Go to the break!' while we all just sat there with our mouths open. Jackie Brambles very quickly apologised to the audience and got us off air.

The producer, Sue Walton, then appeared on the studio floor and asked Miss Rivers to leave. Joan was professing her innocence, saying she thought we had a delay system that bleeped out any swear words on a live show. There were mixed messages from the production box, too. First they were saying she had to go. Then they decided to carry on and were telling Jackie to apologise again at the top of the next half.

The floor manager in the studio prepared to give the count-down to going live for the next part of the show as we all tried to compose ourselves, and Joan Rivers was being very funny and cracking jokes and telling everyone not to worry, her lips were sealed and she would not use any more swear words.

The countdown started. Ten, nine, eight ... suddenly there was a decision to take Joan off! The producer appeared and literally dragged her out of the studio! I later heard Joan Rivers on a talk show describing being thrown off the set, and her Manolos dragging on the floor!

As the show started again, we were all sitting in a row absolutely speechless. Emily was shouting in our ears, 'Say something, say something!' I turned to Carol and asked her a question about something we had talked about earlier, but she very quickly turned it back to me and thankfully I was able to talk sensibly for the next few minutes, while everyone sorted themselves out.

It's amazing, really, that we do not have more scary moments like that. I must say it gets the old heart racing.

In the three years I have been doing the programme we have had a couple of changes. There are more of us ladies now. I think this gives the producers a chance to keep things fresh. Jackie Brambles left in July 2009 to do other things. She was great and had masses of journalistic experience, which I think was very good for the show. Since I joined in 2007, both Jane and Carol have ended their reigns of celibacy: Carol has a lovely young man called Mark and Jane has rediscovered her old flame, Ed. Coleen got married to Ray and Denise is still married to Tim Healy! And apart from being a fantastic job with lovely people, it changed my profile virtually overnight. That is the power of television. All the theatre tours and plays are great, but the general public generally do not really register you until you are on the box!

I WAS ENJOYING MY new life, sober. And I had one wonderful moment of recognition at this time: I was offered an Honorary Doctorate of the Liverpool Institute of Performing Arts.

Thanks to Nik Grace, I had done a workshop for the school a few months earlier. I was so nervous about it but Nik and Mark Featherstone-Witty, the principal, persuaded me and I had a ball. I talked about comedy, my favourite subject. So now I was going to go up to Liverpool and be presented with my diploma by Sir Paul McCartney. A Beatle!

We were all waiting to go into the hall and forming an orderly line behind Sir Paul, and I made a rude joke. What a surprise. Everyone laughed and Sir Paul said something about how that was very like me, or something, and I replied, 'But you don't know me.'

To which he replied, 'Ah, but Lynda, we all feel we know you as we have grown up with you.'

I was so thrilled. Him grow up with me? I don't think so. Me grow up with him? Of course. I had every LP ever made of the Beatles. I have one of their songs for every event in my youth.

Sir Paul was incredible at the ceremony that day. It had just hit the headlines that he was going through a divorce from Heather Mills and you could see he was very wobbly. I was sitting next to him and asked if he was OK.

'Yes, as long as you're not too nice to me, because then I might start crying.' I gave his arm a squeeze to show I understood.

The students were amazing that day. Each one either hugged him or shook his hand and he did it all with such good grace. What a wonderful example to have at the beginning of a career. I found him inspiring and I was three-quarters of the way through mine!

In 2007, I continued with my new broom to sweep my life clean. I also appeared in a fantastic play called *Vincent River* by Philip Ridley. It starred myself and a young actor called Mark Field.

It was very dark and dramatic, and ran for an hour and a half without an interval. It was a marathon for both of us. I have never been so frightened as I was on the first night. We opened at the Trafalgar Theatre Studio, a tiny studio holding seventy people. All the leading critcs came and I was very aware of them because they were so close.

Well, it was a triumph. I got the best reviews of my career. I was thrilled. Typical of my luck, though, we only played for three weeks so hardly anyone saw me and once it was over I was back in my box.

Michael and I decided to move. I had always said that as I got older and the boys left home I would want to move into a place that was serviced and safe. Having lived in old houses for the last thirty years, I had always had to deal with leaky roofs and all sorts of maintenance. So I wanted a, preferably, modern house, where all outside repairs were done for me. Mind you, I had Michael now, which made a big difference. Men who can actually 'do' things are few and far between: one afternoon he was repairing my gatepost, and got several offers from various ladies in the neighbourhood to do odd jobs!

So I found my present home, which is in an old converted hospital. I had passed it many times and seen the board advertising luxury apartments and done nothing about it. As usual it was Michael who suggested we take a look. I fell in love with the whole place straight away. The apartment we wanted had lovely big floor-to-ceiling windows, so the light was fantastic. There was also a courtesy bus, every fifteen minutes, to take people to the station and the local supermarket. How perfect was that? Michael organised a 'For Sale' board and within two days had sold my flat. The man is a miracle.

We had also decided to get married. Michael had thought about it a while before and had proposed, but I had said no. What a silly woman! But my life had changed so dramatically, so quickly, after all those years of misery, that I did not trust that Fate was at last being kind. Also, having made such a huge error of judgement with Nunzio, I still didn't quite trust my instincts now. I also wanted to make sure that I was truly in love with the man, and not just a little grateful to him for helping me through the deaths of my parents. I had been so vulnerable then, emotionally, that it would have been easy to mistake my feelings. But now, having given up the drink, and able to see clearly for the first time in years, it just felt right.

The night I said yes, we were having dinner at the Ivy, as we are wont to do. Since giving up alcohol our bill was positively tiny! Suddenly the waiter brought us two glasses of champagne. I raised my hand to stop him putting them down but Michael stopped me.

'That's fine. Thank you.' I looked at him in amazement. Was he going mad?

'But that's stupid, Michael. We don't drink.'

'Go on, just this once, have a sip,' he prompted. 'One won't hurt you.' He raised his glass and clinked it against mine. 'Here's to us!'

I took a small sip, unconvinced it was a good idea and actually thinking how horrible it smelled. Something brushed my lips and I put my finger to my mouth as the champagne spilled a little. There was something in the glass. I fumbled around in it and found the object causing the trouble. A ring. An engagement ring. Rather a big ring! He is such a romantic and also the master of surprise. He gets me every time.

The journey to my finally saying yes had been a bit rocky. The first time Michael proposed to me, I was so confused. I was embarrassed because I could not say yes spontaneously. I tried to make light of it and explain how I felt but I could tell he was disappointed. Then he mentioned it another time, but in a more jokey way, which made it easier to refuse, but even so, he pointedly announced he was not going to ask again.

Then, one day, we went to see a solicitor to organise our wills. Because we were now sharing property together I wanted everything very clearly set out. What was his and what was mine. I had always been very clear that I could never go through what I went through with Nunzio again. I needed the security of knowing what was mine would stay mine. I know that is not very romantic but, believe me, when you have lost everything once you are never going to do it again.

Michael was great about it and completely understood. However, while we were with the lawyer going through everything, it became abundantly clear that it would all be so much easier if we were married and that if we were, the taxman would not reap all the benefits. I made a comment to that effect and caught Michael's eye. We just sat there looking at each other. I loved him so much in that moment. It absolutely seemed the right thing to do.

'OK, let's get married, then,' I said. The solicitor looked horrified.

'Oh, no!' she said. 'You can't get married just because of the taxman!'

We laughed and explained to her that we had discussed marriage before but that I had been reluctant to take that final step. Now, we could move ahead. It was a great feeling and we started to make plans straight away.

We decided we would get married at Christmas. Embarrassingly, it would be my third time and Michael was determined to make sure it was the last and the best! I had only ever been married in registry offices so it was going to be a white wedding, in every way, even if we had to manufacture the snow.

Tragedy struck, however, when my sister Barbara was diagnosed with lung cancer. The wedding plans were put on hold.

I must say I was very conscious at this time that as my life was coming together, my dear sisters were going through hell. Jean was struggling with her divorce – what could have been a civilised split as far as the money side was concerned turned into a nightmare, thanks to her husband's selfishness and cruelty. It never ceases to amaze me how people that one thinks one knows can change overnight. So Jean had to deal with Barbara's illness and the betrayal by the man she loved. She gave up her job to nurse Barbara and help David, Barbara's husband, keep things together.

Barbara was incredibly brave during the next six months. She was determined to set her house in order. I was full of admiration because she chose to be positive and realistic at the same time. The prognosis was not good but she really tried to fight the disease. Never did any one of us concede the fight was hopeless and she fought right to the last, God bless her. I have so much to thank her for, not least because her death put a whole new perspective on my attitude to life. Similarly to when my parents died, her death made me want to *live*. I wanted to grab Michael and hold on to him tightly and never let him go.

Barbara passed away on 31st October, 2007. It was devastating for David and her two children, Louis and Bonita, but also for Jean. Of course, we had both lost a sister, but Barbara and Jean had been especially close, right from birth. Jean had not only lost our parents two years ago, but then her marriage and now her sister. It was a devastating time for her and I was acutely aware that I was about to embark on a new life with Michael.

CHAPTER THIRTY-THREE

THIRD TIME LUCKY!

I HAVE TO ADMIT that I was embarrassed. My first wedding had resembled a press call for the film, *Confessions of a Driving Instructor* (I really had nothing to do with it at all and can only plead, in my defence, that my intentions were good, even if I was completely naive). My second wedding was a romantic attempt to dispel my first wedding day and show the world that love could conquer all, which was also incredibly naive. So why the hell, at nearly sixty, would I want to risk repeating it all? And what kind of wedding do you have at my age?

I desperately wanted to do the right thing for Michael, but in a way, I felt he had had his big day the first time around and I was not sure how he felt about doing it all again. It is difficult to explain my confusion. I loved him with all my heart, and I believe that one of the main reasons for getting married is to make that commitment to a person in a church before God, and to show the world you are prepared to share your life with this person, so it should be enough to just go off and get married with a few friends privately. But there was still a bit of me, deep down, that wanted the wedding I had never had. Michael knew this and encouraged me to go for it.

I had also always wanted a big party. I had tried to organise it for my fiftieth birthday but just could not afford it at the time, so now Michael suggested we do it for my sixtieth and have the wedding at the same time. Michael does not do things by halves! I feel that part of the success of our partnership is that Michael is just bigger and braver than me. We have the same dreams and aspirations, but whereas I tend to think they can never be more than just dreams, Michael makes them happen.

He swept me up in the plans and set me tasks to do. I spoke to Richard Barber, a good friend but also a journalist who works a lot for *Hello!* magazine, and one thing led to another, and we arranged a deal to turn my wedding fantasy into reality. I was very wary about teaming up with a magazine because I always felt that it would turn into a circus: much as I appreciated now having the resources to make the day special, I wanted to make sure it remained personal. I have to say that the Editor and staff at *Hello!* were terrific and never tried to influence any of my decisions.

We were incredibly fortunate to have the perfect man to perform the ceremony. Dearest Peter Delaney was now an archdeacon. It is odd sometimes to regard close friends as others would see them. Peter is someone I respect and trust like no other. But he is also a venerated man of the church and works incredibly hard in the community in the City of London. After he left All Hallows by the Tower, where he blessed my marriage to Nunzio, he took St Stephen Walbrook under his wing. This is the most exquisite church, next door to the Mansion House, nestling in the heart of the City of London. Built by Sir Christopher Wren, it was the prototype for St Paul's Cathedral. It has a domed ceiling and has an unusual altar, designed by Henry Moore in 1987. It is also the home of the Samaritans founded by Dr Chad Varah in 1953. Could there be a more perfect place to be married?

We went to talk to Peter, who told us that with permission from the Bishop of London, we could be married in St Stephen's and there would be no need to have a civil ceremony in a registry office.

He talked to us intimately about our reasons for wanting to get married and our faith and I surprised myself by how much it meant to me to have this service.

So we started to work towards the big day, 31st May, 2008: the very day I would be sixty. However, I still had my reservations about just how far to go with the whole 'white wedding' thing. Would folk think I was deluded? Did it matter what they thought?

Peter had suggested we went to look at the Coq d'Argent for our reception, a restaurant opposite St Stephen's. It had a roof garden and looked out over London. There were the most incredible views over the City and it was so close to The Gherkin (or No 30, St Mary Axe to give it its rather bizarre full title) you could almost lean over and touch it. The City has that fantastic mix of old and new: the Bank of England stood opposite mocking me; if only I had unlimited funds to spend on the reception! But money is not everything, and between us and the restaurant, we had great fun choosing canapés and wine. Quite a difficult thing to do when one no longer drinks: I did try some wines but all I could taste was alcohol! I put my trust in the sommelier.

The most exciting news was that the restaurant had permission to have firework displays: I love fireworks. I decided against a sit-down meal because I knew that so many old friends would just want to mingle and rediscover each other. Part of the joy for me, about having a party, is to unite everyone from every different part of one's life and see how they all get on.

Dear Jean made me a birthday cake. I had no idea, but Michael was giving me a Zimmer frame with a personalised number plate for my birthday, so she made a little model of me with said Zimmer frame, standing on top of a cake in the shape of a bus pass. Well, no point in ignoring the obvious! The local bakery in Crouch End, Dunn's, made me a wedding cake, so I had the best of both worlds.

The flowers in the church were peonies and sweet peas. Their pale pinks and whites were so delicate and the fragrance was wonderful. We also designed a kind of bower to stand where the guests arrived, where photos could be taken.

My wedding dress was to be my biggest headache. Once again, I was torn between my secret desire to be a real bride in a white dress and my secret fear of looking like mutton dressed as lamb. I tried to cover all eventualities by choosing a dress that could double up as a party dress at the reception.

I went to seek the advice of a well-known designer. I am not going to name names but they were completely unhelpful and unfortunately not that interested. They deal with quite a few society weddings and are quite trendy: I had met the designer several times at charity functions, and he was always very charming, saying that if ever I wanted something special to wear to give him a call. Well, there I was, with his assistant giving me the brush-off. She was so snooty and disinterested it made me feel really inhibited. I chose a dress, off the rail, and suggested they make me an evening coat similar to one I already owned, which was his label. Hardly loads of work.

I had a fitting and the seamstress was lovely but I just didn't feel comfortable. I explained it had to be right because the wedding was going to be in *Hello!* but the assistant just dismissed that, saying they were not bothered about the publicity as they had enough clients. The worst kind of fashion snobbery.

While all this was going on, Michael had organised a trip to the Gambia. No, not a honeymoon, but a pre-wedding week to rest in. How amazing was that? He felt that because we had not had a holiday and I had done the play *Vincent River* and we had lost my sister Barbara, we should take a break and get some sun.

The morning we were leaving I had an appointment to see the

dress designer people. I had told Michael all my worries and he basically told me to tell them to get stuffed. A man of few words. I tried my dress on and still did not feel comfortable in it. This was my wedding dress and I was supposed to feel special, but I felt like a sack of potatoes, and I was being charged a fortune for the privilege. So I told them to forget it.

So now I was on my way to the airport with two weeks to go to my wedding, and I had no dress! Mr Positive sitting beside me said that surely there was a bridal shop we could call in at on the way to the airport? We had lots of time! Well, really, there is hardly an abundance of shops at all on the M4, is there? But we were passing out of London via New Bond Street and I remembered that there was indeed a bridal shop there called Pronovia. It had a window full of the most amazing wedding dresses. The real thing, with trains and lace and everything.

Suddenly it was like being in a sweet shop. I wanted everything. All my thoughts about being too old to wear a white gown vanished until the assistant approached me and asked: 'May I help you, madam? Are you the mother of the bride?'

I nearly ran away! But Michael kept me firmly in the shop. After this initial hiccup they were fantastic and couldn't have been more helpful. I gave them the list of things I couldn't wear because my arms were too fat and my boobs were too big: all the negatives. I tried on three dresses and the third was it: everything I had ever imagined a wedding dress should look like.

As I work with a profession that does glamour to perfection, on this occasion there could be no mistake, and Jean had wisely pointed out that if I had a dress that doubled as a party dress, I probably wouldn't look any different to everyone else at the reception. I was the bride and should look like a bride. Now, thanks to Pronovia, I certainly did.

They told me to go off on my trip and relax. I should come in to pick up the dress the day after I returned and it would be waiting for me. And that is exactly what happened.

Michael and I had a fabulous week in the Gambia. Eating healthy food, sunbathing, sleeping and reading. It was bliss and just what I needed. I came back ready to blaze a trail.

J EAN WAS MY bridesmaid, or matron of honour. Ladies in waiting was probably a more apt description for my entourage, which consisted of Pat Hay, Flic McKinney, Alena and her daughter, Katy, Stacey my stepdaughter (and her son, Cooper) and Lynda La Plante (and her son, Lorcan). We had a hysterical morning getting ready. Pat Hay did my make-up; for the third time! Carol Hemming flew in from Brussels to do my hair. She was doing a film with Michelle Pfeiffer and had got the day off to come and set me up. She couldn't even stay for the wedding, just did my hair and left. How luvvy is that?!

I was up and down the stairs like a yo-yo, trying to make coffee and sandwiches for everyone. My brother-in-law arrived with my nephew and niece, and Karel (yes, we are still friends!) My stepdaughter arrived late, so Pat was doing her make-up instead of mine, and then did not have enough time to do her own!

I had bought all my girls jewellery to say thank you, so we had a little present-giving moment. I look back on it now and feel so proud of everyone, and so lucky to have so many good and kind friends. I also had bracelets made of flowers for the girls to wear instead of the more traditional bouquets; it was a good idea, but impractical as they kept breaking.

Because *Hello!* was involved we had to be careful that there were no photographers around as we got in the cars. I felt such a fool covered in a large sheet as, finally, we set off for the church.

Michael and Bradley, who was best man, had been staying at the Athenaeum Hotel the night before to ensure we would only see each other at the church.

I just kept thinking about my mother and father and my sister. How strange it was not to have them with me. Death is such a big deal in these important Life moments.

Getting into the church was another absurd moment. Keeping under the sheet while big burly men hustled me inside. I thought it was all very unnecessary but I suppose that if a photo had been taken it would have spoiled the whole thing.

AND SUDDENLY EVERYTHING just stopped. All the noise and the bustle seemed to sink into the background. I saw Peter Delaney coming towards me and felt like bursting into tears. This was the real deal. This was what I was here for. To make my vows: vows to be kept for life. For a fleeting moment I saw again my other wedding memories. Not so much because of the men involved but because I felt so keenly how much I had wanted to make things work and how deep down I had at both times felt a niggle at this point; a tiny sense of dread. But not this time. I was truly excited and, deep in my heart and soul, I knew I had got it right. I just wanted to get on with the service and share my love with Michael.

Christopher Biggins and Nik Grace were at my side; I had asked them to give me away in place of my dad. The girls were lined up behind me and we seemed to take a group breath as the organ exploded into my processional music, the prelude to 'Te Deum' by Marc-Antoine Charpentier. I looked up and round the beautiful church. Because it was in the round I could take in everyone's faces, and everyone's smiles.

And then there *he* was, turning to meet me. Michael looked so nervous! Michael Pattemore, Mr Spain, Jack the lad. It is an incredible moment to stand in front of the man you love and prepare to make those vows.

Dear Peter is the best in the world, and knew exactly how to settle everyone. He looked me in the eye and said, 'Lynda, this is absolutely the last time we do this!'

He took our hands and the service began.

I had vowed I would not get tearful but it was impossible not to be overcome with emotion. Saying the words of the vows and singing some of the hymns just made me cry. Biggins provided the comedy relief by tripping up at the pulpit as he went to do a reading! Bless him. I could feel Michael shaking as we held hands and I just wanted to hold him. He is such a man, usually. Not sloppy at all but very sensitive. I think he must have been so hurt when his marriage broke up and he had tried so hard to brush it off. But that is why I love him so much, because he feels things so deeply.

The moment arrived to turn and face the congregation. The music swelled and Michael took my hand and we did a tour of the church. One big circle, stopping and kissing friends and shaking hands and feeling the wonderful vibe in the place. The register was signed and photos taken. Then the main party of people left to go across to the restaurant while we stayed and had more photos taken.

We had to part at that point, as Michael went in one door of the restaurant and I came in by another, in my sheet! We met at the lift that opens into the roof garden. Then it all began; the whole meet and greet. It was a blur really. I didn't eat a thing all night and, as neither Michael nor I drank, we were sober – the best way of remembering your wedding day!

I was concerned that *Hello!* would impinge on the guests' privacy. But it was all done very discreetly and nobody seemed to mind.

Michael had been in charge of the entertainment side of things. His best friend, Steve Markbride, who has a company called Big Bang, is an agent up in Blackpool (he and Michael became friends when Michael had the Palace nightclub there). He had found us a wonderful quartet that played at the beginning of the evening, and then a group that played all the old favourites. It is amazing to me how much people love dancing to all the seventies stuff. Michael and I never dance but we did start the proceedings with a first waltz – well, shuffle! By that time I was so overcome by the whole occasion I didn't know if I was coming or going.

As usual Michael surprised me, with the most brilliant video of all my friends talking about me. I had once told him that at my fiftieth I had so wanted a video, and he'd remembered and done this for me now! So there I was, surrounded by everyone, watching old friends doing their spiel to camera. It meant so much to me that they had bothered. People who were not able to come to the actual wedding, like Robert Lindsay and Maureen Lipman and Christopher Timothy. Michael had driven all over the country to get these interviews. He had gone to so much trouble and I never had an inkling. He had worked with an actor called Nathan Amzi, who is a computer whizz-kid and does videos to make money when he is out of work. It was just too much and I was completely overwhelmed.

I was sitting watching all this on a big screen, clutching my Zimmer frame. Then I became aware of what I would look like in the photos and hastily abandoned it. Too early in my life to be using that just yet!

While in the Gambia, Michael had spent the week writing his speech. I feel so guilty now because I had kept dismissing him: 'Don't worry about it, Michael. Nobody's going to listen to you!'

How crass. But I really did not think he had to worry too much. Little did I know he was writing a confession. A tell-all.

The room in the restaurant was quite difficult to speak in because it was a strange shape, and most people were outside on the roof terrace when we called for silence. As usual at these events, everyone had already had lots of champagne and were not in the mood to stand and listen to a speech. But Michael started speaking like a pro, and within seconds the room had gone quiet.

Most of the guests knew nothing about Michael or his past, and some of my friends were probably quite hostile, having judged Michael from newspaper reports, without even meeting him. Worse still, some were snobs, and thought he wasn't good enough for me. I appreciate that, after all I had been through, my true friends were protective of me, but suddenly, they were able to see for themselves why I loved this man.

He told his story simply and with enormous candour. He was witty and funny and, most importantly of all, he expressed his love for me so openly and truthfully there wasn't a dry eye in the house! I looked round and saw my two boys with tears in their eyes and just felt full to bursting.

Michael and Robbie hadn't come to the actual wedding service in the church because of their father. Nunzio had given them a hard time and told them it was a betrayal of him if they went to my wedding. To try and explain to them that theirs was misplaced loyalty was impossible. I understood just how much they had had to endure to be there at the reception at all. But now, looking at them listening to Michael's speech, I knew it would be OK and we could move on as a family. It's something that means so much to me and always will.

Michael's speech was a revelation. The room broke into spontaneous and appreciative applause after it had finished. Biggins and Nik Grace were on next, but he was a difficult act to follow.

The reception was of the theatrical variety. Full of life and laughter. So many dear friends turned up for me and I will always be so grateful. It was a mix of really old friends, some very new ones and some that I work with. I was very lucky because everyone seemed to get on. The famous faces mingled with the not-so-famous. There was a wonderful moment when Cilla Black met Michael Redfern, my Oxo husband, and completely confused real life with the commercial. She was convinced I had married my Oxo husband. It didn't help that they are both called Michael!

I wandered round all night in a daze. It was like seeing my life paraded before me. All the memories of the good times we had all had. I missed my parents and Barbara so much; my joy would have been complete had they been there. Thank goodness I still had Jean.

The fireworks were spectacular. My dream come true. Paul O'Grady stood next to me, and pronounced they were 'Fucking fantastic'!

I tried to speak to everyone which was quite a feat as there were over three hundred people there. As we finally waved goodbye and descended in the lift, I just wanted to sit down and take it all in.

We were staying at the Athenaeum that night, which was very special as it had been the venue for so many of our rendezvous in the last three years. I am sure many couples find that the moment when you get into the bedroom after all the razzamatazz is weird. Even though we had been living together for the last three years, the sense of occasion demands one pays attention. The hotel had put a bottle of champagne in the room with beautiful flowers and choco-lates, and a gift of a glass vase from Tiffany. It was all so perfect. We left the champagne but ate the chocolate-covered strawberries and I had a bath because the bathroom was so lovely that I was determined to enjoy it! We had an enormous four-poster canopied bed and we consummated out marriage in style.

Michael is determined we live life to the full for the rest of our days, and I agree with him one hundred per cent. I fell asleep determined to keep the Zimmer frame in the cupboard for as long as possible.

CHAPTER THIRTY-FOUR

BACK IN THE LIMELIGHT AND LOVING IT

I HAD BEEN ASKED to do a rehearsed reading of a play called *Calendar Girls* by Tim Firth. Tim had co-written the screenplay, with Juliette Towhidi, of the very successful film of the same name, based on the story of the ladies of a Women's Institute in Yorkshire who had stripped for a calendar to raise money for the Leukaemia Trust.

Angela Baker and Tricia Stewart were the two friends who made it all happen when Angela lost her husband, John, to non-Hodgkin's lymphoma. The calendar was launched on 12th April, 1999 and the rest is history. It has been an unprecedented success and raised over £2,000,000 for the Leukaemia Research Fund.

A rehearsed reading is a way of showing the play to the money men or a theatre producer or, as was the case with *Calendar Girls*, so that Tim could listen to his play, with the producers – David Pugh and Dafydd Rogers – and see what state it was in, and what, if anything, needed to be done to improve it.

My agent told me they wanted me to read the role of Chris, which was the part played by Helen Mirren in the film. I had expected them to ask me to read Annie, the role played by Julie

Walters, because that is always the way I am seen – Mrs Nice Mum – so I was thrilled to get the chance to play the lead, and also the slightly edgier character. I spent hours going through the script and getting things straight in my head. I had a feeling that if I did this reading right it could mean a chance for me to do the play.

The day before the reading my agent rang, and said would I mind changing roles and playing Annie, as the producers felt that would be a better role for me. I was so upset, and rang Michael.

'Tell them to fuck off,' came his response.

'I can't, Michael. They'll stop me playing the other part and then I'll have lost the chance of doing the play.'

'No, you won't, Lynda. Be strong. Don't keep taking shit all your life.'

Well, what could I say to that? So I said, no, I wanted to do the part for which I had prepared. 'Fine,' came the response. A victory!

We all assembled in a room in Waterloo. Barbara Flynn was going to play Annie to my Chris which, I have to say, would normally have been the other way round.

As we did the reading it was obvious that I was one of the few actresses there who had really worked on the script beforehand. It was interesting because part of Chris's character is that she is bossy and gets all the other women organised. During the reading I was doing that in spades in order to keep the energy up for the sake of the play, as some of the actresses were losing their places in the script and fluffing their lines through lack of knowing it.

After the reading Tim Firth came and thanked me for all my hard work, and lovely David Pugh was also very complimentary. David told me later that, based on my performance that day, they decided they wanted me, no matter what, and realised it would have been a terrible mistake for me not to have had the chance to show them what I could do with the role of Chris. At the time, though, nothing happened and I heard no more about it until, just as I was getting into my real-life role as Bride to Be, David Pugh rang and offered me the role. We were going to open in Chichester in September. What a wedding present!

We started rehearsing in London in July. The first day is always scary: you sit around thinking everyone is wondering why you got the part. I knew some of the other actresses a bit, and I knew Patricia Hodge from way back when we did *Waterloo Bridge Handicap*. Our director was Hamish McColl, who did *The Play What I Wrote*, amongst other things. He is a really lovely man but if I have one criticism, it is that he should have put his foot down from the beginning, because with all those egos it was a nightmare sometimes, in rehearsal. Everybody knew best! However, I think that, bearing in mind the world expects conflict from a group of women, we did remarkably well over the next year to never have a real falling out!

WHEN WE OPENED at Chichester we were barely ready. For one thing the set had been built for the tour and not for the theatre here, which was on three sides. Almost like being in the round. It made life very awkward at certain points in the play, especially the scene where we all had to strip off. Everything had to be choreographed with great care. In a way it was the making of the piece because the audience were just waiting for a carefully placed bun to drop, or blanket to fall away. In the film it would have been so much easier because the camera could just focus on a certain part of the anatomy but, live on stage, we were all very vulnerable.

In one scene I had to turn upstage and stand at the top of a hill and take my bra off. I then had to turn round with my hands covering my breasts to show the other ladies that they could take their clothes off without actually showing anything. I had to turn again, keeping my back to the audience, and look out across the dales. You then heard a car horn toot and next the sound of a car crashing, obviously because the driver had been distracted by my bosom. Well, that was all fine and dandy when we were in a normal theatre on tour because the audience is in front of the stage. At Chichester, however, with the audience on three sides, they got a very good view of my tits! Word got out that the view was very 'unrestricted' and, unlike normal where the seats with a restricted view cost less, I wanted the theatre to charge more!

During the early days we were performing, we kept changing things all the time which made everything difficult to remember. The play also had many quick costume changes as well. One night, I ran off to get changed, forgetting I had another scene to do first. Suddenly, just as I had removed my bra I heard my cue. There was no time to get dressed again so I stood in the wings completely naked, except for a G-string, and called out to Pat Hodge who was onstage waiting for me: 'Annie, you had better come out here a minute!' It was the only way I could think of letting her know I would not be coming on again. She responded with, 'Are you all right, Chris?' She was worried there had been an accident.

'Yes, but you must come out here,' I replied. She did, she saw, she understood, and we continued the play. It was hysterical and very scary at the same time!

It was ridiculous that the press made such a fuss about actresses taking their clothes off on stage. There was nothing to see out front; but if you had been a fly on the wall in the changing room, you would have been shocked by the goings on! Nudity in abundance and panic, usually. It was like a bad day at the Harrods' sale, only in the nude.

*

WHAT WAS GREAT for me on the tour was that Michael came with me, so I had a companion, driver and lover all rolled into one. It made the whole process so much more pleasant. When I was younger, touring was great fun because I never knew where I was staying and most of the time I didn't care. But as you get older you need your creature comforts.

The original agreement had meant we toured until Christmas and then went into the West End. Christmas arrived but there was no theatre free, so we had to do another eight weeks which brought the total to twenty-two weeks. Had I known that at the beginning I might not have agreed as through all these weeks I was also trying to fit in *Loose Women* as I did not want to lose my slot.

We finally hit the Noel Coward Theatre, St Martin's Lane on 20th April, 2009.

It is such a wonderful feeling arriving at the stage door with all your gear and setting up home. Because that's what it really is like, making a home in the theatre. Sometimes it can be for only a few weeks, even a few days, but an actor's dressing room is a sacred place.

The Noel Coward is a beautiful theatre and Cameron Mackintosh had had it all recently refurbished so it was shiny and bright. I had waited forty years for the moment I walked into the number one dressing room and put down my make-up on the dressing table. As I came through the stage door there were some building workers opposite and they all cheered me and raised their hard hats. I did feel like a star.

During the run I gained the added bonus of a small mouse. Theatres are notorious places for mice and often there is a resident cat to deal with the problem. This mouse got very brave during our run and would often pop out to say 'Hi'. I bumped into Sir Cameron Mackintosh one evening in Sheekey's restaurant and thanked him for my lovely dressing room, adding that I shared it with a mouse. The next day a huge Fortnum & Mason hamper was delivered to my door, full of the most delicious cheeses. The note said: 'Dear Lynda, Something for you and your little friend to enjoy!'

When our company arrived, the play running at Wyndham's Theatre, opposite, was *Madame de Sade*, starring Dame Judi Dench. The stage doors of the two theatres are directly opposite each other, across a passage that runs between St Martin's Lane and Charing Cross Road. Judi has a wicked sense of humour, and she and the cast sent us a good-luck card saying: 'Welcome to vagina alley.'

It was, indeed, a female-dominated alley through the next three months! Then Jude Law arrived with *Hamlet* and we welcomed him in much the same way. I don't think we got a reply! It always made me smile because after the shows, our stage door was surrounded by women of a certain age, and opposite waiting for Jude Law were girls of a certain age. But we held our own, I am proud to say.

All through our run in the West End and when we were on tour, our audiences were just fantastic. So many wonderful women. The discussions that rage about ageism are all pertinent, but I still say that so much of it, in television, has been created by the advertising giants. They only want to attract youth because they think that is where the money is. I would like to point out that the money is with the grey pound – their mothers! If you run advertising campaigns that ignore that fact, you do so at your peril. My sons need me to buy that car or those trainers. We were playing to eight to ten thousand women a week on tour, and that represents a lot of money.

It was also inspiring to listen to all the stories, and all the heartbreak, that so many folk have had to deal with in life. Cancer is insidious. I had a line in *Calendar Girls* that said: 'If it means the end of this shitty, sly, conniving, cheating, silent bloody disease, that cancer is…' Silent bloody disease is exactly what it is, and so many millions of people have to deal with it every day. We used to have standing ovations at the curtain call and it never ceased to amaze and move me. I felt very honoured to be part of such a strong body of society. Invisible they may be to the kind of media that deals in dreams and unreality, but we women are the silent movers and shakers, and should stand up and take a bow.

The producer wanted us all to leave the show at the end of July. It was like the end of a love affair. Very poignant and emotional. In a strange way, during this run, I had been less emotionally involved than I used to be, because I had Michael in my life. When things were so bad at home my work was my salvation, a place to go to get away and forget my troubles. Now, however, I have a beautiful life and I can enjoy my husband and my family, and have my work as an added bonus. So when I left *Calendar Girls* it was sad, but I was looking forward to the next chapter. And just before the end of July I found out exactly what I would be doing for the next few months. Dancing!

I FINISHED *CALENDAR GIRLS* on 25th July, 2009. My plan was then to spend a month in Spain and finish writing my book, but this had all changed after I was summoned to the BBC to meet the producers of *Strictly Come Dancing*.

I had always vowed I would never do a reality programme but everyone kept telling me *Strictly* was different. I had a long talk with the makers of the programme and thought it might be fun as it's not like those shows that set out to make fools of the contestants. And it's all about learning to dance, they said!

I went home and talked to Michael and Jean, who was thrilled as she was a fan. 'Do it!' they cried. I didn't hear anything from the show, though, so decided that was the end of that and prepared to go to Spain. But then, two weeks before I left, the call came through that they wanted me.

My initial reaction was a bit mixed, but everyone else was so pleased for me that I was swept along by their enthusiasm. It also meant I would have to come back from Spain for a costume fitting, and cut short my month away to two and a half weeks.

But it was worth it! On my return to England, the first port of call was the costume department. Sue Judd, the programme's costume designer, was there and we went through several dresses. It was so bizarre, sitting in a room surrounded by sequins and tulle and talking about waltzes and the cha cha cha. I had no idea what was involved. They showed me dress after dress and I just nodded. I was given two pairs of flesh-coloured satin dancing shoes to practise in. One pair was strappy for Latin dancing and one pair was for ballroom. Both pairs had three-inch heels. I was told to wear them in and make them comfortable. But I was not going to walk round the villa in them, no matter how keen I might be! So I left them in my bedroom in London and flew back to Spain.

In a way it was a good job I was closeted away in the villa, because once I had accepted the job I was sworn to secrecy until the BBC announced the line-up at the press call. This is not easy for an actor, let me tell you! We spend half our lives unemployed, trying to pretend we have got work on the horizon when people ask, and suddenly here I was with an amazing job and not able to tell a soul.

The day of the launch of the show finally arrived and I was driven to a secret location to meet the other contestants and the press. We all met in a hotel in Holborn. There were cameras everywhere, filming everyone's tiniest reaction and this became the norm for the next two months. I found it very irritating, I have to say.

All the contestants were nervous. I had a long conversation with Zoe Lucker and Jo Wood about the bits of our bodies we wanted to hide and how difficult that would be with the flimsy dresses we would be wearing, not that that stopped us getting stuck into the coffee and croissants on offer. Then we lined up in a corridor to make our entrance to the press.

I've done some press launches in my time, but nothing prepared me for the sight that awaited us in the ballroom. There were at least ten tables of journalists and it was wall-to-wall with cameras. It was all rather unreal and weird – we were being asked about dance steps and dresses when we had no idea of what was to come.

The same afternoon we filmed a trailer for the show. It was great fun being given a wonderful dress to wear and fabulous make-up and hairstyling. The men were so funny because most of them had never been near a sequin, let alone wear a shirt covered in them. There was a wonderful moment while we were all sitting around and Ricky Whittle was showing off some spins. Joe Calzaghe was watching him and asked if he had danced before. Ricky tried to play down his dancing expertise but couldn't help giving us all the moves. It was so obvious he had done this before. Joe told him, 'If I find out you've had training, I'll knock your block off!'

Looking round at the celebrities that first day, I could see the different categories we'd fall into even then. The sportsmen and the actresses. The pretty woman and the old person – me! I was determined to fill the role with aplomb. If John Sergeant could do it, so could I. When I told Darren Bennett, my partner, that I was going to provide the humour he was not impressed at all: 'Not on my watch,' he said.

By the end of the day's filming we had all bonded. I loved Jade Johnson because she had such a wonderful attitude, not to mention the most incredible body and the longest legs in the world. Zoe and Laila were good fun and Ali Bastion was just so lovely and gentle. I knew Ricky Groves a bit because I have known his wife, Hannah Waterman, since she was born, having babysat her on occasions. Her mother Patricia and I were in *General Hospital* together in the seventies. All the professional dancers were great and the girls, in particular, were gorgeous. Throughout the entire time I was in the show, I never got over feeling inadequate whenever I stood next to the girl dancers. Their bodies were amazing. So tiny, and perfectly formed. Natalie Cassidy and I used to joke about wanting to touch their perfect bottoms, but that really would have set the gossip-mongers going. Maybe that is what I should have done to make me look more interesting: when Joe and Kristina were kissing in car parks, I could have been photographed grabbing a dancer's bum!

The training began in earnest and it was relentless. Every day, Darren and I met around two o'clock and worked for three hours. I really could not do any longer. Some celebrities worked all day but for me it was just too much to take in.

The producers had changed the format of the show and so for the first two weeks, we were divided into two groups. One week Group A would dance two nights in a row, doing a ballroom and a Latin dance, while the other group did a group dance all together. Then the following week Group B danced the two dances and A did a group dance.

To learn one dance as a novice is tough. To learn two is horrendous. Not only are you learning dance steps, but you are also having to learn to dance physically! Every night I would go home and lie in a bath and find new blisters and bruises. Every morning I woke up unable to move for the first few minutes. As the weeks went on I woke up exhausted because it felt as though I had dreamed my dance all night. Certainly I would go through my dance every night before I went to sleep, and first thing when I got up. It took over my entire life. And throughout all this, I was also doing *Loose Women* twice a week and finishing my book. This meant I sometimes had to get up at four in the morning to write as it was the only spare time I had!

The studio days were the highlight of the week, and came round wonderfully quickly: hardly had I stepped out of one frock than I was stepping into the next. We were all offered a spray tan every week which added to the overall look and feel of being in the greatest show on earth. And the level of maintenance needed was unknown to me before this – one's nails had to be painted every week, and in order for the tan to look smooth I had to exfoliate regularly and moisturise every night!

It was all taken very seriously. When I arrived at the studio on a Saturday, before filming was to take place that evening, someone escorted me to my dressing room, all the while inquiring if I was feeling OK. Obviously I was not feeling great. Nerves would always take over by Friday and I just felt sick all the time.

I would be left in my dressing room in the bowels of the BBC until someone else came to take me to make-up. This was fun because the make-up was glorious. I had a wonderful make-up girl called Rozelle who was fabulous and very good at her job. I loved the false eyelashes and the glittery eye shadow: I felt like I could hide behind the face a little.

Once make-up was done, I would be taken to the hair department. This was not quite such a successful experience, because I felt they tried too hard to give me a 'look' – less is more I find, but as regards my hairstyles they tended to be rather big and set until I asked if I could look more natural.

Then I would be taken back to my room and offered the lunch menu. The first week I ordered a large lunch only to discover that I couldn't eat a thing because I was so nervous!

I will never forget the first show. Back in my dressing room, I kept leaping up and going through the dance steps every five minutes, while my phone kept bleeping texts at me. So many dear friends were sending me wishes of good luck but every time I read

'Knock 'em dead' or 'You'll be great!' it made me feel even worse. In the end I had to stop reading them.

By four in the afternoon my lovely dresser, Lena, arrived to sew me into my dress. Because we had to wear microphones they were in a material pack sewn into the back of the dress. This meant that going to the toilet could be a nightmare. God knows how many microphones went down the toilet.

Once Lena had finished, I would be in my dressing room at 4.30, sewn into the frock and all dressed up and ready to go, but still with three hours to wait. I would go upstairs and join the other celebrities pacing the corridors and doing their steps over and over again. The trouble was that as the nerves set in, I would go completely blank. It was terrifying because unlike forgetting lines in a play, when I could always fill in with something, I had no 'muscle memory' to fill in with steps in a dance.

Finally we were called to the Star Bar, a kind of holding room (definitely *not* a drinking establishment). It was extraordinary to feel the tension: each person would be going through their steps or stretching tight muscles or adjusting a curl. We would all give each other a hug or a squeeze of encouragement, then it was into the studio to line up on the stairs to make our entrances at the top of the staircase going down to the ballroom floor. Then the familiar *Strictly* music would start and my stomach would crash to the floor, but I would be buoyed along by everyone else laughing and jostling for positions and it was out into the bright lights and roar of the audience and we were off!

The evening would pass in a flash. The actual moment one goes and performs is a nano-second in the great scheme of things, but the build-up is just unbelievable. That moment when you wait in the wings to go on, and the camera is there for a close-up of your face, is something I never want to experience again in my life.

I couldn't breathe. In fact I never really did breathe throughout the whole dance! Nor did I hear the judges' comments because I was usually in another world – it was like being underwater: voices seemed very far away. When I was finally voted off I could hardly respond, except to follow Darren down to the red mark on the floor to do our last dance. Then, suddenly, it was as though I had come up and broken through the surface of the water into air. The noise of the audience hit me and I woke up and was in the daylight again. I was so relieved it was over!

As far as my husband was concerned he appreciated having me back inside my comfort zone because I was hell to live with for those two months. However, he loved the dance practice in the bedroom at night. Especially the time I had forgotten to go through the steps of the group number and jumped out of bed, naked, to go through it once before I went to sleep. All was going so well until I reached the bit where I had to jump up and down...

Strictly was an amazing experience and I'm pleased I did it. Nothing can be as nerve-racking again, surely? I conquered my body issues and proved to myself I do not crack under pressure. Best of all, the public have been so kind and supportive. I have had such positive feedback that I really feel I have a place in their hearts, and that means everything to me.

CHAPTER THIRTY-FIVE

'I AM NOT AFRAID OF TOMORROW, FOR I HAVE SEEN YESTERDAY AND I LOVE TODAY'

(WILLIAM ALLEN WHITE)

S ADLY I HAVE one other, far more poignant, last chapter to tell, before I close my story.

In January 2009, Michael and I were to be found sitting in the lounge of Edmonton Airport. Outside it was 30 degrees below zero, as we looked out on to a snow-covered runway and, beyond that, a flat, ice-covered prairie. Inside the airport lounge it was hot, sanitised and very Canadian.

We were both in shock after a week spent with three people over ninety. Impending death had seemed to hover constantly. Quality of life, positive thinking and a healthy lifestyle describe another planet; they are words that belong to another language, another time. They are not words that describe the life of a senior citizen.

I had looked into a deeply disturbing place, a place that is unavoidable to all of us. Old age.

Since my divorce from Nunzio in 1996, I had only managed to visit Marjorie a couple of times. She and Shirley lived in a block of apartments close to Milton's home. They each had their own flat. Marjorie would visit Milton every evening. He was still just about compos mentis but it was no life for either of them. When Marjorie talked about Milton, she gave the impression he was right on top of things but the reality was a long way from that.

The first time I took Michael, in November 2005, to meet my birth mother, things were already going downhill. Marjorie had stood in her kitchen, chatting away to us, when Michael noticed the microwave was on.

'What's in the microwave, Marjorie?' he had asked.

'Oh, nothing, dear, I'm just warming it up before I put our dinner in!'

Michael and I were both still drinking at this time and thanked God for the oblivion, because it was utterly bizarre being with these two old birds. They had to shout at the top of their voices to converse and, in Shirley's case, repeat the same conversation several times, because Marjorie had forgotten it five minutes later.

We spent a lovely week with Marjorie and Shirley on that occasion, nevertheless, and I cooked up a month's worth of food and left it all labelled in the freezer. But alarm bells were starting to ring even then. I had thought that Marjorie was forgetful and put it down to old age (she was, and is, very good at disguising the seriousness of her condition).

When I got a call from Marjorie in October 2008 telling me she had Alzheimer's, I was not completely surprised. It just seemed very harsh, though, as I knew what things would be like for her as I had been through all this with my mum only four years before.

Michael and I discussed the situation and we both agreed that if I did not go and see Marjorie as soon as possible, I would regret it. The only week I had free was the week after Christmas, before we started back on tour with *Calendar Girls*.

So Michael and I had to travel to Canada in the middle of winter. Actually, Michael quite liked seeing the snow! We stayed in the same hotel as before, The Macdonald, which was like being in an old-fashioned station hotel in Britain in the 1950s. It just all added to my general feeling of sadness throughout the trip.

Marjorie tried so hard to hide the effects of the dementia but I could see the change in her. The apartment was no longer spick and span. Poor Shirley, who was ninety-four, seemed to walk around with a bill permanently glued to her fingers, trying to sort out Marjorie's finances.

Michael was so good and went through everything with them. Shirley had gas and electricity bills going back years. It was very apparent that they needed proper help. Milton's daughter, Sylvia, lived a thousand miles away, in Ottawa. She rarely came to visit, and it seemed that she had not done very much to try and sort out her aunts. Marjorie was still talking about Milton as though he actually knew what was going on, but when we visited him in the home we realised just how bad the situation was. He had no idea who I was, at all, and yet we all played Marjorie's game that everything was all right and nodded along with her in agreement.

So, here was Marjorie at ninety years old trying to come to terms with the finality of Alzheimer's, and the inevitability of her mind deteriorating, while visiting her husband who was lying in a bed in a home for the aged. He was ninety-eight and lay hour after hour in a dementia ward, staring into an abyss.

When we went to see him, Marjorie led the way through the ward dismissing the other lost souls as they crowded in on us. She rushed to Milton's bedside and kissed him passionately on the lips, caressing him like a young lover. He lay inert, his eyes staring off to another place. She held his hand and kept up a constant flow of chitchat. She tried to coax him into some kind of response to her, to me or Michael. She told him over and over again that she loved him. His lips moved but he wasn't looking at her. Marjorie seemed more and more desperate. It was as though she could see him fading, and was scared he was trying to take her with him.

But her sense of survival kept her clinging on to her few remaining shreds of reality. She was not ready to go yet, no matter how much she cared about him. She had told me that morning that she had terrible dreams now. She had a sense of her dementia and described it as like having constant déjà vu. She found it hard to distinguish between what was real, what was dreamed and what was remembered. I used to see this helplessness in my mother as she turned to me sometimes. Looking into her eyes, I could see the Alzheimer's forcing its way into her sanity. It is a disgusting disease. Poor Michael just couldn't cope. He had to leave the room. But I found him later trying to ask the way to the toilet from a nurse who did not speak a word of English. His anguish and frustration was getting the better of him and he was shouting at her, 'Where's the bloody toilet?'

When we got back to the hotel he sat on the edge of the bed and wept. He was just so bowed down by the whole situation. The other person involved in all this was dear Shirley. What about her life? Here she was at ninety-four and profoundly deaf. She sported a constantly whistling hearing aid, which must have done exactly the opposite from aiding her, as it filled her head with noise. She weighed eighty-seven pounds and was like a tiny bird. Arthritis had bent her fingers round each other and the only shoes she could wear were children's trainers because her feet were so narrow. Her little sparrow's ankles peeked out over the tops of the trainers like sticks, holding up her waif's body. But her eyes were bright. Dark brown, warm and intelligent. Shirley did not miss a trick, God bless her. Without her, the other two would not have coped.

We spent the rest of the week trying to set things up to visit various nursing homes. Michael was amazing and just took over. When we spoke to Social Services they explained that Marjorie was being less than co-operative and they would have to take over very soon if the two old ladies remained on their own. So Michael returned a few weeks later and managed to persuade them both to go with him to look at places, and eventually he found them a lovely place to which they have now moved.

That week for me was about saying goodbye. I knew from the experience with my mother that the Alzheimer's would slowly remove all memory of me from Marjorie's brain. How ironic that I had found her, only to lose her again.

I have had plenty of time to reflect on my brief time with Marjorie over the twenty years I have known her, and the one powerful thought that keeps coming back to me is that my dear parents, the Bellinghams, truly changed my life. I would never have survived without them. Literally. I may have lost them too, but their love and advice has been the driving force that kept me going throughout my life, and still does today.

Looking back, perhaps the single biggest problem was fear. Fear of failure, fear of other people – but mostly fear of myself. It has taken sixty years to discover who I really am. It's never too late to find yourself, however lost you may be.

EPILOGUE

OVER THE LAST five years my career has really come together and blossomed. *Calendar Girls* showed me that much, as I wanted to prove to everyone that I can be a serious actress. And actually it really doesn't matter what anyone else thinks because I have proved to myself that I can lead a cast of actors and make a success of a play. Making comedy work is hard, and I have shown I can bring it to life for people in my own unique way.

My sons are carving a life for themselves and, despite all the traumas, they seem to be reasonably normal! My stepchildren couldn't be lovelier and I hope that in the years to come I will take up the challenge of being a grandmother, not only to their children, but to my own boys' children as well. *Loose Women* has given me the chance to keep a handle on what is going on in the world and that keeps me young, as does my gorgeous husband. This book means so much to me and I am just so grateful I was given the opportunity to write it. I could never have believed in a million years I would be having so much fun in my sixties. It is positively immoral!

It has taken me a long time to get it right, but I have finally cracked it and I intend to hold on to it. I have so much more to do, though ... so watch this space.

ACKNOWLEDGEMENTS

I would like to thank: my sister Jean, for all her help; my editor, Charlotte Cole; Gordon Wise, for encouragement and support; and Sue Latimer and Oriana Elia for keeping faith with me. And finally my thanks to anyone and everyone who has read my story.